STONE CIRCLES OF THE PEAK

John Barnatt

STONE CIRCLES OF THE PEAK

A search for natural harmony

Turnstone Books, London

Published by
Turnstone Books
37 Upper Addison Gardens
London W14 8AJ

© 1978 John Barnatt

ISBN 0 85500 088 0

First published 1978

Phototypeset in 10/11½ pt Palatino
and printed by
Lowe & Brydone Printers Limited
Thetford, Norfolk. Bound by
G. & J. Kitcat, London.

Contents

Table of figures (maps, diagrams, plans)   7
Acknowledgements   9

1. **Introduction**   11
2. **The Peak District**   17
    The Landscape   Man in the Peak   Stone Circles
3. **Research and Interpretation of the Circles**   41
    Geometry & Measurement   Astronomy
    Relationships to the Landscape   Macrocosmic Geometry
4. **Itineraries**   59
    Tour 1: Arbor Low; Nine Stones Close; Nine Ladies; Barbrook I
    Tour 2: The Bull Ring; Staden Henge; Arbor Low I & II
    Tour 3: Barbrook I; Barbrook II; Barbrook III; Stoke Flat.
    Tour 4: Offerton Moor; Wet Withers; Ciceley Low.
    Tour 5: Nine Stones Close; Nine Ladies; Stanton Moor – Central, North & South; Doll Tor; Park Gate
    Tour 6: Bamford Moor South; Bamford Moor North; Hordron Edge
    Tour 7: Ewden Beck.
5. **The Henges:**   74
    Arbor Low; Gib Hill; Arbor Low II
    The Bull Ring – Doveholes; The Staden Henge.
6. **Circles of the Central Area**   94
    The Stoke Flat Circle–Froggatt Edge; Barbrook I; Barbrook II; Barbrook III; Barbrook IV; Barbrook V; Brown Edge Circle; Barbrook Circles' Relationship; Wet Withers – Eyam Moor; Offerton Moor, West & East; Burbage Moor – Ciceley Low, North & South.

7. **The Southern Circles** 137
   Stanton Moor: Nine Ladies, Central Circle,
   South Circle, North Circle,
   Doll Tor Circle, Other Features;
   Nine Stone Close, Harthill Moor; Park Gate Circle, Beeley Moor

8. **The Northern Circles** 162
   Bamford Moor: South Circle,
   North Circle; Hordron Edge Circle;
   Ewden Beck Circle, Broom Head Moor

9. **The Great Triangle** 180
   Relationship to the landscape

Appendix A: The Circles of the Peak District 186
   B: Symbolism of Numbers 188
   C: The Zodiac 192

Chapter Notes: 198
How to Use the Map References 201
Keys to the Figures 202
Bibliography 204
Index 206

List of figures

1. Topography and geology of the Peak District   21
2. The distribution of stone circles in the Peak District   34
3. Major roads and the tours of the region   60
4. Tours 3 and 4 Map.   64
5. Barbrook circles Map.   65
6. Stoke Flat circle Map.   66
7. Ciceley Low circles Map.   66
8. Wet Withers and Offerton Moor circles Map.   66
9. Tour 5 Map.   68
10. Stanton Moor circles (Nine Ladies, Doll Tor) Map.   69
11. Nine Stone Close Map.   69
12. Beeley Moor circles (Park Gate) Map.   69
13. Tour 6 Map.   70
14. Tour 7 Map.   72
15-22. Arbor Low Henge   15. *Location*   75   16. *Plan*   77
17. *Geometry*   77
18-22. *Alignments*   83-87

23-26. The Bull Ring Henge   23. *Plan*   88   24. *Location* 89
25-26. *Alignments*   89

27-30. The Staden Henge   27. *Plan*   91   28. *Location* 92
29-30 *Alignments*   92

31-35. The Stoke Flat Circle   31. *Plan-geometry*   95
32-35. *Alignments*   98

36-53. The Barbrook I Circle   36. *Plan-geometry*   100   37. *Plan-balance*   103   38-43. *Alignments from the circle*   105
44. *Plan-outliers*   107
45-53. *Alignments from the outliers*   108

54. The Barbrook II Circle   54. *Plan-geometry*   110
55. The Barbrook III Circle   55. *Plan*   114

56. Relationships between the Barbrook Circles 118
57-64. Wet Withers

57. Plan-geometry 120
58. The horizon 123
59-64. Alignments 124-6

65-69 The Offerton Moor Circles

65. Plan of the west circle-geometry 128 66. Relationship between the two circles 131
67-69 Alignments 133-4

70. The Ciceley Low Circles
71-72. The Nine Ladies, Stanton Moor

70. Plan 135

71. Plan-geometry 138
72. Plan-balance 140

73. Stanton Moor – Central Circle
74. Stanton Moor – South Circle
75. Stanton Moor – North Circle
76-77. The Doll Tor Circle

73. Plan-geometry 143

74. Plan-geometry 147

75. Plan-geometry 147
76. Plan 150
77. Alignments 152

78. Stanton Moor – The prehistoric sites 153
79-81. Nine Stones Close. 157
82-83. The Park Gate Circle

82. Plan-geometry 159
83. Alignments 161

84-92. The South Circle – Bamford Moor

84. Plan-outliers 162
85. Plan-geometry 163
86-92. Alignments 165-6

93-97. The North Circle – Bamford Moor

93. Plan-geometry 168
94-97. Alignments 172

98-102. The Hordron Edge Circle

98. Plan 175
99-102. Alignments 175

List of Figures

103-106. The Ewden Beck Circle
    103. *Location* *178*
    104. *Plan* *178*
    105-106. *Alignments* *178*
107. The Great Triangle *181*
108-111. Sections along the Great Triangle lines *184*
112. The Zodiac *193*
113. How to read map references *201*

Acknowledgements

To the works of Thom, Critchlow, Michell, Radley and others, whose books provided the inspiration and groundwork which made this work possible.

To Eric and Norah Heaf for much advice and guidance, and to Eric for checking the macrocosmic geometry with his own research.

To Mr. Perrett for checking many of my celestial observations with his own research.

To Paul Hewitt for many hours of help with the fieldwork.

To Lydia Johnson for help with the presentation.

To all my family for practical help and support.

1
Introduction

Stone circles are some of the most intriguing and enigmatic relics of our distant past. They are basically rings of erected upright stones, the majority of which are small simple circles of unshaped stones unobtrusively placed in the landscape. This is not always the case and at the other extreme are such well known sites as Stonehenge, Avebury and Callanish with massive stones and complex designs. Between the two is a complete range of circles with many variations and regional characteristics, some very impressive, others hardly ever noticed by the casual observer. They are frequently found in isolated spots in areas of natural beauty; this enhances the mysterious atmosphere of power often present in these structures which were obviously of great importance to our prehistoric ancestors. Over 900 circles have survived the ravages of time and they are predominantly found in upland areas in northern and western England, Wales, Scotland and Ireland. The only place outside this region where similar monuments exist is Brittany, although these are rarely circular.

The average visitor to stone circles has very little information readily available to explain them, as only at Stonehenge and a few other major circles are guide books for sale. In recent years much has been written about circles, but this is usually in scientific journals, or books such as those by Professor Thom which are so technical that great staying power is needed fully to understand them. In 1976 A. Burl published the only book which is close to a comprehensive study, but even this monumental work only gives minimal information on most circles and is not adequate for the person who wants the specific site in front of him explained. The visitor is therefore usually left guessing at the circle's origin and function. Even if widely read and familiar with the many current theories, especially those connected with geometry and astronomy, one is left wondering how they relate to the site one is looking at. This book is an attempt to rectify the situation for one area of the country. The research which has made this possible was first started as an investigation of the theories of Professor Thom who in the last few years has revolutionised our understanding of circles. In his work he used a selection of well preserved circles throughout Britain. There was clearly a need to study a small area in depth. The Peak District was chosen because it is in the centre of Britain and is a well defined geographical region with a group of circles which have a variety of forms and sizes. This book is drawn from the conclusions of the research and covers every circle in the area worth visiting, describing each in turn with an interpretation based on all current theories which have been shown to be founded in fact. It is written primarily as a guide for anyone wanting to visit the Peak District circles, but also to stimulate research of this kind in other areas.

Stone circles have always fascinated man. Until relatively recently they were venerated by country people who regarded them with awe, telling many strange tales about them and visiting them in the hope of miraculous cures. The study of the folklore connected with circles shows that these legends and practices are degenerate relics of pre-Christian beliefs; and that they represent the fragmentary remnants of a continuous tradition of worship at circles, the significance of which had been lost in the distant past due to supression by Christianity. The Church's early policy was to integrate pagan religion with Christian beliefs so that the new faith was easier to accept. The old practices therefore continued in a corrupt form, becoming more and more mechanically performed as their meaning was lost. Perhaps the reason that some of them have survived today is that they have a relevance in this environment. Stone circles have had long-standing connections with witches, who actually practiced the pre-Christian beliefs based on nature, a perfectly wholesome tradition misinterpreted in most people's minds because of Christian propaganda. Today witches' covens still meet here, but one suspects that nowadays many of them have little in common with the old ways, being corrupted by fanciful modern inventions often of a perverted nature. Another group who meet at Stonehenge calling themselves Druids are eccentrics following rituals invented in relatively recent times, which are claimed to be an intuitive reconstruction of druidical rites.

In the last 350 years there has been a growing scholarly interest in stone circles and many attempts have been made to interpret them. It is a curious paradox that more circles have been destroyed in this time than in any other era in history. The reason for this is the gradual breakdown of the veneration of circles with the spread of logic and reason, later escalated by the Christian revival of the Victorian era which made country people lose their fear of disturbing ancient sites. The impressive circles like Stonehenge and Avebury were the first to be noticed, and John Aubrey in the seventeenth century expressed the opinion that they were temples built by the Druids, a theory that was to dominate the next two centuries. The main source of information about prehistoric Britain available at the time was Roman writings; these gave only the names of their immediate predecessors, the priesthood called the Druids. Until the science of archaeology was developed by the Victorian scholars in the preceding centuries they had to rely on guesswork. The circles were ascribed from time to time to every period, from prehistory to the Danes.

In the eighteenth century William Stukeley noticed an important fact—that the Heel Stone at Stonehenge had astronomical significance. This connection has been developed in more recent times to give a much fuller understanding of stone circles. In this century it became fashionable to tour the wilder parts of Britain and gradually more and more circles became known. The first documentation of Peak District sites, including some which have now been destroyed, was made towards the end of the century by Rev. Pegge and Major Hayman Rooke.

In the nineteenth century many over-enthusiastic amateurs began to dig into prehistoric sites to look for artefacts. One of the foremost of these was Thomas Bateman who opened hundreds of Peak District burial mounds. As a result of their findings it was concluded that there were three ages in prehistory which they named the Stone, Bronze and Iron Ages. By today's standards these first excavators used methods which were very crude and much valuable data was unwittingly destroyed. In spite of this they laid the foundations for the understanding of British prehistory which still holds today although modified in many ways. These studies showed that stone circles were much earlier than was thought, dating from the late Stone Age or the Bronze Age and the name Druid gradually became detached from circles.

At the turn of the century there was a great revival of interest in stone circles and many were visited, measured and regional lists were made, including one for Derbyshire by J. Ward. Precise excavations began, such as the one at Arbor Low in 1901-02 which was carried out by Gray. At this time there was also renewed interest shown in the astronomical alignments of stone circles throughout Britain, by men such as Lockyer and Somerville whose findings attracted a great deal of attention, and many other people took up this study. Unfortunately only a few of these understood astronomy well enough to collect accurate data, with the result that stone circle study sank into a quagmire of supposition and wild theories and was abandoned by serious archaeologists. In the light of present knowledge we can see that some intuitive workers at that time were clearly on the right track.

After this period circles were largely ignored except for a few isolated excavations such as those in the Peak District round Stanton Moor by Heathcote. After the second world war, interest again began to revive and excavations were undertaken, including four in the Peak District to date. With the aid of modern archaeological methods it was now possible to discover more about circles. Radio carbon dating together with tree ring dating has shown that they were built over a period of about 2,000 years with the earliest before 3000 BC and the latest well after 1500 BC. Circles themselves often yield few artefacts, but comparison with other sites of the same period show that they were built by skilful farmers who lived in dispersed settlements, perhaps divided into tribal areas. These people possessed many basic skills including husbandry, agriculture and building, making many finely worked artefacts of stone, wood, leather, bone and in the later part of the period, metals. One thing that seems not to have developed at this time, however, is writing and information was probably passed on by word of mouth.

In the last 20 years the controversial research of Professor Thom has stimulated the interest in stone circles and divided opinion into two camps. He has revived the astronomical theories, but this time based on sound scientific fieldwork proving their validity, and also shown that the circles have sophisticated designs based on simple geometric shapes constructed with a standardised measure. Many archaeologists are vehemently opposed to these findings and they argue that they conflict with the other evidence from this period.

Thom mainly used small circles for his research rather than the large complex circles which have always been recognised as communal sites. Because these small circles often contain burials, they have been argued by some to be only complex sepulchral cairns. This argument however is based on too many assumptions. It is also argued that the sophistication of Thom's solutions would be beyond the simple farmers of the era. Logical modifications of the theories dissolve this objection.

The over-technical approach of Thom is limiting, though understandable, as he is a product of this age. His arguments have not been helped by a number of people who have taken up his theories as a starting point for flights of fancy of their own, some of which are obviously untrue, for example the claims that they are built by the Egyptians or even by extraterrestrial beings. Some writers like Critchlow and Michell working on a more intuitive level have proposed very interesting theories that are worth investigating. There is also 'ley line' research, which seeks significance in the alignment of ancient sites, although the traditional world of archaeology has dismissed these as pure supposition. However some of these more subjective approaches are surviving the test of scientific investigation.

The traditional approach of the archaeologist is very limiting because of the scarcity of finds in circles; it can offer no convincing answers to the function of stone circles apart from vague generalisations. The only conclusions which can be reached are predominantly about mundane aspects such as their method of construction. The new approach instigated by Thom proves to be much more productive, giving insights into the way prehistoric man thought, and why he built these circles. The archaeological approach is useful in conjunction with the other as it can help give a clear picture of the original form of circles which today are often damaged and cannot be studied without reconstruction.

At present we are entering a new era in stone circle study as the rift of the last few years is beginning to close and the theories of Thom are being at least partially accepted by many archaeologists. It is now apparent that although the builders of stone circles led simple lives, in some ways they were by no means primitive in the accepted sense, but were capable of complex and creative thought just as we are today. They had the added advantage of lacking the overwhelming distractions of modern society. Indications are that as in any society there was an elite group, probably a priesthood, composed of learned men chosen for their merit. This group was responsible for the design and construction of the circles. The standard unit for length and similarities in purpose and architecture imply that most of the tribal groups in the country were linked at least culturally by these priests and that there was a free interchange of ideas between communities. Possibly the guesses of early scholars such as Aubrey and Stukeley were wrong in name only, as the Druids could be distant descendants of the same tradition based on knowledge passed down orally from generation to generation.

This book reflects current attitudes put together with detailed evidence to support the new outlook, namely that circles were built by intelligent men involved with interpretation of the world about them, using a mixture of objective observation and magical ritual aimed at harmonising the forces of nature. Aspects of the research described here reveal forgotten knowledge about the landscape around us, with implications which take the study of stone circles beyond historical curiosity as they have great potential relevance today.

2
The Peak District

The Peak is in the centre of Britain at the southern end of the Pennines and is a naturally defined region with a central block of limestone moors dissected by deep valleys. Surrounding these on three sides are high bleak moors covered in peat and heather which separate the communities of the Peak District from the populated regions to the east and west. Only in the south do the moors gradually drop down to the lowlands of the Trent valley. Today the man-made boundaries do not follow the geographical divisions exactly, and although most of the region is in Derbyshire, other counties administer the edges of the area. In the north-east large areas of the bleak uninhabited moors east of the river Derwent are in Yorkshire. In the south-west all the land west of the river Dove is in Staffordshire and the foothills of the moors north of this are in Cheshire.

This region is one of outstanding natural beauty with a very variable character, and in 1950 after many years of discussion it was officially made a National Park having authority to control activities within the area. The main concern is to preserve the beauty of the region with its fauna and flora so they can be enjoyed by everyone. The area is well used, being close to large industrial conurbations which include the cities of Sheffield, Manchester and Derby.

The Peak District park has much to offer. The most frequent visitors are those with no specialised interest, the motorist and the walker who come just to enjoy the contrasting scenery. The uplands of the bleak northern moors give way to the tamer limestone moors with their network of drystone walls forming complex patterns on the landscape. The deep vallleys in the north around Ladybower reservoir drop down to the settled valleys downstream, and to the rocky gorges in the limestone, among the most spectacular of which are the Winnats near Castleton, the Wye valley, Lathkill Dale, Dove Dale and the nearby Manifold Valley, all of which are well known beauty spots.

Scenery apart, there are many interesting things for the visitor to see, such as the great house of Chatsworth with its fine state rooms and extensive gardens and Haddon Hall which is a rambling house of many different periods in a beautiful setting. At Castleton there are fine show caves and a medieval castle. Bakewell, set picturesquely on the River Wye, has many old buildings. Eyam is famous for its associations with the great plague. Many of the other villages of the Peak are quiet and unspoilt, though in the limestone area some have their peace shattered for a few days once a year by hoards of people visiting the well dressings. In this unique custom, wells are decorated with large religious pictures formed of flower petals. The date varies from village to village, though it is always in spring or summer.

The area is popular for outdoor sports. The serious walker would have difficulty exhausting the multitude of footpaths. The southern end of the Pennine Way starts in Edale and climbs onto Kinder Scout, the highest moor in the area. The frequent natural cliffs and old quarry faces attract many climbers, and cliffs like the ones at Stanage on the gritstone moors are very popular. The limestone area attracts people going downwards, as it contains some of the best potholes in the country. Fishermen frequent many of the rivers which are well known for their trout and the gritstone moors are well used in the autumn for grouse shooting.

For people with specialist interests the region has a lot to offer. The rocks and minerals are very interesting. The geologist can spend many hours collecting fossils in numerous exposures of limestone and fine mineral specimens are to be found in the old spoil tips of the lead mines. For the naturalist there are also many sights which are rewarding, such as the colourful blankets of flowers which are prolific in the spring and summer on the limestone.

The area is one of the richest in the country in varied remains of man from all ages, and for those interested in archaeology and history many sites are well worth visiting. There are prehistoric remains such as Neolithic chambered tombs like the one at Fivewells and hundreds of fine mounds of the Bronze

Age. Some of the most interesting are the stone circles which are the main topic of this book and these alone can provide the visitor with many days of fascinating exploration. Other remains of a slightly later date are the hill forts such as the one on Mam Tor above the Hope Valley. Roman sites are scantily preserved. There is a fort at Brough but little can be seen above ground; the course of various Roman roads can be followed but none of their original surfaces remain.

Of the later periods many interesting relics survive. There are Saxon crosses, fine examples of which can be seen in the churchyards at Eyam and Bakewell. Mediaeval churches in many villages, including large ones at Tideswell, Bakewell and Wirksworth. Peveril Castle at Castleton, built by the Normans, is well worth a visit because of its spectacular location. Interesting buildings of post-mediaeval date include a large number of halls and manor houses and also old mills and mines studied by the industrial archaeologist.

There are many problems to be considered in the management of the Peak District by the National Park Authority, some of which conflict and call for compromises. Employment for the local population is just as important as the tourist attractions. Many local people have always been employed in farming and still are, and the boom in tourism has provided jobs for others; but one of the main occupations has always been the exploitation of the rocks and minerals beneath the soil. Because of this a strip of land around Buxton and another area of the uplands near Matlock and Wirksworth were left outside the National Park. These areas are now being extensively quarried for limestone which is one of the basic raw materials of modern society, used in the chemical industries and also for fertilisers, cement and steel making. One has only to look at these eyesores to be thankful for the National Park Authority which has saved most of the region from a similar fate. Unfortunately these areas alone are not enough to satisfy the demand for limestone and employment and a few quarries also exist within the Park, particularly at Hope with its prominent cement works and others at Eldon Hill and Stoney Middleton.

The other main rock of the region is a coarse sandstone called Millstone Grit which used to be quarried for grindstones. This ceased many years ago and most of the quarries now blend with the scenery. The minerals of the region all occur in the Park itself and the mining of these is widespread on a small scale. Because of the nature of their occurrence the lasting scars on the landscape are less noticeable, as the workings are backfilled after mining has ceased and soon blend with the surrounding landscape. At the present time the most extensive workings are on Longstone Moor and parts of Bradwell Moor. Another large scale change brought about by man in the region is the building of reservoirs which provide water for the towns and cities on either side of the Pennines. These were mainly built before the creation of the Park and in many cases enhance the beauty of the area, as with the largest group of reservoirs in the upper Derwent Valley. The sides of these valleys have been covered with extensive plantations which help to ensure a pure water supply. These large lakes surrounded by dark conifers create a landscape which is alien to the region, but which has a special beauty of its own.

THE LANDSCAPE

The variety of scenery found in the Peak District is the result of the different rocks and the way in which they are folded. They are all from the Carboniferous age, and have three distinctive layers. The lowest and oldest are massive beds of limestone which were formed in shallow sea conditions and often contain many fossils such as shells and corals. This limestone is easily recognised by its colour, often virtually white or light grey. They are not however consistent and are sometimes darker and also occasionally contain thin irregular beds of chert, a mineral similar to flint.

On top of the limestone are beds of dark grey shale layered with coarse sandstone. Upwards the sandstones soon become predominant, in thicker beds of coarse Millstone Grit. This rock forms a contrast to the limestone, for although its colour is usually a yellowish brown, it quickly turns dark grey when exposed to the air, looking almost black from a distance. These rocks were formed as the shallow clear sea of the limestone age was invaded by rivers depositing sediment from nearby land masses, mud forming the shale and heavier material the sandstones. These beds gradually get thinner as they run southwards so that there are no high gritstone moors at the southern end of the Peak District, which gradually drops down into the lowlands of the Trent Valley.

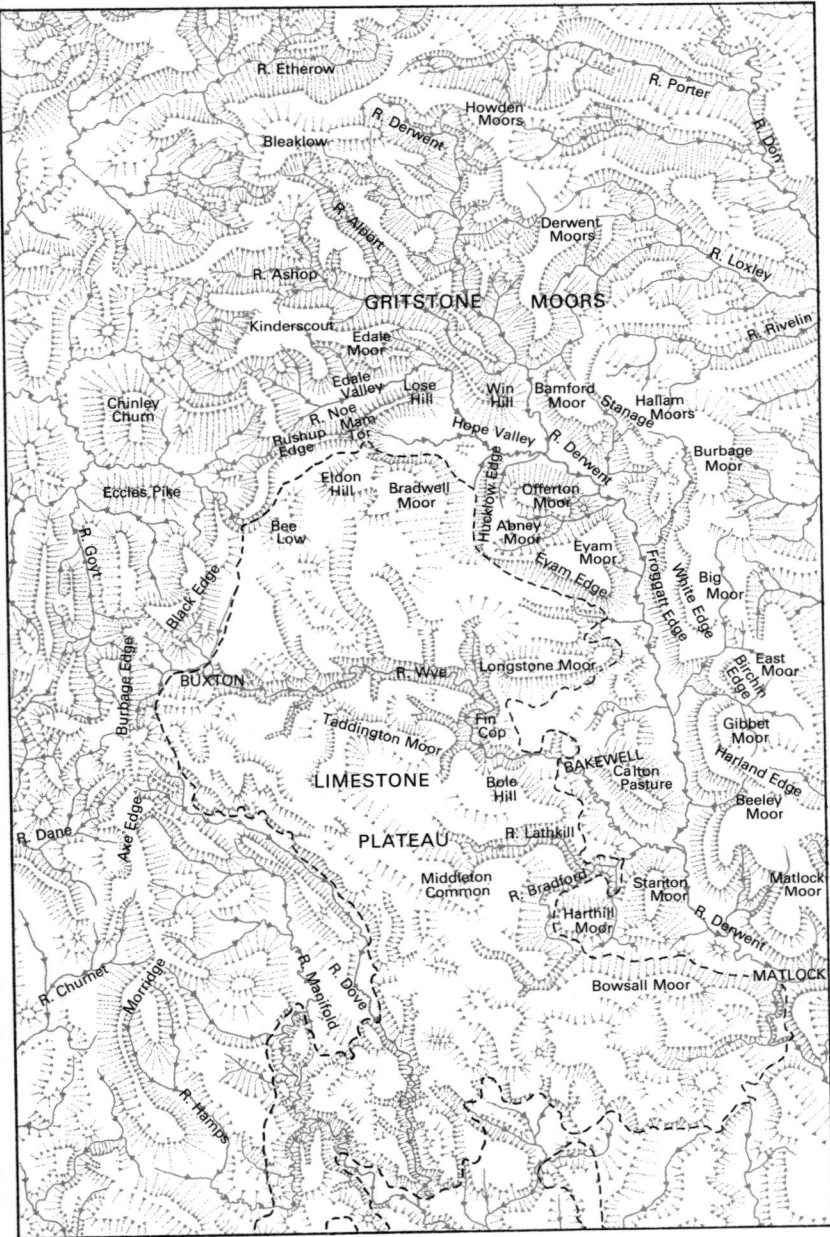

FIG. 1

The margins of the Peak District are formed from the layers above the Millstone Grit which are known as the Coal Measures. These are finer sandstones with occasional layers of coal, deposited when the shallow sea had virtually been filled, and delta-like conditions prevailed with the coal formed from compressed layers of luxuriant vegetation.

Due to earth movements these rocks have been pushed upwards to form the southern end of the Pennines. In the Peak it resulted in a massive dome with the rocks dipping to the east and west and to a lesser extent to the north and south. This folding took place many millions of years ago and subsequent erosion has exposed all the different layers. In the centre of the Peak District the limestone forms a high plateau with many interesting minor geological variations. Around the edges of the limestone, the soft shale layers above have been eroded away to form the main valleys of the region, notably those of the rivers Derwent and Dove.

Surrounding the valleys are the gritstone rocks which have steep escarpment slopes locally called 'edges' facing the central area. These are formed by erosion cutting away the hard rocks along vertical lines of weakness. In the east, softer layers of shale between the gritstone bands form steps in the escarpment, with wide shelves of flat land between steep slopes. Above the escarpment the land falls away very gently following the dip of the rocks until the coal measures are reached. As these are slightly softer the land has eroded more and drops away steeply to the lowlands on either side of the Pennines.

There are also many minor folds which govern more localised features of the landscape. In the limestone there is buckling at right angles to the main fold, forming ridges running from east to west. The most noticeable of these created Longstone Moor on the northern side of a central dip with Taddington Moor and Bolehill on the south, the dip between forming a wide low-lying area between Great Longstone and Ashford. To the north of this another fold forms the northern end of the limestone outcrop creating a steep slope around Castleton with the limestone dipping steeply under the shales to the north.

Large folds in the south form other ridges such as Elton Common and Bonsall Moor and the limestone plateau is at its widest here. Connected with this folding are small domes which cause the limestone to outcrop in two tiny patches on the eastern margin of the Peak at Crich and Ashover, surrounded by gritstones. The western side of the dome has many folds running north to south which causes the gritstone to form ridges rather than flat-topped moors, this is especially noticeable around the river Goyt upstream from Whaley Bridge and in the Manifold Valley further south.

All this folding caused many lines of weakness in the rocks and vertical splits or faults formed. These allowed molten rock to penetrate the limestone and to follow horizontal weaknesses in the strata, forming thin beds of dark igneous rock which often outcrop in the limestone valleys and have a significant effect on drainage and settlement.

At a later date hot fluids seeping up these weaknesses contained a variety of minerals which were deposited to form rich veins up to twenty feet wide, locally called 'rakes'. These have been a source of wealth since prehistoric times and the main mineral which has been mined from them is lead, although zinc and copper have also been worked in smaller quantities. The main trend of the rakes is east/west, following the direction of the folding. Often they are a few miles long and today can be traced by long lines of old waste tips following the veins. Although the faults themselves continue upwards through later rocks, the shale covering the limestone stopped the fluids going higher, so the minerals only occur on the limestone plateau. The mines of the eighteenth and nineteenth century, however, followed some of the larger veins under the edges of the shale for over a mile until the veins become too deep to make mining practical.

Erosion has played a major part in the formation of the Peak District landscape. The main river of the region is the Derwent which starts as a small steep-sided valley in an area of dissected gritstone moorland. It soon enters the wide Hope Valley formed from the erosion of thick layers of shale. The river continues to flow southwards in a deep valley formed along shale bands. To the west of the limestone plateau the smaller river Dove follows the shale, again flowing southwards in a deep valley. Between the two rivers the plateau rises to around 1500 feet above sea level; because limestone is pervious there are very few streams in the area—most of the drainage is underground in numerous cave systems.

This area has two very different types of scenery. The top of the plateau has gentle slopes and wide shallow valleys, with occasional east/west escarpment slopes. The plateau is highest in the north around Bradwell Moor and in the west where there is a series of ridges running from north-west to south-east. The tributaries of the Derwent have eroded the eastern side of the plateau which slopes towards the valleys.

The other type of limestone landscape is the large number of steep sided gorges which cut through the plateau. These are usually deep and narrow, following the floor of the shallow hollows of the plateau; good examples are the Winnats near Castleton and the Wye Valley with its many tributary valleys.

Millions of years ago the Peak was not as high above sea level as it is today and the undulating top of the limestone was part of a large plain which had been eroded to form typical lowland scenery with wide valleys and low hills. A few million years before the last ice age there was a relatively sudden second uplift of the whole region which caused a dramatic increase in rainfall. This caused upland drainage to develop, quickly cutting deep gorges in the base of lowland type valleys. Because of the pervious nature of the limestone the streams soon developed underground drainage which left the landscape in what can be described as a fossilised state, with the gorges never widening to form large valleys as in the gritstone areas. This is well seen around Monyash where Taddington Moor, originally a lowland hill, drops gently southwards to the village at the base of a lowland valley. Here the narrow Lathkill gorge with its steep cliffs begins, and above this, down the valley on either side, are gentle slopes which were the original valley bottom.

Today the only running water on the limestone is in the larger gorges. The river Wye starts in the west draining the slopes of the gritstone moors, and forms a valley in the shales around Buxton. From here the river flows east across the limestone plateau in a very deep gorge which formed here because of a dip in the east/west folding. The other river in the region, the Lathkill is in a similar dip. In the southern part of the Peak District the folds formed a much wider area of limestone which traps the rivers draining southwards in the shale valleys. This caused similar gorges to form; on the east the Derwent passes through a 1½ mile long gorge immediately south of Matlock, and in the west the Dove passes through one which is five miles long with spectacular cliffs. Further west its tributary the River Manifold passes through a similar gorge.

The gritstone moors which surround the limestone can be divided into three areas with different features. North of the limestone plateau are vast expanses of flat moorland such as Kinder Scout and Bleaklow which in places exceed 2000 feet above sea level. They are dissected by a multitude of small steep sided valleys locally called 'cloughs' which come together to form the upper Derwent valley and similar tributary valleys, all draining to the south-east. These have narrow floors and very steep sides up to 800 feet high because of the hardness of the gritstone. Similar streams drain off the periphery of the moors coming together in the east to form the river Don and in the west the river Etherow. At the southern extremity of these moors, near their junction with the limestone, larger valleys have formed in the shale beds, such as the Hope Valley (the largest), the Edale Valley and one to the south of Rushup Edge.

The second main area of moorlands is a wide strip running down the eastern side of the Peak. The Derwent cut the main escarpment on the east where one finds the main moors and shelves. These are relatively intact with only small streams running off them, dissecting the shelves. To the west of the Derwent are isolated blocks of moorland formed by hard layers of gritstone between the shale beds of the Derwent Valley and those at the limestone junction. The largest of these, Eyam Moor, has steep escarpment slopes on the west and south. To the south are others, such as Calton Pasture and Stanton Moor with Harthill Moor to the west.

The third area of gritstone moor is on the western edge of the Peak. This is much more irregular because of the complexity of the geology and consists of high ridges with only a few areas of wide flat-topped moors such as those above Black Edge and Axe Edge. The north/south folding has led to various rivers draining the area, like the Goyt, Manifold and Hamps, all of which follow dips in the folding.

To the south of the limestone plateau there are no moors, and a number of small streams drain gently sloping sandstone ridges which gradually drop to the south.

The vegetation varies according to different soils and altitude. Today large areas of the more hospitable regions of the Peak have been altered by farming, but enough remains to show what the natural vegetation was like in the late prehistoric times of the stone circle builders, when the climate was warmer than it is today. Although the same species have remained, trees would have grown at slightly higher altitudes than they can today and many of today's bleak upland areas were suitable for habitation.

The limestone plateau has the richest soil and today is virtually covered with enclosed fields which are used for livestock and arable farming. The natural vegetation is open woodland with a predominence of ash and sycamore which grow to an altitude of about 1000 feet. Above this the land is mostly open and covered in coarse grasses. Evidence suggests that as early as about 5000 BC the relatively open woodlands of the plateau were beginning to be cleared for pasture. These clearings were probably substantial by the time circles were being built in the area. The tops of many moors on the plateau, well above 1000 feet, were natural open moorland. As one descended, the hollows and shelves above the gorges were probably a mixture of woodland and large open clearings with only the gorges and low shelves like those above Bakewell with a thicker intact wood cover.

The large valleys on the shales and gritstones were entirely different in character. Their sheltered floors, often only between 300 and 600 feet above sea level, enabled a thick forest of predominantly oak and birch to grow. This was so thick that it was beyond the technology of Bronze Age man to make substantial clearings. These valleys probably remained unaltered until the Iron Age, although they were likely to have been inhabited by a small number of people taking advantage of natural clearings, using the forest for hunting. As one went up the slopes and onto the gritstone moors the trees would become smaller and stunted. Today the oak stops at 1000 feet and the birch at 1250 feet above sea level.

Before about 6000 BC there was a very dry climate and trees grew on even the highest moors. As the climate became wetter, peat gradually replaced the woodland in the highest areas, and most of the moors above about 1400 feet were probably open peat moorland by the stone circle era. Below this level there were patches of peat moorland alternating with open grassland or heather, with a scatter of low stunted birch trees passing into thicker woodland at lower levels. At the time of the circle building man spread onto these moors and started clearing them, although it is not clear how much was removed. Most of the circles were probably on land which was at least partially cleared and fairly open.

By around 600 BC the colder climate of today had set in, and these moors were abandoned except for sheep grazing. Large tracts of heather moorland established themselves which are still characteristic of much of the moorland today. The fact that many of the shelves below the tree line are open moorland perhaps indicates that they were substantially cleared in the prehistoric period, remaining open to the present day because of continued sheep grazing. Later clearance of timber for lead smelting also created many moors—so if an area is now open it should not be assumed to have a prehistoric origin.

MAN IN THE PEAK

Man has lived in the region since earliest times and the area is rich in remains of his presence from all periods. In early prehistoric times man was a nomadic hunter following game around the countryside, and he probably never built any kind of permanent structures. He is known to have frequented the Peak District, as many examples of his flint implements lost while hunting have been found.

The first men to have permanent bases were those of the Neolithic period which started in this region in the third or fourth millenium BC. These people were pastoralists who moved onto the limestone plateau because its light wood cover was ideal for grazing their animals. They were probably semi-nomadic, moving their animals to new grazing with the seasons, but unlike the hunters, keeping within a relatively small area. This limitation of movement eventually gave incentive to build permanent structures acting as focal points for meeting and worship, perhaps based on tribal ownership of land.

The earliest of these structures are chambered tombs of which there were at least ten in the area. These are large mounds of earth or rubble containing chambers built of stone slabs, and were used over a long period of time for burials. Each tribal group probably used its own mound as a meeting place and for performing ceremonies. Chambered tombs which occur throughout the western half of Britain vary in design, indicating different cultural waves. However those in the Peak do not fit well with any of the recognised groups, but appear to be a mixture of different elements. The reason for this is the Peak's unique isolated position in the centre of Britain, which in prehistoric times was surrounded by vast forests.

The area has never been subjected to large influxes of people, but rather, any cultural advance was gradually absorbed and the few immigrants who did arrive were soon integrated with the existing population. The region was at the crossing of trade routes to many of the centres of prehistoric population including the Lake District, Ireland, North Yorkshire and Wessex, and these would have brought new ideas and cultural advances from all directions to be fused together in the Peak District. These conditions prevailed throughout the prehistoric period and all changes should be seen as cultural innovations and fashions rather than violent invasions.

In the late Neolithic a new development was the building of circle henges of which three or four have survived in the area. These result from a fusion of ideas from both sides of Britain. The henges were great focal points for the population and were probably in use for over a thousand years.

The advent of the Bronze Age in about 2000 BC brought important changes. As the name suggests, the use of metals was introduced, but these were not common, and throughout the period only a few people owned bronze objects which would have been very precious and probably given ceremonial or magical significance. The commonest of these were wedge-shaped daggers and later axes which were occasionally buried with their owners. The most frequent material used for weapons and tools was still flint. This must have been brought a great distance from the east as its nearest source was in Lincolnshire and the largest known exploited region was Norfolk. On the limestone, chert, an alternative to flint, was often used, although it could not be worked to such fine shapes as flint and was therefore a poor substitute for some purposes. Another important type of stone in use for implements from Neolithic times onwards was volcanic rocks of various kinds, which were used to make beautiful polished axes and maces. This is found locally but these artifacts were also commonly imported from the Lake District and North Wales.

The technological advances in metal working could have brought the first exploitation of the minerals of the limestone region. The mineral veins are often exposed in natural cliffs and so would have been known, although there is no direct evidence of mining at this date. It seems probable that the people would at least have investigated the minerals to find their uses. Lead would have had only limited use but was probably mined in small quantities. The copper occurs in large quantities only around Ecton in Staffordshire and it is not known if this was exploited. Copper is one of the two constituents of bronze;

the other, tin does not occur anywhere in the region and no evidence exists to indicate bronze was made locally. The main source was probably Ireland from where gold was also imported.

New fashions in burial methods were also introduced in the Bronze Age, all of which had one thing in common—individuals were buried in their own mounds. This indicates a tribal system was now well established with an elite probably comprising of chiefs and their families. The theory of an elite is supported by the examination of the burial mounds where often secondary burials are placed in the edges of the mound with very few grave goods, as if they were of people of lesser importance. No special form of burials exist which would indicate a priesthood, but perhaps the chiefs also fulfilled this role. At the beginning of the Bronze Age a distinct group of graves is classified as of the Beaker Period, named after their characteristic pottery. These were probably built by a small group of people who entered the region with many of the new ideas. It is thought that they soon became integrated with the local inhabitants and a form of pottery called 'food vessels' became common. These were probably produced by the indigenous population. In the mid Bronze Age the burial customs were modified again with cremation in urns rather than inhumation becoming the predominant custom, a practice which continued for the rest of the period. There are many hundreds of Bronze Age burial mounds in Derbyshire, indicating a thriving community and a period of expansion.

The pastoralists of the Neolithic and Beaker periods appear to have confined themselves to the limestone plateau. During this period many of the indigenous hunters continued their old way of life in the forests and on the moors of the gritstones. In the Bronze Age the more advanced limestone cultures spread onto the gritstone areas and large-scale exploitation of the region took place, with many areas cleared and used for pasture.

By the mid Bronze Age there was probably one totally-integrated population throughout the Peak District, and the spread of cremation was perhaps due to the influence of the hunters. This was the time of the construction of the many small stone circles found on the gritstone moors, although some could be earlier. These are shown later to be directly connected culturally with the circle henges of the limestone and are part of the spread of similar religious ideas throughout the region.

Towards the end of the prehistoric period there were new advances in metal working when iron was discovered. This enabled the thick lowland forests to be cleared and ploughed for the first time which radically changed the pattern of settlement centres in Britain. At this time the Peak District was becoming a cultural backwater because the deterioration of weather conditions was making upland habitation less attractive, and the gritstone moors were virtually abandoned. The foothills at either side of the Pennines with their sheltered valleys were now much more suitable. A new structure introduced at this time was the hill fort: seven exist in the Peak, the largest covering 16 acres of Mam Tor above the western end of the Hope Valley. It is not clear why these were built, but if they were defensive, perhaps the tribal system was now so well developed that large bands of warriors could be organised, and the population so large that expansion was not possible without hostility. In the century before the Roman conquest large waves of invaders crossed the English Channel and conquered most of southern Britain, establishing a number of small kingdoms which may have given incentive to fort building in this region. Doubt is now being cast on the nature of hill forts, as it is clear that many of the larger ones would be impossible to defend with the population that existed, so perhaps they were built for symbolic or magical purposes.

By the end of the Iron Age the basic pattern of settlement which is still found today had probably been established. Being predominantly uplands, there are only a limited number of spots which are suitable for habitation. On the limestone plateau the main problem is a water supply, and springs only occur in a few places. Some are at the limestone-gritstone junction and supply a string of villages such as Eyam and Great Longstone. Other springs on the shelves above the gorges served settlements situated to exploit these fertile areas of land. The occasional outcrops of horizontal layers of igneous rock which exist in the limestone create springs and such spots are usually chosen for these limestone settlements. The individual farm was the most common form of prehistoric settlement, but on the limestone because of the shortage of suitable sites, villages probably developed at a very early date. In the infertile gritstone valleys it is more usual to find a scatter of small hamlets and farms equally spaced along the valleys, each with is own area for pasture, many probably established in the Iron Age. These patterns have remained constant until the present day, with only the size of certain settlements changing.

The Roman occupation made very few lasting changes to the area and after their departure life reverted to the natural pattern with the Roman settlements being abandoned. Their main civic settlement was at Buxton where natural thermal springs made the place a spa of some importance. There was also a fort at Brough near the centre of the Hope Valley which was part of a network crossing the Pennines. The presence of this fort and the Iron Age fort on Mam Tor indicate that the Hope Valley had by this time become an important centre of population. The Romans exploited the lead mines of the area right from the start of their occupation, suggesting that the mines were well established on their arrival. We do not know where the main Roman lead smelting centre was, but many people have suggested it was somewhere near Wirksworth as this was the chief centre for Saxon mining.

The Saxon invasion came late to the area, starting in the seventh century, and was not a conquest but a gradual infiltration by a few people who soon intermarried with the local population. They probably made very little difference to the pattern of settlement and in the north, in areas such as the Hope Valley, the Celtic patterns are clearly seen after the Norman Conquest in the Domesday Book, the first comprehensive survey of settlement. Here the main village of Hope is in the centre of the valley, surrounded by a large number of isolated satelite farms. However the Saxons exerted a strong cultural influence with their customs and language becoming dominant. The villages have Saxon names although the sites are often older.

By the beginning of the mediaeval period the villages on the limestone had become well established, practising mixed farming. They had large open fields which can still be traced from the relatively recent enclosure walls which follow the field strips; animals would have been pastured on the higher areas of open plateau. The settlements in the gritstone valleys were much smaller, mostly small hamlets and farms, with the exception of a few regional centres. They were predominantly based on sheep and cattle farming and no open fields developed.

A number of sites began to expand in Saxon or earlier times and developed into market centres, chiefly Bakewell and

Wirksworth but also Hope, Tideswell, Youlgreave, Hartington, Matlock and Parwich. With the exception of Hope and Tideswell they are all at the junction of the limestone and gritstone where the two types of economy could exchange products, at points where there is also easy access to other centres along the main valleys. Hope is a similar type of settlement, but placed in the centre of the valley at the crossing of important routeways rather than at the exact geological junction. Tideswell only developed as an important centre in the late mediaeval period because of its central position in connection with the wool trade which flourished at this time and to a lesser extent because of lead mining.

In the mediaeval period two changes took place. Large expanses of the northern high open limestone plateau and moors to the west were made into a royal hunting park which inhibited expansion, except for centres for the foresters in charge of the park, such as Peak Forest and Chapel-en-le-Frith. Also monks from abbeys all over the country acquired land on the high bleaker areas of the limestone, establishing granges, sometimes on new sites, which concentrated on sheep farming, creating a boom in the woollen industry. This has had lasting effects on the farming of the region, resulting in much of the land today being used for pasture.

In the seventeenth and eighteenth century the lead mining industry reached its peak with hundreds of people employed, and many of the villages close to the richer veins expanded to accommodate the miners, notably Bradwell, Stoney Middleton, Eyam, Youlgreave, Winster and Brassington. Soon after this quarrying was expanded, and large quantities of Millstone Grit were removed in the eighteenth and nineteenth centuries above Hathersage for grindstones used in the cutlery industry of Sheffield. Another village to expand was Stanton where the gritstone was quarried for particularly fine building stone. This century limestone is being quarried in great quantities, particularly around Buxton. The eighteenth century also brought the rediscovery of thermal springs at Buxton and Matlock. They quickly expanded from villages to the large towns they are today, and although the spas are no longer popular, their populations have found alternative employment in quarrying and tourism which are two of the main industries of the whole region today.

Due to the drastic improvements in communications this

century many of the villages on the gritstone closest to Sheffield have expanded with many houses built for commuters in Bamford, Hathersage, Grindleford and Baslow. This breaks the tradition of local natural resources governing settlement and is a worrying sign of the times where true harmony with surroundings is ignored. Fortunately the National Park authorities have now stemmed the flood to a large extent, controlling the types of building allowed, and their appearance.

THE STONE CIRCLES

The sites of the Peak District are of two basic types which differ in their size and construction. These are the larger henges and the smaller stone circles.

Henge is a name adopted by archaeologists from the most famous of this type of site, Stonehenge, and is used to describe a variety of large ring structures of the Neolithic and early Bronze Age. Stonehenge, however, is not a typical henge which usually consists of just a bank with an internal ditch. These are broken by entrances, the earliest type having one, and the later two, which are usually diametrically opposite. They were probably built as tribal centres where many communal activities took place including meetings for secular and religious purposes. Sometimes they contained wooded huts built for ceremonial rites which have been found by excavation. These henges are found throughout eastern and southern England, predominantly in relatively low sheltered locations and usually on main trade routes.

When the tribes of the east were building these henges, those in the west of Britain were building equivalent communal structures but out of stone, usually in the form of large open rings of tall standing stones such as the one at Castle Rigg in the Lake District. One of the main reasons for this difference is that in the east there is very little good hard stone and it is easy to dig deep ditches, while in the west the situation is reversed. However indications are that the difference is greater than this, with the western circles favouring a cult connected with astronomy while the henges in the east have locations which are unsuitable for this. Here the cults probably emphasised the earth and fertility. It is not clear how much should be read into this, as recent study of stone circles shows that both cultures

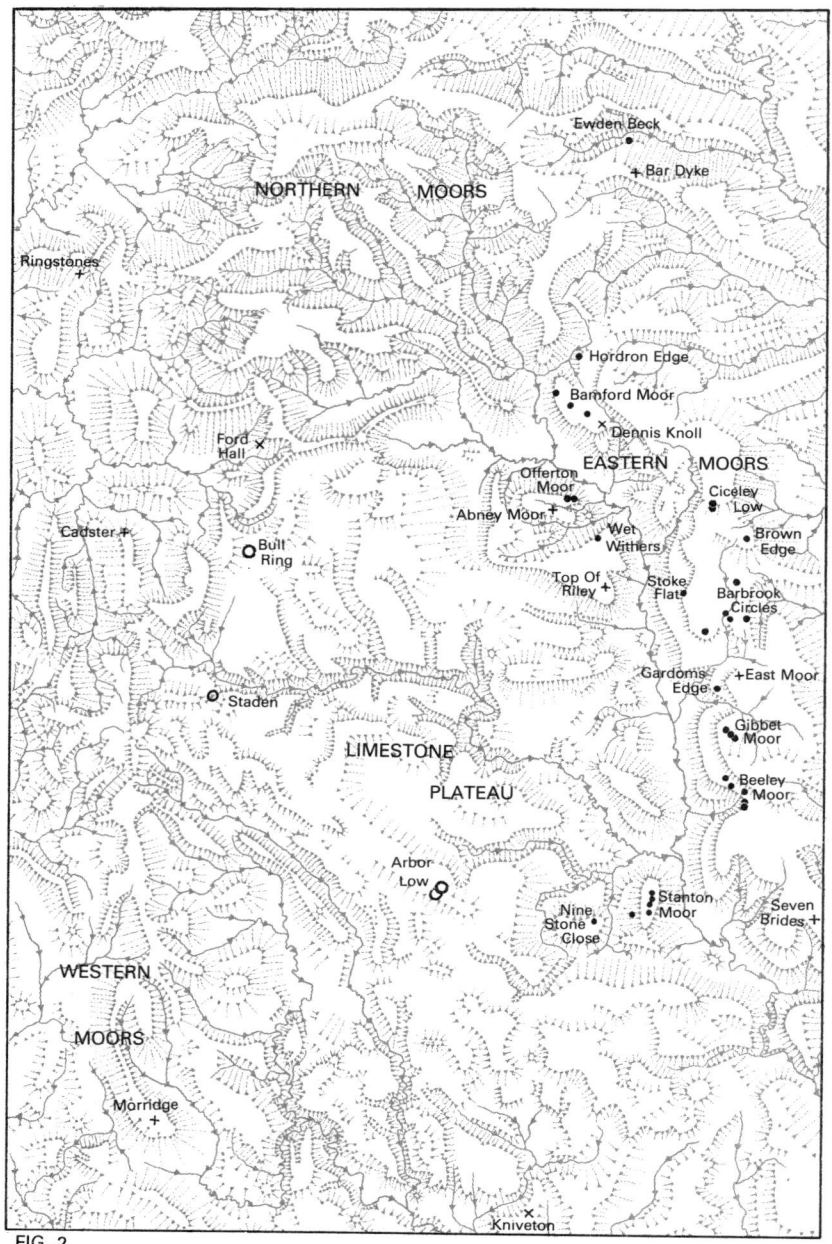

FIG. 2

The Peak District

were to some degree concerned with the veneration of all natural phenomena around them.

Running up the centre of Britain are a number of henges which are obviously a fusion of the two cultures with elements from both, having the bank and ditch from the east surrounding a ring of upright stones or timber posts from the west. This interesting group of circle henges includes some of the most impressive and complex constructions of prehistoric man in Britain such as Stonehenge and Avebury which is one of the largest sacred areas in the world. The henges at Arbor Low and the Bull Ring in Derbyshire are part of this group.

In their original states they were probably very similar with impressive banks and ditches of nearly 300 feet total diameter and rings of standing stones in the central area. Today however the stones of Arbor Low have fallen and those at the Bull Ring were removed over two hundred years ago. They both have two entrances, which shows they were built in the late Neolithic or Beaker period and their size and locations show they were communal centres of some importance. Both are on the main trade route from Ireland and the Lake District to the rich region of Wessex with Avebury at its centre.

The Bull Ring is in a typical location for a henge in a sheltered spot at just over 1000 feet above sea level and is at the head of the main pass through the western moors to the wooded ridges leading to the coast and Ireland. This site probably served as a centre for all the people in the half of the limestone plateau north of the river Wye.

Arbor Low is within an easy day's journey (12 miles) from the Bull Ring, south along the high ridges which avoid the limestone gorges. This henge probably served the population of the plateau in its southern half. It is more impressive than its counterpart, which possibly reflects a larger population in this area, living in the more fertile areas of land around here. It is located in an unusual position for a henge, being on the top of an exposed ridge at 1230 feet above sea level, the highest henge in Britain. There are many likely reasons for this. It is on the ridgeway trade route at a position that was central for its population, if the division at the river Wye is correct. It is also connected to a Neolithic mound, Gib Hill, and the excellent astronomical alignments from this spot made this exact exposed position desirable. From Arbor Low the trade route continued southwards past the southern limit of the limestone, then crossed the thick forests of the Vale of Trent before reaching the upland ridgeways leading to southern England.

There are two other henge sites. A few hundred yards from Arbor Low is a second, smaller site that is very badly damaged. It is probably a henge which may never have been completed. It is not clear why this was replaced by the larger one although it is possible that it was too small, or that a better design was adopted. The main site was a masterpiece of planning that would have taken a long time to perfect, as is shown in the description of this site.

Four miles south of the Bull Ring there is a probable henge at Staden. This is a slightly smaller site than the other two with very low banks and ditches in a sheltered hollow on the plateau. It needs to be excavated before anything definite can be said, but it looks as if it could be an earlier site than the others, possibly with only one entrance and no stones. If so, this site was probably the original meeting place of the Peak District, as it is also on the main trackway near the head of the Wye which divides the plateau in half. Only later was the area divided in two, possibly with the coming of the Beaker people and perhaps this site was abandoned as it was not well placed for the study of astronomy which was developing in the late Neolithic period.

The second type of site in the Peak District is the smaller embanked circle. A typical circle consists of a ring of standing stones each about 2 to 3 feet high, set at the internal edge of a retained rubble bank which is between 6 and 10 feet wide, sometimes broken with one or two entrances. The diameter of these circles varies between 15 and 100 feet at the internal edge of the bank. Today they are often badly preserved, the standing stones are fallen, or even removed in some cases, and it is often difficult to determine the original number. In well preserved sites it varies from 6 to 26 depending on the diameter of the ring. Often there are few signs of stones, as they have become buried. This was the case at the Barbrook II circle which, on excavation, was found to have a complete ring of stones. No excavations have revealed sites in this area originally without standing stones but it is probable that some exist. A midway stage has been discovered at the Brown Edge circle which was found to have only two standing stones. Surrounding some of the circles are outlying standing stones which are from 50 to a 1000 feet away. However, problems often exist identifying them in a landscape which is frequently scattered with many natural stones and only when these stones can be proved to have important astronomical alignments are they included.

Some of the circles have small burial mounds in their flat centres which has led some archaeologists to regard them as nothing more than a complex form of burial mound. However, as I show later, the circles obviously are sacred sites, used for ritual and observation, and there are many indications that these burial mounds are secondary features, perhaps placed here because of a wish to be buried in a sacred spot, as is the custom in many cultures. Four thousand years from now, a visitor to Westminster Abbey might conclude that its principal use had been for burials.

Variations from the typical construction do exist and notable ones are Nine Stone Close, which is the only circle with significantly larger standing stones. These are seven feet high and free-standing, without a bank. The only other stone of similar size in the area is the Old Woman's Stone which is an outlier of the Bamford Moor Southern Circle. This is now fallen.[1]* Two other sites possibly have free-standing stones as they have no banks today. These are the Hordron Edge and Doll Tor circles. The second main type of variant is seen in two more complex sites, the Stoke Flat and Ewden Beck circles, which have standing stones on both edges of the bank. Other circles on Stanton Moor appear to be simpler forms of this type.

The circles that remain are nearly all spread along the eastern moors, on the flat tops and large shelves of the still unenclosed open moorland, flanking the river Derwent. Between 31 and 33 circles survive and at least 5 more are known to have been destroyed in the last 200 years. They are on relatively flat land generally between 900 and 1100 feet above sea level with good views to distant horizons. The flat shelves below this level were probably too densely wooded and have no circles. At the one exception, Nine Stone Close which is at 750 feet, the large trees nearby probably explain why it has large stones. The more northerly sites such as those on Bamford Moor are slightly higher than the rest at 1200 to 1350 feet above sea level. However, this difference only reflects the height of suitable flat land in this area.

On the higher moors north of the limestone plateau all the flat

---

* These numbers refer to notes which start on page 198.

areas of land are covered in peat, and together with the lack of wide valleys, this made these areas unsuitable for settled communities, resulting in an absence of circles. There is evidence, however, that the wooded valleys and ridges at either side of the area had a small population, and a few isolated circles exist there. In the east the Ewden Beck circle, and another nearby whose location is now lost, can be seen as a northerly spread from the main eastern group. In the west nothing survives, but a farm called Ringstones could indicate a similar isolated community with a circle, evidence for which is also provided by nearby prehistoric cairns.

On the western moors there is evidence of circles, with a definite example on the Morridge which has now been destroyed and two dubious ones at Ford Hall and Cadster. The flat tops of these moors are higher than those in the east and often peat-covered, making the area far from ideal for habitation, with only relatively small suitable shelves and ridges. The population here was therefore probably much smaller with only a few circles, but this is uncertain because much of the land has been enclosed and sites may have been destroyed. Small circles make ideal quarries!

The main centre of population throughout the prehistoric period was the limestone plateau. This has no small circles and it is not clear if it ever had. It could easily have done so because the area has been subjected to large scale agricultural activity for many centuries, and most of the land is enclosed, so that it is to be expected that much will have been destroyed. On the other hand there are pointers which suggest that they never existed: one would expect traces of at least one to have survived; the rolling landscape of the limestone area is not as suitable for the study of astronomy; and the difference between henges and circles discussed below could indicate that only henges would be built in this area.

All these circles have always been ascribed to the mid Bronze Age, corresponding with the large scale spread into the gritstone areas at this time. This is probably true in the majority of cases but there are no good reasons why some of them could not be earlier and be contemporary with the Beaker period henges on the limestone. Archaeologists have placed them in the mid Bronze Age for two main reasons, but doubt can be cast on both.

The first is that of radio-carbon dating, which although

relatively accurate, in the case of stone circles is usually based on remains from the central burials—often the only source of datable material. As I have already mentioned, however, these burials are secondary features and not necessarily contemporary with the circles, which makes this method tenuous to say the least.

The second argument is that these stone circles are of a different construction to henges, and therefore cannot be contemporary or from the same culture. When this is examined however, the apparent differences between the two types of site are not as great as they first appear. The type of embanked circle common in this area is typical of the whole of the Pennines, where they occur more frequently than elsewhere. The common form of small circles in western Britain is different with most of them being free standing. The regions with embanked circles are those where the fusion between the large circle and henge cultures was taking place, and these small sites can be seen as part of the same tradition. The difference between the henges and small circles can be explained by geological factors: the gritstone is a very hard rock and it would have been virtually impossible to dig large ditches to construct a henge; the nearest thing possible to this must be something close to the actual design of the circles.

The difference in size is also not as great as it seems for the ring of stones at Arbor Low is 140 x 120 feet, while that of Wet Withers on the gritstone is only slightly smaller, (101 x 98 feet). Another factor showing that they are of the same tradition is that of their astronomical alignments and geometry, discussed in the next chapter. These reveal no differences in the preoccupations and methods of the builders.

The main difference between the two types of site is that the henges appear more impressive than the circles and different factors point to reasons for this. It is not clear why so many circles were built in such a small area on the eastern moors. There are obviously too many to serve as just religious meeting places for the population, as less than half this number would have sufficed.

It is possible that they were not all in use at one time, some becoming obsolete and being replaced by others. This is probably true in some instances, but this reason is not valid as a complete answer and others must be sought. Another possibility is that individual sites were used at different times of the year, but the general evidence in this area does not support this.

The most likely theory that can be put forward is that many of these circles were not for the use of the general population, but for the priesthood, where they could carry out complicated observations of natural phenomena and also perform secret rituals. They were however, probably multi-purpose monuments with the local populations also using some of them. The sites are distributed irregularly across the eastern moors—some on their own, and others grouped closely together. Where the circles are grouped in complexes with many associated burial mounds, there could be a case put forward for communal worship and perhaps focal points of separate tribal units who built them because they found it was too far to travel to the henge centres further west. These centres are Stanton Moor, Beeley Moor, The Barbrook Valley, Eyam/Offerton Moors, Bamford Moor and Ewden Beck.

Although the limestone plateau remained the centre of population through the Bronze Age, perhaps no small circles were built here because the henges were close enough for communal worship while the priests were prepared to travel the longer distances to the west for their study, as the landscape was more suitable.

3

Research and Interpretation of the Circles

Due to the revolution in thought primarily instigated by Professor Thom, we are coming for the first time close to an understanding of many important aspects of stone circles. Thom's great breakthrough has laid the foundations for further research in many directions connected with geometry, measurement and astronomy. My own work in the Peak District convinced me that his theories were basically sound, but it became apparent that many of the aspects of study can be advanced further than Thom has taken them.

In order to prove to the archaeological world that circles were sophisticated monuments, Thom had to be scientifically exact and prove his theories statistically, never letting unprovable data enter the argument. This approach unfortunately has made his work rather inaccessible to the layman and presented a somewhat disjointed impression of the many facets of stone circles he investigated. My modifications to his theories link together the different aspects of circles in an attempt to create a more unified picture. In some cases the links cannot be statistically proved because of the present lack of confirming evidence from other regions, though they are always kept within the realms of probability. All the field work was undertaken with a high degree of accuracy (usually using the same techniques as Thom). It is therefore possible to say 'these things happen', though their importance to the builders is sometimes open to question.

Thom showed that Bronze Age man was capable of complex projects and was interested in mathematics and astronomy, whilst my work points to at least some of the reasons why the builders had these interests and presents an overall picture of man at that time trying to live in harmony with his environment. Preoccupied with this, the circles were a conscious effort to express harmony in all its facets. Indications are that the sun, moon and earth were regarded as linked parts of 'the whole', and circles express the way in which they relate to each other. Evidence suggests that they believed these bodies emanated forces which created the harmony in the world around them and the circles were an attempt to bring these together, possibly to channel them to try to combat disharmony and hardship. They probably made no distinction between science and religion as there was no conflict between the two. There is evidence however that some of the functions and rites connected with the sites were secret known to an elite only, with a more simplified form of knowledge being passed on to the common people.[1]

The chasm which has existed for the last few years between the views of Thom and the traditional archaeological world is hopefully narrowed by the concepts proposed here; for the evidence of their simple way of life suggests a people trying to live in harmony with the world, perhaps striving for it, due to the hard conditions around them. This chapter lists below all the facets of the stone circle study undertaken in the Peak District. While it must be stressed that only the complete picture gives an insight into the circles, the different aspects are dealt with separately for convenience, including a simplified summary of Thom's findings as they are the basis of the others.

GEOMETRY AND MEASUREMENT

Professor Thoms research establishes three principal points:
1) Stone circles have sophisticated geometric designs which are carefully constructed to obtain the maximum accuracy possible with the methods available to prehistoric man. The shapes he found fall into the following basic groups: true circles, ellipses, circles flattened on one side, circles elongated on one side (egg shaped) and a few more complex forms only detectable in large well-preserved sites. All these are easy to build using only

Research and Interpretation

stakes and a rope to draw the arcs. The modifications from a true circle are based on a few standardised constructions, and usually have right-angled triangles placed in the centre with the points used as centres for the arcs. All the basic variations exist among the Derbyshire circles. Referring to their descriptions later in this book will clarify the principles on which the geometries are based.

2) After establishing the geometry of a large number of circles he was able by statistical analysis to determine a unit of length used for building the sites, which appears to have been standard throughout Britain. This is 2.72 feet, now generally called the megalithic yard (MY). For long distances and also many circumferences he also found evidence for a larger unit which is 2.5 MY (6.8 feet) called the megalithic rod (MR).

3) Once the dimensions of the geometries can be given numbers, it becomes apparent that they usually have integral (whole numbered) diameters and circumferences, which is obviously significant. Thom came to the conclusion that this was the main reason for conceiving geometries which deviate from true circles, as these are difficult to keep integral because of the irrational number π which relates the diameter to the circumference. π is an approximation to $\frac{22}{7}$ which means that only circles with a diameter of 7 or a multiple of this will have whole numbered circumferences. The numbers also show that the central triangles have whole numbers and are therefore pythagorean, the commonest is the simple 3, 4, 5 triangle.

There have been developments of Thom's basic theories, some suggested by him or other researchers but not investigated thoroughly.

4) It always seemed illogical to me that when the geometry was constructed with such care, the stones did not appear to have any kind of symmetrical arrangement. An investigation of this problem showed that the geometries as formulated by Thom were not complete, which lead to the most significant development. Thom's geometries are enough to define the ring, but do not satisfactorily explain why the deviation from a true circle was made. If it was only to overcome the problems of π then multiples of seven would have been usable without too many problems. It turns out that nearly always there has been a last stage missed from the construction which is the most

important in the geometry, the earlier stages being just a means to this end. This last stage is always a simple geometric shape such as a pentagon or hexagon drawn inside the ring, transforming the geometry from being complex for no convincing reason to an expression of simple harmony. These shapes could have been placed inside true circles, but it would have been impossible to create integral numbers in this way.

The modified circles are probably the best solutions the builders could find, combining simple shapes and integral measurements, and the main reason for deviation. The only compromise which had to be accepted is a slight flattening or elongation of the shape which on site is hardly noticeable. Many of the different types of construction are probably conclusions from a continual search for an ideal solution to particular requirements. In the Peak District the following shapes have been found:

True circles—square: e.g. The Stoke Flat circle

Ellipses—a confusing group which appears to have four, six or eight-sided figures but these are rather tenuous e.g. The Offerton Moor Western circle

Flattened circles—'type A': always a hexagon
'type B': always a pentagon: e.g. The Barbrook I circle
'type D': always a twelve-sided figure: e.g. The Bamford Moor Northern circle
others: hexagon: e.g. The Barbrook II circle
(note that the 'types' are Professor Thom's classification).

Eggs—no good examples of simple eggs are found in the Peak (the only site worth looking at in this context is Arbor Low which appears to be a hexagon). I have found that some of the circles are more complex types of eggs enclosing hexagons and pentagons: e.g. hexagon: Wet Withers; pentagon: the central Beeley Moor circle.

Complex circles—two unique sites exist which are the central and southern circles on Stanton Moor both of which create triangles.

5) Several new geometries which differ from Thom's standard constructions have been found; these are all egg-shaped except for the Barbrook II circle which is a peculiar type of flattened circle.[2] All Thom's eggs have a first arc of 180° or more (see the

Bamford Moor southern circle), whereas the new types have arcs of less than this because different points in the internal triangles are used to draw the arcs. This is well illustrated at Nine Ladies. This new type of construction is found at Nine Ladies, the Beeley Moor central circle and probably the Staden Henge and the Ciceley Low main circle, (another modified type of egg is found at Wet Withers). These eggs have much in common with the two unique complex constructions in the area, the Stanton Moor central and southern circles which are more extreme forms of the eggs. The only circle with similarities to these is one found by Thom at Kerry Pole in Powys[3] which can be compared with the central circle.

6) When the simple shapes in the geometry are related to the stones, it shows that they form logical patterns. These take the form of a series of balances round the axis of the geometry which divides the circle into two identical halves. The balances are of two types—stone against stone—and stone against a point midway between stones. These are often combined in circles with the changes from one to the other being made at the points of the simple shapes (e.g. Barbrook I circle). Unfortunately there are very few circles in Derbyshire with intact rings of standing stones, but study of others throughout Britain confirms the theory. Two complete circles in the Peak, Nine Ladies and the Barbrook II circle, have one or two stones which spoil the absolute symmetry of the arrangement. This indicates that other considerations, perhaps connected with alignments, sometimes compromised the pattern.

7) One thing that always intrigued me was, how did the builders find the geometric centre once a circle was built, and why was it not marked with a standing stone as this would have been necessary for using the site for accurate alignments? The answer to this is that four or more stones in the ring are always arranged so that if one knew the correct points to use, then by holding two taut ropes across the central area from these, they would intersect at the exact centre. The use of this method rather than a direct marker implies that there was an element of secrecy involved in the use of circles.

8) There is strong evidence for a unit of measure of ¼MY (8.16 inches) Which unfortunately is too small to be statistically proved. It often creates measurements which are numerically more satisfactory than 1 MY and also makes sense of the megalithic

rod which as 2.5 MY seems an unlikely multiple to use but as 10 × ¼ MY is very convincing. The analysis of Bronze Age cup-and-ring carvings by Thom also confirms this, as he concluded a unit of 0.816 inches. The basic measurement of ¼ MY was therefore probably the stone circle builders 'one' and possibly it had its origins in the human body as 8.16 inches is close to many people's handspan.

9) Thom's third point about integral numbers can be expanded to say that the builders tried to make intregral as many numbers in the geometric construction as possible. The diameters, simple shapes and internal triangles were especially important, and the last to be compromised. Indications are that the builders' geometry was a purely practical science and their solutions were arrived at by drawing rather than calculation. The result of this is that they would be unaware of small errors that can be found by trigonometry, regarding their constructions as perfect.

The simple shapes were probably considered to be numerically important—for example: square = 4, pentagon = 5, etc. These numbers relate to the overall length of their sides, which is often a multiple of the sides of the shape. The number of stones also relates to this when the balance points are included from the sections of opposite balance, although there is not enough evidence as yet to indicate any general tendencies, and various arrangements have been found (e.g. the Barbrook I and II circles).

10) When looking at the geometry and numbers in all the sites it becomes apparent that the builders had an obsession with the basic numbers 1 to 10, and that the chief aim when determining the shape and size of a circle was to combine as many of these as possible in an integral whole. The way in which this was done has many variations, but one common factor is that the geometry's simple shape is of prime importance and the measurements are to complement it. This use of number implies a concern with building a structure that was a symbolic expression of harmony and integration, a theme running throughout the many aspects of stone circles. The constant use of numbers in similar ways indicates that they had some meaning for the builders, and an examination of number symbolism gives great insight into this. This is a complex subject about which a great deal has been written—mostly with one bias or another.

There are, however, basic threads running through writings

on the subject, which indicate certain universal deep relationships applying to all cultures. These therefore would have been just as applicable to the stone circle builders as to us today and they throw new light on their beliefs. The arrangement of the geometries so that they emphasise 4, 5, 6 and 7 is especially significant, and the relationships with the landscape, sun and moon fits perfectly with the concepts revealed by this approach to numbers. The detailed interpretation within each number is rather tenuous, but looked at as a whole, a picture emerges which approaches the way in which the builders' minds were working. The analysis of numbers given in appendix B should be used as a guide to an intuitive understanding of each number rather than known truth.

11) When the use of numbers is realised, it becomes apparent that for some geometric solutions there were problems building a circle of practical size as the unit of ¼MY was too small and the megalithic rod too large. In some cases circles were apparently conceived in units of 4 (the megalithic yard) and also possibly 2 and 5; this overcame the problem. It also explains why Thom's statistical analysis revealed the megalithic yard.

To summarise the geometry, it indicates that stone circles are carefully constructed monuments that are primarily concerned with combining a circle of stones with a hidden simple shape such as a pentagon or hexagon, in such a way that all the other aspects of the design complement this shape, fitting together to form a 'temple' of symbolic harmony. It is interesting to note that the pentagon and other shapes found in circles are used throughout western cults concerned with magic. These cults are basically remnants of pre-Christian religion, which could indicate that the execution of some kind of magical rites was an important function of the circles. Today these cults emphasise secrecy and initiation, and the hidden elements of stone circle design indicate that this was also the case here.

ASTRONOMY

Professor Thom proved that stone circles often align to the sun and moon. Before discussing these alignments, it is necessary to explain the movements of the sun and moon as they have passed out of common knowledge today now we are no longer so reliant on the elements. The scientific explanation is described in detail by Thom, but in the context of the world of prehistoric man it is important to understand the apparent motions of these bodies as observed in these latitudes.

The movement of the sun is relatively simple with its cycle of one year. At the midpoints of the year (the equinoxes) it rises in the east and sets in the west, with twelve hours' daylight. After the spring equinox it rises and sets further north every day and the hours of daylight get longer, until it reaches its maximum at the summer solstice (midsummer's day) where it rises in the north-east and sets in the north-west with about sixteen hours of daylight. After this day the sun moves south along the horizon to the autumn equinox and on to the minimum position, the other solstice (midwinter's day) where it rises in the south-east and sets in the south-west with only eight hours of daylight. From here the cycle is completed with a return northwards to the spring equinox. The daily movement along the horizon varies from a maximum at the equinoxes where it changes $0.7°$ per day, to a minimum at the solstices where for a few days the movement is so small that it is undetectable with the naked eye. This is called the 'standstill' and is only $0.003°$ per day. The standstill must initially have created problems when trying to determine an exact solstice, but it is easily solved by taking a nearby point marking the horizon, counting the number of days between each successive rising or setting of the sun and then dividing the total in half. The fact that a year is only approximately 365 days must have created confusion, and counting methods must have needed periodic adjustment by rechecking observations.

The moon is much more complex in its movements with three cycles all working at once:
a) The basic cycle is its revolution round the earth, taking nearly 27 days 8 hours, the lunar month. At midwinter the new moon rises in the south-east and sets in the south-west. Every day it rises and sets further north along the horizon; at half moon it rises in the east and sets in the west and at full moon it rises in the north-east and sets in the north-west. After the full moon it moves south again until the cycle is complete. This swing up and down the horizon every month gradually changes through the year until at midsummer the situation is reversed with the new moon rising in the north-east and the full moon in the south-east. This is caused by the movement of the sun because a

full moon is the result of it being diametrically opposite the sun. Therefore as the sun swings from winter to summer, the apparent shape of the moon for any one position in the sky also changes.

b) Imposed on this cycle is another which takes 18.6 years. From observations this would have been easily detectable at the solstices. On midwinter's day the full moon at the minimum point of this cycle (the minor standstill) would rise and set somewhat south of north-east and north-west. The next year on the same day the moon would rise and set further north than before. This continues every year until 9 years later at the maximum of the cycle (the major standstill) when the rising and setting points will have changed by 10°-15° and the moon is in the sky for 2¼ hours longer. After the major standstill the moon goes south again to complete the cycle. At midsummer this cycle would also be detectable and here it is visually reversed, the moon at the minor standstill being further north on the horizon than at the major standstill. The situation described above is made more complicated because the cycles of the sun and moon are not in phase and the full moon often misses the solstice by a few days.

c) The third cycle would only be detectable at the major standstill as a slight change of rising or setting position of only about 4 minutes of an arc. This needed very careful observation and could only be made at the same position on the horizon once every 18 or 19 years (changing because the actual cycle is 18.6 years).

One of the major events in the sky is an eclipse, the prediction of which appears to have been one of the astronomical preoccupations of the stone circle builders. This would have been difficult, and was only possible with precise observation. To predict these the builders would have to find the date of the major standstill and also detect the 9 minute wobble which has a cycle of 173.3 days. Only when this is at its maximum are eclipses possible. If the full moon is observed at the major standstill with the 9 minute cycle at its maximum, then an eclipse is imminent within a danger period of 3 weeks. If 173 days (174 days every fourth period) are counted from this observed point, then another eclipse will occur. If this is at the time of a full moon then it will be eclipsed; if a new moon, the sun will be eclipsed, although this is not always visible at these latitudes. This counting method would need adjustment periodically by reobservation which was only possible once every 18 or 19 years. There are complex problems with this method of observation and the above is a simplification; anyone wishing to know more should refer to Thom's book *Megalithic Lunar Observatories*.

To study the phenomena described above, differing degrees of accuracy were needed. Both the sun and moon when rising or setting usually define a little less than 1° of horizon. To mark this general direction at a particular day of the year, the following applies: a stone set endways to a site (say 1 foot wide) would need to be over 120 feet away to define half a degree; or if set facing the site (say 3 feet wide) it would need to be 350 feet away to define the same arc. This is perhaps the minimum degree of accuracy that would be required for accurate observations. For more precise work, especially connected with the moon and the prediction of eclipses, an arc of less than 1 minute needs to be defined, which would require a stone about 5000 feet away, and none have yet been found in the Peak District at this distance. An alternative was the use of distant horizons which have defined features marking the necessary small arcs. This obviously involves a very careful choice of site so that the required directions are correctly defined by natural features.

It must be noted that since the time circles were built, the tilt of the earth's axis has changed slightly, and alignments are thrown out by approximately one width of the sun. This makes direct accurate observation of stone circle alignments impossible today, and all work has to be done by calculation of the positions of the sun and moon in prehistoric times. This change however is not so drastic that it makes visits to circles on the correct days pointless. With a little imagination, the correction to the original position can be made, and a powerful atmosphere still lingers at such times.

Professor Thom's four main observations on astronomy are:
1) The stone circle builders were concerned with the study of the sun, moon and possibly first magnitude stars. This was carried out by the use of outlying stones placed near circles which were in the required direction from the circle centre. When more precise lines were needed, the builders used the outliers to mark the direction of prominent horizon features which gave the required accuracy. Thom noted that the observation of the planets was also a possibility but, because they have very

variable cycles, almost any position on the horizon would mark one planet at some time or another, and therfore their study is now not possible.

2) The main reason for the study of the sun proposed by Thom is that of establishing a calendar. This was found to have 16 months based on the solstices, equinoxes and sub-divisions between these, arranged so that each month lasts for between 22 and 24 days. This calendar was marked on the horizon to show the rising and setting positions at these divisions. This required a minimum of 9 markers (not necessarily all at one circle) each serving two points, one in the spring half of the year and one in the autumn half (except the solstice with only one point).

3) The study of the moon was undertaken to try to understand its complex motions, and perhaps more importantly to predict eclipses. Thom has proved that this problem was solved in specially designed sites in Scotland. Once the method for prediction was established, it was possible to mark horizon lines to the major standstill which were accurate enough to observe the eclipse wobble correctly.

4) Some of the stones are used as time indicators. Stones due south marked midday, and stones to the rising and setting points of first magnitude stars were used to tell the time at night. Work in Derbyshire does not support this theory as the star lines claimed by Thom have been found to have more convincing lines to the sun and moon using other outliers rather than the circle as backsights.

Developments and observations on Thom's work which have been studied are:—

5) The 16 month calendar proposed by Thom is probably correct, but it appears that 8 main divisions are more important, and those between them are secondary for timekeeping purposes only. The main divisions have interesting connections with the remnants that survive today of the festivals concerned with the natural cycle of rural communities. The names and dates given are Thom's:—

i) **Midwinter Solstice** (21st December)
Connected with fire rituals concerned with the renewal of the sun, to ensure its return the next year, transformed into Christmas.

ii) **Candlemas** (the end of the first week of February)
The Celtic festival Oimelc which celebrates the beginning of spring and the rebirth of nature.
iii) **Spring Equinox** (the end of the third week of March)
iv) **May Day** (the end of the first week of May)
The Celtic festival Beltaine. This is the beginning of summer and the time of the planting of the main crops. This May Day festival has many surviving relics and has been christianised as Rogation. It is also the time of Walpurgis night.
v) **Midsummer Solstice** (21st June)
The longest day of the year and a solar festival celebrated with fires.
vi) **Lammas** (the end of the first week of August)
The Celtic festival Lugnasadh. This is the beginning of the harvest and a great period of celebration.
vii) **Autumn Equinox** (the end of the third week in September)
viii) **Martinmas** (the end of the first week in November)
The Celtic festival Samhain. A fire festival at the beginning of winter to ward off the hardships of the coming season. Also the time of Halloween.

6) To prove that stone circles were connected with the sun and moon, Thom had to limit his analysis to accurately defined astronomical lines marked with outliers. Now that the connection is proved, many other lines can be considered. One important type is 'symbolic alignments' which align through the standing stones and along the axes of the circles themselves. These probably had ritual significance as the stones always define an arc larger than that required for accurate pin-pointing of one particular day. However, they are shown to be important as their centre or point is directly in line with the position for the required day. When stones mark an axis, they often reveal a slight compromise made by the builders, the astronomical line being offset from the axis, but remaining well within the stone. Other stones show a slight offsetting from their position of balance, so that they are exactly in line with an astronomical position.

This type of alignment is obviously significant, but conclusions on how these are arranged are more difficult because only twelve circles in the Peak District have enough stones surviving, with clear horizons, to enable a complete study to be made. With the present evidence it can be seen that several types of arrangement exist, which possibly indicate different

Research and Interpretation

functions or dates for individual sites.

a) The main axis of the geometry is often orientated to the most important alignment of the circle, usually in the direction of the distortion from the true circle, as at Arbor Low, the Stoke Flat, Barbrook I and Wet Withers circles. At the Barbrook II and Bamford Moor south circles the opposite direction was used.

b) In a few cases the site has been carefully chosen in relation to the relative height of the horizon, so that a right angle is formed between two connected alignments on which the axes are based. This is the case with the midwinter sun at the Barbrook I circle and midsummer sun related to the midwinter moon at Wet Withers. At Arbor Low all four directions of the axes align to the sun at the solstices. This was made possible by the high bank and stones forming intersections with the sun.

c) Most circles incorporate significant alignments to both the sun and moon. The only definite exception to this is the Barbrook I circle which is solar only.

d) In many circles there appears to be a significant difference between the way the solar and lunar alignments are marked, with the standing stones marking sun lines, while the moon lines are hidden, marked by the geometry or horizon only. This is the case at the Stoke Flat, Barbrook II and Nine Stone Close circles. At the Barbrook I circle stones mark solar lines but there are no moon lines. At Arbor Low the situation is more complicated with the solar lines marked with the geometry and stones while the lunar lines are marked by the entrances and stones.

e) Some circles have sites which are chosen so that the horizon and standing stones mark a solar calendar with all of the main rising or setting positions for the year included. The only circle with rising lines is Nine Stone Close, setting lines are marked at the Stoke Flat, Park Gate and Bamford Moor North circles.

7) Other significant alignments resulting from the points mentioned at the beginning of group 6 are those to horizons not marked with outliers. If a prominent feature of the horizon defines a celestial alignment accurately, there is no need to mark the direction, as the knowledge of its existence and use could be passed down from generation to generation. With this group of alignments problems arise in deciding which lines are significant and which coincidence. Three guides have been adopted. Firstly, lines which are marked with symbolic alignments in the circle formed by standing stones or the geometry. Secondly, lines which go to particularly prominent features in the landscape

which dominate the skyline. Lastly, lines which are the missing link in a group of alignments obviously being studied at a particular circle.

8) Occasionally circles occupy the exact horizon position of the setting sun or moon in circumstances which are not coincidence. From the Stoke Flat, Barbrook I and probably the Ciceley Low circles, the main alignment is to Arbor Low. This indicates that the sites of the circles were carefully chosen for their relation to the main sacred monument of the region. These circles could be connected with rituals to rejuvenate the setting sun or moon, which apparently disappear into the henge from the circles. Other alignments of this kind are found from Wet Withers to the Offerton Moor circles, and possibly from Arbor Low to the Staden henge, although these two sites are not intervisible.

9) Only two circles in the Peak District have collections of outliers—the Barbrook I and Bamford Moor South circles. A careful study shows that these outliers are there not only to mark directions from the circle, but also more often between each other. In both circles they are arranged so they mark the complete range of sun and moon lines for the year, at rising, setting or both. The way they are arranged shows that the main use of outliers is for accurate study, possibly for a calendar. This contrasts with the two circles themselves which have alignments indicating a ritual use at a particular time of year.

RELATIONSHIPS TO THE LANDSCAPE

Evidence is now coming to light which indicates that the stone circle builders not only used the landscape around them for astronomical foresights, but had an interest in its intrinsic nature. The way in which the circles' geometry and stones often align with landscape features without celestial alignments, gives clues to the form of this interest. Comparison with astronomical alignments shows that similar arrangements were often used, and a combination of alignment with appropriate landscape features was probably even more desirable. The general impression gained from a prolonged study of this aspect of stone circles is that the builders believed in underlying patterns and forces governing the landscape, which they then tried to integrate into their circles by careful positioning. The visible shape of the land was thus harmonious from the spot they had chosen, especially in the direction of places they regarded as significant. This theory is difficult to prove as it is often impossible to separate the landscape from its relationship to astronomy. It is undoubtedly the most logical answer to many alignments. The following list shows the different expressions of their concern with landscape:

1) Circles are very rarely placed on the top of hills where the maximum number of accurate celestial alignments can be achieved. They are placed on gentle slopes so that there is a combination of distant and close horizons. This is often about half of each, with junctions between the two orientated approximately north/south (e.g. Park Gate circle), or alternatively east/west (e.g. Wet Withers). These arrangements relate to the astronomy, with the former separating the rising and setting lines and the latter the winter and summer halves of the year. It is interesting to note that at Arbor Low a similar situation to this was artificially created by building the high bank which obscures some of the distant views.

In some circles the arrangement is more complex: at the Barbrook II circle there are only two small sections of distant horizon to the north and south, where there are two breaks in the ring of standing stones. To the east and west are two relatively close horizons which contain all the astronomical alignments. At the Hordron Edge circle there are three equally spaced dips in the horizon with high featureless moors between them, the standing stones forming three groups marking each of the dips with no stones in the direction of the moors. The most complex arrangement is at Nine Stone Close where short sections of near and far horizons alternate, each close horizon marked with a stone.

2) Individual features of the landscape are also used in similar ways in many circles. The centre of the visible far horizon often has a prominant feature, as at Arbor Low with Taddington Moor rising above the more distant hills. Another good example is at Wet Withers: looking above the large cairn next to the circle, the northern end of Stanage Edge is very distinctive. This is at the approximate centre of the far horizon and almost exactly marks true north. The choice of circle sites as an expression for concern for the visual harmony of landscape features is well illustrated at the Wet Withers and the Offerton Moor circles, all of which relate to Higgar Tor. This hill is flanked by equally spaced hills

rising above flat moors. Another example is the arrangement at Doll Tor circle, where rounded hills flank the direction of Nine Stone Close.

3) The shapes of standing stones often mirror that of the horizon behind them—flat stones to flat moors and pointed stones to hills. This is not always the case though, as pointed stones are also used to mark directions more exactly. A good example of a mirror image is the largest stone of the Hordron Edge circle with Win Hill behind it. A unique example is found on Offerton Moor, where from the western circle, the other mirrors the horizon perfectly.

4) Another important factor in the significance of the landscape is that certain places were obviously regarded as sacred, as shown by the fact that they are frequently marked. These include prominent pointed hills such as Win Hill and, perhaps of most significance, a number of unusual natural outcrops of rock (e.g. the Mother's Cap on Over Owler Tor above Hathersage and the Eagle Stone above Curbar). These freaks of nature are massive isolated blocks of stone, looking like larger versions of standing stones, and are formed by the removal of the surrounding rock by wind erosion. One of these stones, the Cork Stone on Stanton Moor, once had erected stones around it, confirming their importance to prehistoric man.

5) Another type of alignment is to other stone circles often marked with the geometry or stones. Some of these which relate to astronomy have already been mentioned above. Others exist, of which a good example is the Doll Tor circle, which has its main axis aligned to Nine Stone Close clearly visible across a valley. Many alignments also exist where the circles are not intervisible, and these are described in more detail in the section on macrocosmic geometry. These alignments add weight to the suggestion that the circles were seen as part of a network covering the landscape.

6) Many of the factors in alignments connected with astronomy, landscape and other circles show that the site of a stone circle was chosen with great care, so that all the desired requirements were achieved. There are often so many of these that it would seem to be a virtually impossible task to find a suitable spot in the landscape. This implies a great knowledge and understanding of their surroundings on the part of the circle builders. Even

then, by using trial and error, it would take years, although suggestions made in the next section may throw further light on these problems. The harmonious relationships at these spots probably led to them being regarded as sacred, for this alone as they are so rare.

MACROCOSMIC GEOMETRY

When the alignments between circles were investigated, they pointed to a new direction for study, namely geometric relationships between circles. A large number of these have been found, particularly isosceles and right-angled triangles. Preliminary work using only 20 circles revealed over 140 separate triangles, each one so accurate that errors could not be detected on a one-inch-to-the-mile map. When all these are placed together a jumble of lines covers the map, with no obvious overall pattern. This is to be expected, because if 20 points were selected at random a large number of triangles would form by coincidence.

At the moment this study is inconclusive and a more thorough search using a computer has been started by Eric Heaf, a fellow enthusiast on stone circles, who has devised a programme that can investigate all geometric relationships for any area of the country. The indications suggest that the number of triangles found will be more than would form by coincidence. If this proves to be the case, the problem is going to be to determine which of them are significant. Clues here are perhaps going to be reoccurring directions, lengths or angles in the triangles and alignments marked in the circles.

The triangles already examined are all on a large scale with sides of between 1 and 15 miles in length. These are measured along the horizontal, rather than following the contours of the land, and most of the circles are not intervisible. Obviously prehistoric man did not conceive and construct these, as it would have been beyond his resources to measure the lengths without maps of the same accuracy as the Ordnance Survey maps used for this study.

If these triangles are not coincidental and were not conceived by man, then the most likely conclusion is that they are a natural phenomenon. If so, they are probably a manifestation of the 'life force' suggested by intuitive writers, which has a subtle underlying effect on the landscape and on the well-being of its population. Many people have talked about this force, but as yet it remains elusive. Some of the triangles found in the area, illustrated later in the book, are so perfectly in harmony with their surroundings that they support this theory. If the patterns discovered here have a significant effect on their surroundings they could be of considerable importance and if the secrets of the geometry can be unravelled, it may be the first step to understanding how this 'life force' is manifest, if not what its effect is.

There are various other studies which have been carried out in recent years which may relate directly to these triangles. An important one is that of 'ley lines' of which this is probably a development. If individual lines in a triangle are examined they are often indentical to these. One problem which is common to both is that it is not known how wide the lines of force are, so it is impossible to determine the degree of accuracy to work to.

Perhaps the most revealing study is that of the ancient science of astrology. This is basically a belief that the celestial bodies and the earth emanate forces which constantly change their effect as their sources form different relationships to one another. Modern research is now proving that although the oversimplified newspaper type of 'star' column is nonsense, there is much truth in the principles behind astrology, and that a force does have a cyclic effect on people's character.

There are many indications that the stone circle builders probably believed in some form of astrological influence, explaining their obsession with harmony and their attempts to combine the geometry with the sun, moon and landscape. It is not clear to what extent the prehistoric builder was aware of the earth force manifest in the triangles, but since he placed stone circles at the intersections and apexes of these related lines, where one would expect a force to be at its strongest, he must at least have been able to detect the force.

There is corroborative evidence of the existence of this 'life force' in the traditions and practices of many so called 'primitive cultures' throughout the world. They detected it in a more intuitive way with techniques such as dowsing, which was probably used by the stone circle builders. They could detect the power centres but probably did not perceive the complete pattern, although the marked alignments show they had some knowledge of the direction of the lines of force.

4

Itineraries

Of the 40 circles surviving in different states of preservation in the Peak District, only about half are worth visiting by anyone except the specialist. These are described in detail in the next section of the book and include examples of every aspect of the theories expounded in the last chapter, as well as all the main variations in design in the area. This chapter is included to help the visitor find the circles and to suggest a logical order in which to visit them. The sites themselves are fully described in chapters 5 to 8. Many of the sites interrelate; when this is the case they are included in one tour.

The itineraries are primarily designed for the motorist but can be used by walkers with some modification. None, however, could be completed easily on foot in one day and so would have to be subdivided. Because the Peak District is surrounded by highly populated areas and people enter it from all directions, the tours have been made circular, so they can be joined at any point.

When visiting any of the circles it must be stressed that the country code should be strictly observed. Violations will result in access being restricted, even at the circles on open moorland where there is presently no problem. The visitor must remember that some of the circles are on private land and that paths to these are not public rights of way. Wherever this is the case details are given below and permission to visit the circle should be sought whenever possible.

In Derbyshire certain points should be given special care:
1) The moors in summer are often particularly dry. Fires start very easily and are very difficult to put out because of the underlying peat.
2) Avoid taking short cuts over drystone walls as they are old

FIG. 3

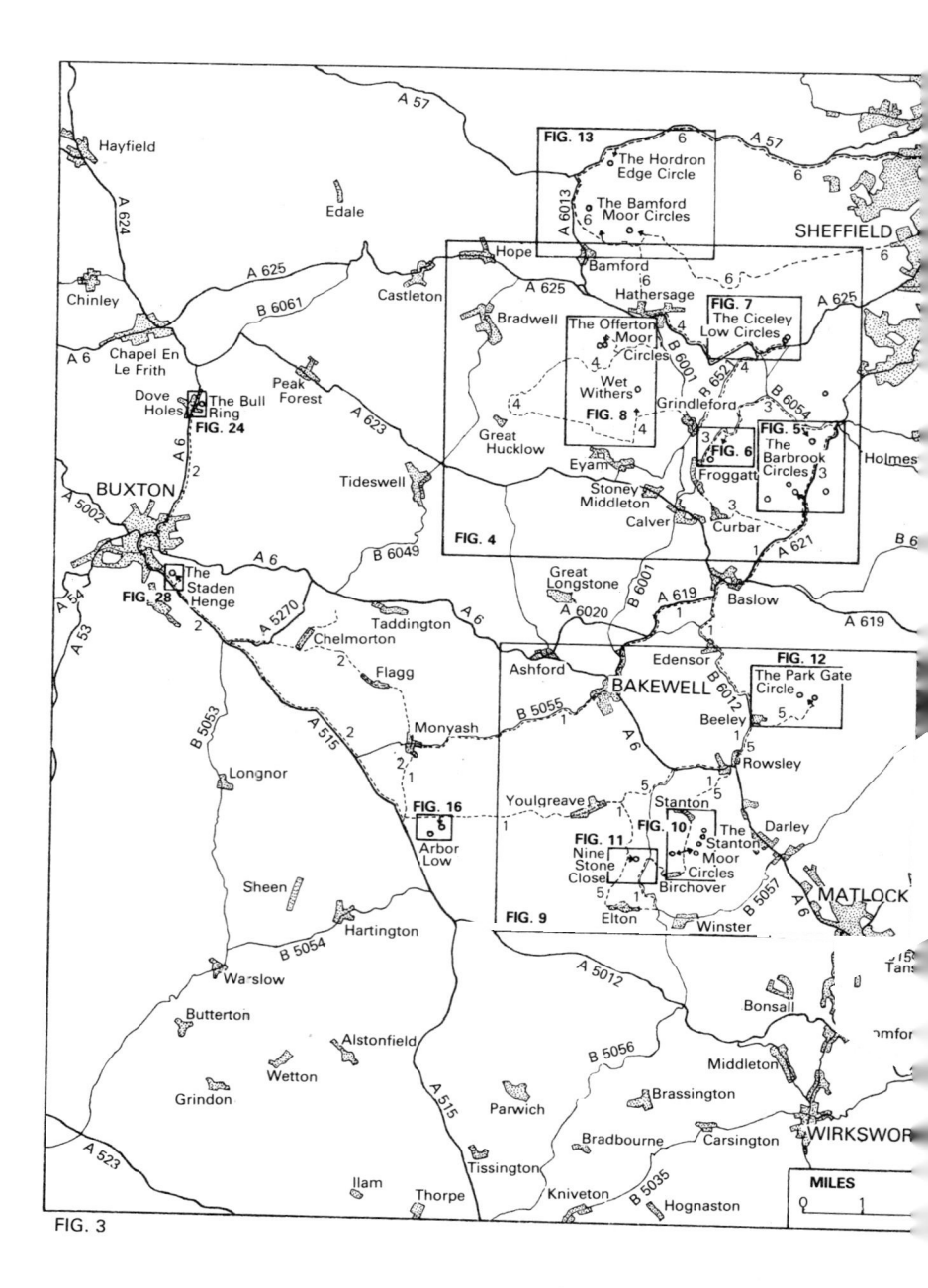

and unstable; collapsed walls create havoc with livestock.
3) Some of the moors are used for grouse shooting and should be avoided during the breeding and shooting seasons.
4) Some circles are on land which drains into reservoirs, so any kind of pollution should be avoided.

TOUR 1

Arbor Low; Nine Stones Close; Nine Ladies; Barbrook I

This first tour is for the person with limited time, and covers a selection which can be seen in one day, including the best preserved sites of all the main types of circle in the area. A good place to start is **Bakewell**, which is itself an interesting place. It has always been the chief market centre of the area and is situated on a picturesque stretch of the river Wye. An ancient bridge leads to the centre of the town where there are many fine old buildings including a Tudor market hall and a much restored Norman church. This has two Saxon crosses in the churchyard and numerous fragments of others in the porch and nave which were found during restoration in Victorian times. From Bakewell take the road to **Monyash;** this takes one through typical limestone countryside with a beauty all its own. As you approach Monyash it is interesting to note the narrow fields surrounding the village. These are the enclosed strips of mediaeval open fields. Monyash itself is a good example of an unspoilt Derbyshire village with unpretentious houses, a church and a green with a mediaeval cross shaft. Turn left in the village, and after about a mile and a half take the first left which leads to **Arbor Low:** be careful not to miss the signposted track to the right. Cars are parked in the field below the farm; a small fee is payable at the farmhouse and the footpath to the site is clearly marked.

After visiting the henge continue down the road in the same direction. On the right in the trees following the road is **Long Rake,** one of the main mineral veins in the Peak. This has been extensively worked for lead in the past and is now being reworked for calcite.

Take the second turning to the right; this leads to **Youlgreave,** another unspoilt village with a small Tudor manor house next to the main road, and an impressive late mediaeval church tower.

Continue through the village on the main road to the hamlet of Alport in the valley below. Here turn right down the small side road and over the bridge. Immediately past the bridge take care on two blind bends as you go up the hill. Continue up this road for just over a mile until the **Nine Stone Close** circle can be seen in the fields to the left with Castle Ring farm on the right.

There are two other sites worth visiting in the immediate vicinity, as well as the circle and **Robin Hood's Stride.** At the base of the eastern cliffs is a mediaeval hermit's shelter which has a crucifix carved out of solid rock. Behind Castle Ring farm is what was probably an Iron Age fort, with bank and ditch defences on a slight hill.

After visiting these, continue along the road to Elton, where you turn left and go through the village to the crossroads. Turn left again here, onto the main road. After a mile take the first right to Birchover. As you enter the village there is the **Druid's Inn** behind which on the wooded hill is an interesting collection of caves, steps, seats and other features cut for a garden in the eighteenth century. Among these is a large natural rocking stone.

Turn left at the top of the village. Nearby are quarries which are being worked for a particularly good building stone. Park a short way along this road, across from the main footpath onto the top of **Stanton Moor.** This leads to **Nine Ladies,** and some of the other circles passed on the way should also be visited if time permits.

From here follow the road to **Stanton,** an unusual long one-street village built on a steep hill. Half way down the village take the small road signposted to Pilhough. From here there are fine views across the **Wye valley** with **Haddon Hall** among the trees.

Follow this road to Rowsley where you turn right, and then left onto the main road going north. You will pass **Chatsworth House,** one of the finest stately homes in the country, surrounded by beautiful gardens, parkland and woods, on the right before reaching **Baslow,** where there is a mediaeval church with a good example of a broach spire.

Take the Sheffield road and follow it onto the top of the gritstone moors. Just before you reach the highest part of the moor there is a white gate on the left and a lay-by immediately past it on the other side of the road. The track from the gate leads onto open moorland and the **Barbrook I** circle, the best preserved site in the Peak. This circle is on waterboard property. If continuing back to Bakewell, return via Baslow from where it is well signposted.

TOUR 2

The Bull Ring; Staden Henge; Arbor Low I & II

This tour takes in the four henges of the Peak, all of which are on the limestone plateau to the west. A good base for this tour is **Buxton** which is an old spa town, fashionable in the eighteenth and nineteenth centuries. The pump-house and Georgian crescent still survive.

Take the road to Chapel-en-le-Frith from Buxton as far as **Dove Holes**; this passes through countryside spoilt by limestone quarries. Pass the crossroads in Dove Holes and park near the chapel on the right of the road. The **Bull Ring Henge** is in a field beyond the sports field.

After seeing this return to Buxton and take the Ashbourne road. Just outside the town you will pass a large cemetery on the left. Take the first side road after this, on the same side of the road, and park just past the bridge over the railway line. From here the **Staden Henge** is only a short walk across the fields.

After a brief look at this barely visible monument, the main stop is **Arbor Low,** a complete contrast, being the most impressive site in the Peak. Return to the main road and follow it south. The quickest route to Arbor Low is to follow the main road, but the scenery is marred by extensive quarries. A much more picturesque route is to take the second turning on the left to **Chelmorton.** This is a typical one street village with a church at the top nestling under the moors above, surrounded by mediaeval fields which are now walled as at Monyash. If you have plenty of time, it is worth making a detour to the **Five Wells** burial mound which is a large neolithic chambered tomb with its two stone chambers exposed, commanding fine views to the north. It is reached by taking the footpath from above the church which goes to Taddington across the moor to the north-east. Where the path crosses a lane turn left along this till the steep northern edge of the moor is reached, the mound is three hundred yards to the right, in fields belonging to Five Wells farm.

From Chelmorton the way on is along the signposted side roads through fine upland limestone countryside to Monyash, and from here to Arbor Low and its associated sites in the same way as described in Tour 1. When returning from Arbor Low, if time is pressing, instead of turning right to Monyash at the end of the road, turn left. This road soon meets the main road back to Buxton.

TOUR 3

Barbrook I; Barbrook II; Barbrook III; Stoke Flat

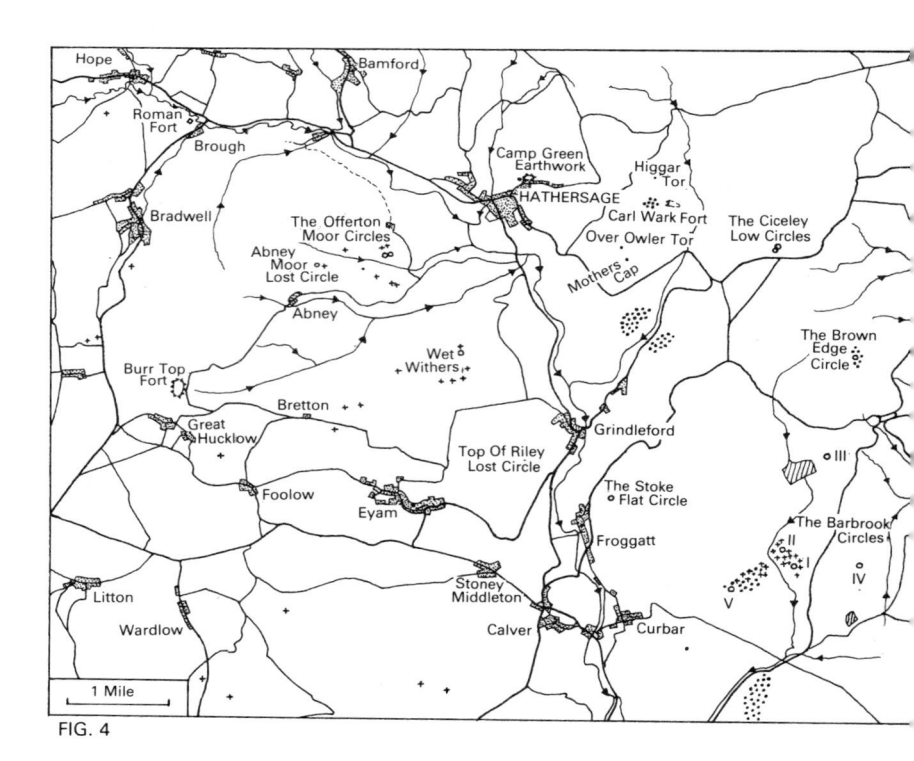

FIG. 4

Itineraries

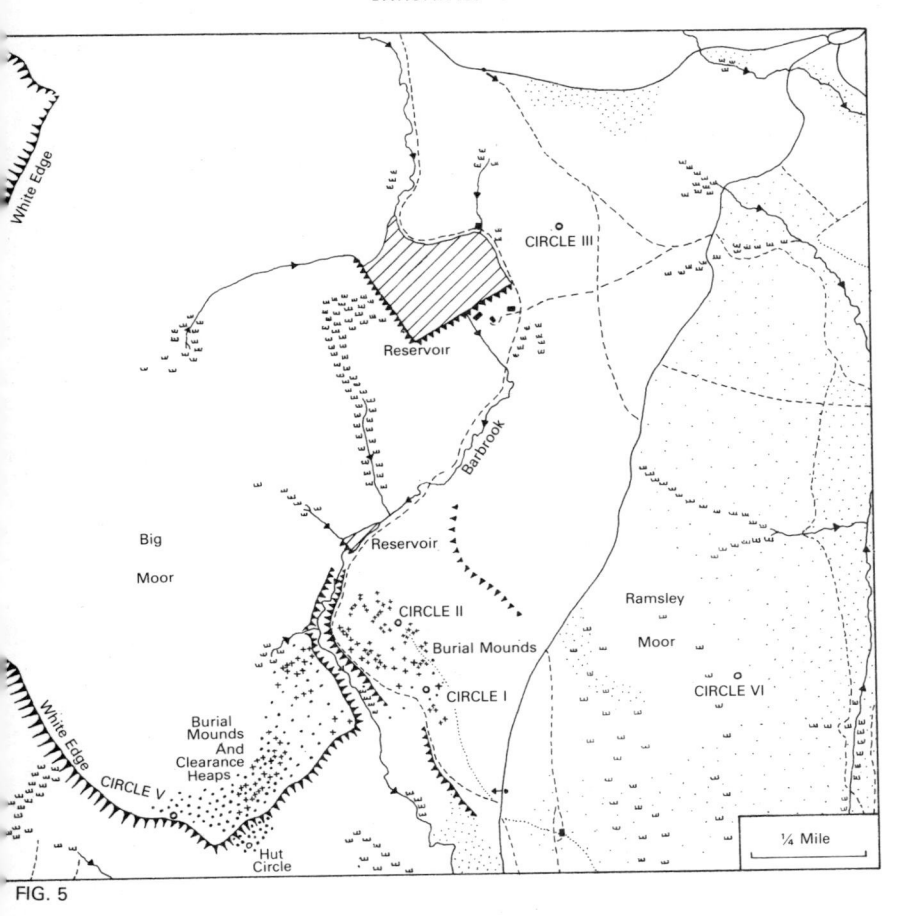

FIG. 5

This tour and the next cover the central group of circles. A good place to start is at the **Barbrook I** circle which can be approached from Baslow (as described in Tour 1), or from Sheffield in the other direction. From Barbrook I, it is only a short walk to **Barbrook II**. Above I near the top of the slope is a large restored burial mound which should be examined. A few yards beyond this is a path which leads to Barbrook II, passing other burial mounds on the way, including a typical small cairn which has recently been restored.

After looking at the many monuments on this moor, return to the car and continue towards Sheffield until you reach the

Owler Bar roundabout. Take the first exit and follow this road to another white gate on the left side of the road. The track from here leads to the **Barbrook III** circle which is also on Waterboard property.

From here continue up the road to the next junction and turn left, unless a detour to the **Ciceley Low** circles is planned. All these roads are old turnpike routes and interesting milestones can occasionally be seen at the side of the road. From the left junction the road twists down across the moors, with fine views across the **Derwent valley** which contrasts with the bleak moors you have just passed through. After passing a pub on the right, there is a series of bends where the car should be parked (or in the new car park just before this). From here you should follow a well used footpath through a gate for about half a mile amongst small silver birch trees along the top of Froggatt Edge. The **Stoke Flat** circle is a few hundred yards past a second gate at the end of the wood.

After this walk, follow the road into the valley and the first

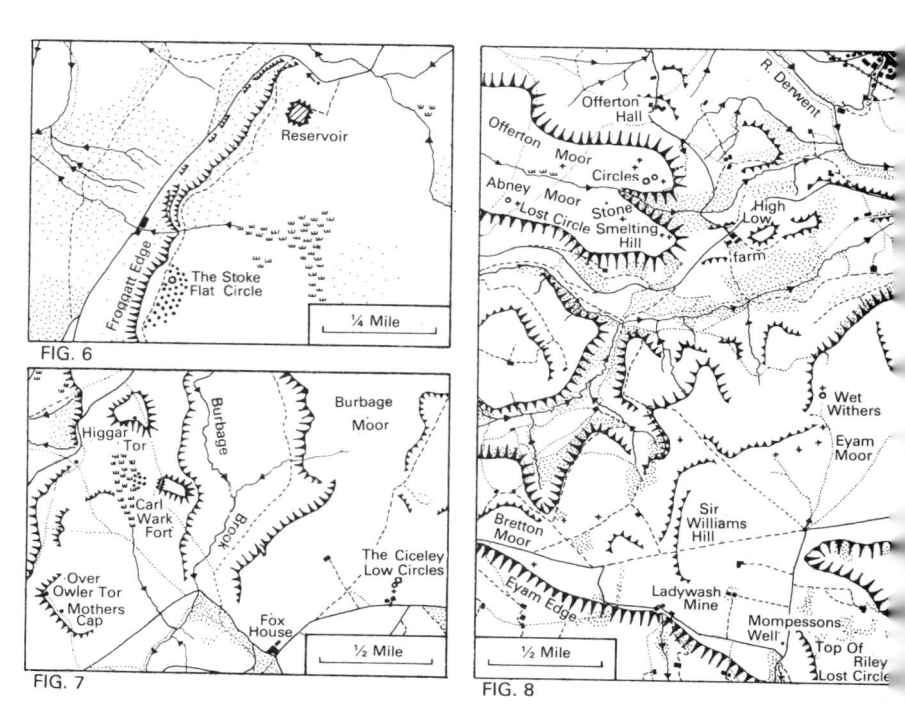

FIG. 6

FIG. 7

FIG. 8

Itineraries 67

side road to the left taken to Curbar. From here, go uphill again to the left. The road passes through a small gap in the escarpment edge and at the top is an old packhorse route guidepost to the left of the road. A detour can be made from here along the edge to the right to the point where there is a massive natural block of stone called the **Eagle Stone,** which, as folk legends indicate, was probably regarded as sacred in ancient times.

Continue along the road to meet the main road half a mile below the Barbrook I circle. A footpath from the crossroads going south onto **Gardoms Edge** crosses an area which is covered in evidence of habitation by prehistoric man in the form of field enclosures, clearance heaps and hut circles.

TOUR 4

Offerton Moor; Wet Withers; Ciceley Low

A good starting place for this is **Hathersage** which has an interesting mediaeval church dedicated to St. Michael. Behind this, in a garden, are fragmentary remains of an earthwork of unknown age. Take the Grindleford road, cross the river, then immediately turn right and follow the winding side road uphill to Highlow Hall Farm next to the road on the left. Here turn down a very narrow road on the right, follow this for about half a mile until **Offerton Hall,** a gaunt Tudor house just below the road, comes into sight. Here there are a few spots where the car can be parked by the road. Near the east end of the very steep slope above, an old trackway should be followed uphill through the grass field. This leads to the open moors and the **Offerton Moor** circles.

From here retrace your steps to Highlow Hall Farm and turn right, passing through Abney to the hamlet of **Bretton** on Eyam Edge. From there is one of the finest views in Derbyshire across the limestone plateau to the south, where dry valleys and sink holes can be traced from the edge, running down towards the deep Stoney Middleton gorge. The whole area is covered in walled fields, with the mediaeval system of narrow strips clearly visible around Eyam, to the left.

Follow the road from here for about a mile and a half to a

junction. The way on is to the left but if you have plenty of time a detour can be made to the right into **Eyam** in the valley below. This village, famous for its plague in the seventeenth century, has a beautiful Tudor hall and a mediaeval church with a fine Saxon cross in the churchyard. Just above the junction, on the left of the road is **Mompesson's Well.** During the plague, money was placed in the well in exchange for food from the outside world. Further up the hill is the **Ladywash mine,** one of the few working underground lead mines in Derbyshire. At the end of this stretch of road is a junction with a track, where the car should be parked. From here three footpaths radiate to the north. The least used, unsignposted, central one leads to the **Wet Withers** circle.

After returning from the circle follow the road to Grindleford and turn left towards Sheffield; this road climbs out of the Derwent Valley, eventually reaching Fox House, an old coaching inn. From here continue towards Sheffield for half a mile. Just past a track to a farm on the right, the low ruins of a house are seen on the same side of the road. The **Ciceley Low circles** are on the slope just behind this.

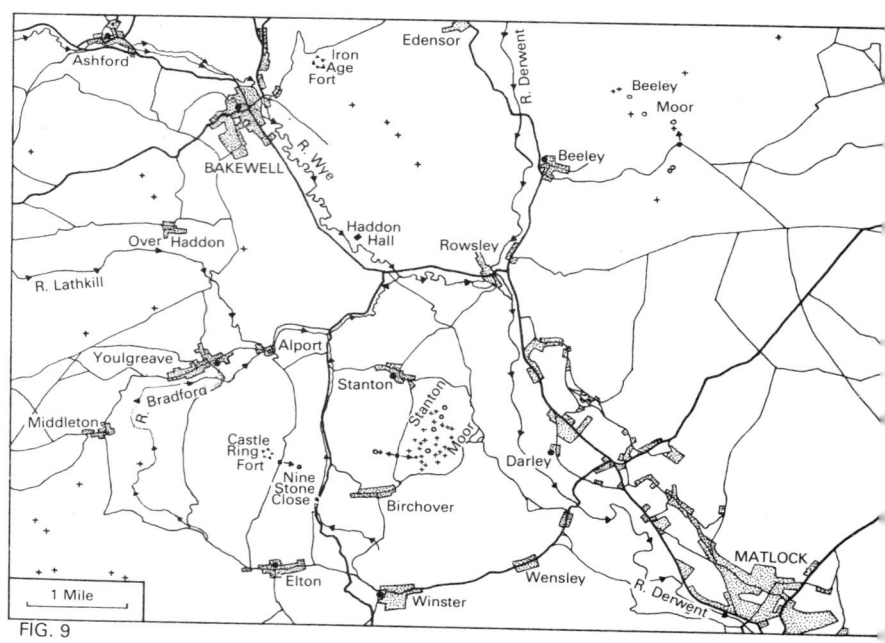

FIG. 9

Itineraries

The road back to Hathersage from Fox House passes some interesting sites which are worth visiting. Towering to the right of the road is the cliff of **Higgar Tor** (its holed rock is described under Wet Withers). Below this is a second cliff which is the **Carl Wark Fort**. This triangular hill has two sides of cliffs, and a third which had a wall built across it in the Iron Age. This was later rebuilt in the Dark Ages, just after the Romans left Britain. It still stands about 10 feet high, and the fort has an inturned entrance in the south-west corner.

Further along the road on the same side is the prominent rock, **Mother's Cap,** and **Over Owler Tor** beyond. (These important alignment points are also described under Wet Withers). As the road is leaving the moor it takes a sharp turn, revealing the 'surprise view', a magnificent prospect over the Hope Valley. From here the road drops steeply into Hathersage.

TOUR 5

Nine Stone Close; Nine Ladies; Stanton Moor, Central, North & South, Doll Tor; Park Gate

This covers the circles at the southern end of the gritstone moors, a good place to start is the village of **Rowsley**. From here take the Bakewell road and then turn left on the Ashbourne road. Take the first turning on the right, signposted to Youlgreave, which after half a mile brings you to **Alport**. From here follow the same route as described in Tour 1 to **Nine Stone Close** and then on to **Stanton Moor,** where a walk to the **Doll Tor circle** should also be included, as well as to some of the less important monuments on the moor.

After returning to Rowsley go on as far as Beeley on the Baslow road and take the first turning to the right. This winds up onto the moors, and at the top you will reach a track going to the left where the car should be parked. Follow the track to a high gate on the right. The track through this leads to the **Park Gate circle,** which is on open moorland owned by Chatsworth Estate.

If there is time a visit to **Hob Hurst House** can also be made. This is a large, well preserved burial mound which has a square

FIG. 10

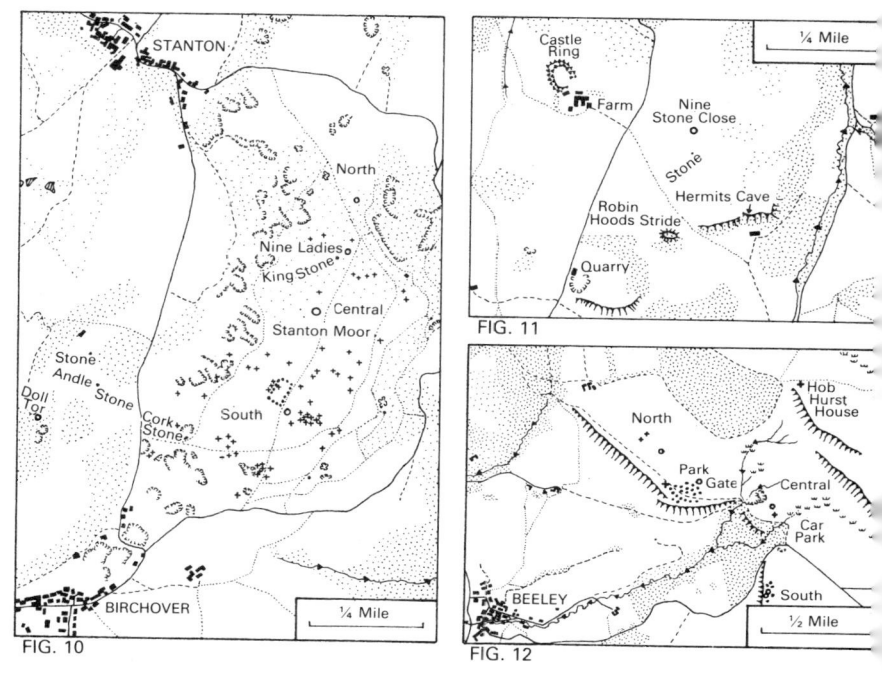

FIG. 11

FIG. 12

central mound surrounded by a deep ditch and external bank. It is reached by walking from the circle to the top of Harland Edge above, keeping just to the right of the wood; the mound is close to the 'edge', just to the south-east of the corner of the wood. On the way back from the Park Gate circle to the car are other sites worth looking at on the moor to the left of the track (see Chapter 7).

TOUR 6

Bamford Moor South; Bamford Moor North; Hordron Edge

This covers the northern circles and can be started from **Sheffield** or alternatively from **Hathersage**. From the former, branch off the main Hathersage road in Ecclesall to **Ringinglow**, where there is a fine old toll house. Carry straight on from here onto the top of the moors, after which the road passes through

Itineraries 71

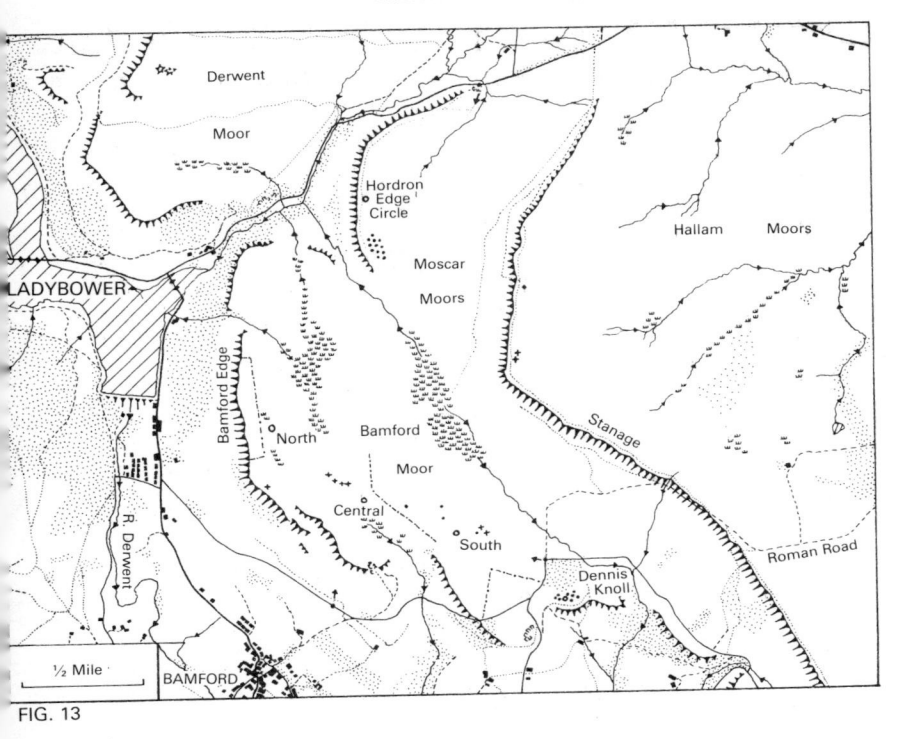

FIG. 13

some of the most spectacular gritstone scenery in the Peak. At the first junction detour for a few hundred yards along the right road and walk onto **Higgar Tor** to examine the rock described under Wet Withers.

Along the left fork the road drops below **Stanage Edge**. Turn right at the bottom, following the road below the edge, always keeping right until you reach a conifer plantation and a sharp turn to the left across a cattle grid. Park the car by this corner. This spot can be reached from Hathersage by Jaggers Lane at the western end of the village.

The **Bamford Moor Southern circle** is on the moor to the north-west of this point. All three circles in this tour are on open moorland owned by local farmers who do not encourage visits, as the land is used for grouse shooting.

After returning from the southern circle drive further along the road, turn right at the next fork and continue for about a mile until **Bamford Edge** is visible, high above to the left. Walk up onto the top, and after nearly a mile along the top of the edge on sheep tracks and across thick heather, you will reach the **Bamford Moor Northern circle.**

Now follow the road as far as the main road. Turn right here and right again after crossing Ladybower Reservoir. This road climbs out of the valley again and there is a layby on the right hand side where the gradient becomes gentler and the shelves below Stanage Edge become visible. From here it is a half mile walk, following the top of **Hordron Edge,** to this circle. If returning to Sheffield from here continue along the main road.

TOUR 7

Ewden Beck

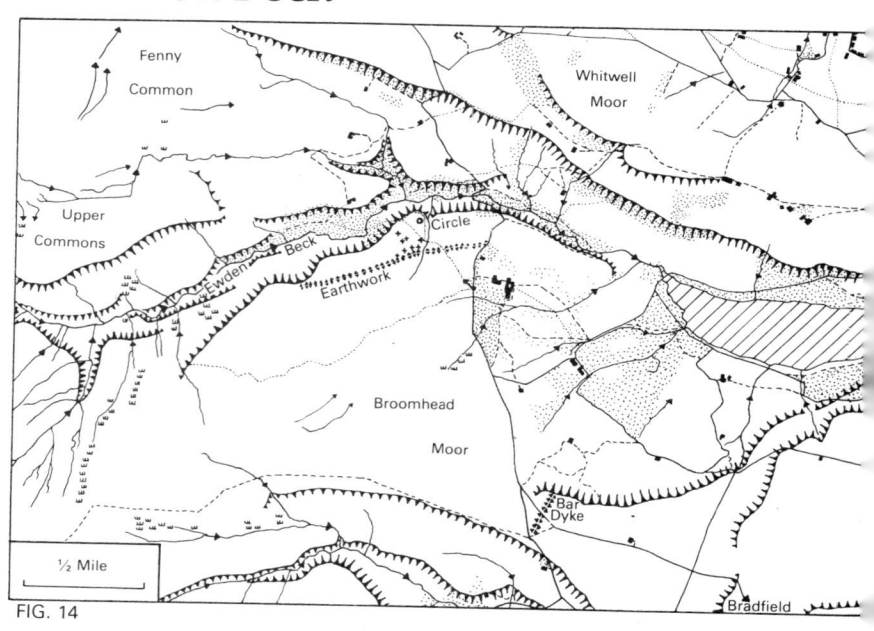

FIG. 14

This trip goes to the isolated **Ewden Beck circle** which is only worth a visit for anyone in the vicinity of Sheffield. It is reached by going up the Loxley Valley to **Upper Bradfield** which has an interesting Saxon cross fragment inside the church and a very good example of a motte and Bailey castle behind the church, covered in trees.

From the village take the road immediately to the right of the lane to the church and then bear left at the next junction. Go straight over the next crossroads and after half a mile, just before the next junction, the **Bar Dyke** is crossed. This is a large ancient bank and ditch of unknown age which is worth examining. It has fine views from both ends. Continuing to the right the road gradually drops towards Ewden Beck, and after nearly a mile a small track goes off to the left. This is the way to walk to the circle. The quickest way to return to Sheffield is by the same route.

5
The Henges

Arbor Low (SK.1603.6355)

This well known henge monument is one of the most important sites in the north of England. It is situated at the centre of the high limestone ridges in an exposed position on Middleton Common, a flat-topped hill which is over 1200 feet above sea level. The henge is on a slight northern slope, open to the worst of Pennine weather, with panoramic views over this half of the horizon. Many moors are clearly visible: the Morridge on the west, Taddington Moor dominating the horizon in the north with more distant views on either side, and the main eastern block of moors, including Stanage and White Edge, to the east.

The name Arbor Low is probably of Saxon derivation, originally 'Eorð burh Hlaw' meaning the earthwork mound. The site comprises a large bank and internal ditch with two entrances leading to a central area. This has a ruined ring of stones, a central cove and other features of lesser importance. It was partially excavated in 1901-02 by Gray, who inferred from what he found that it was built in the beaker period, the transition between the Neolithic and Bronze Ages.

The bank has an external diameter of 280 x 295 feet elongated to the north-east, is 7 feet high and the ditch is 5 feet deep. From the excavation findings, the original height of the bank from the ground surface can be reconstructed as approximately 9 to 10 feet, with a total vertical change of about 18 feet. Together the bank and ditch have a width of 55 to 60 feet on the eastern side and 65 to 75 feet on the west creating a central area with an approximate diameter of 150 x 170 feet. This is rather irregular, because less care was taken with the ditch, which appears to

The Henges

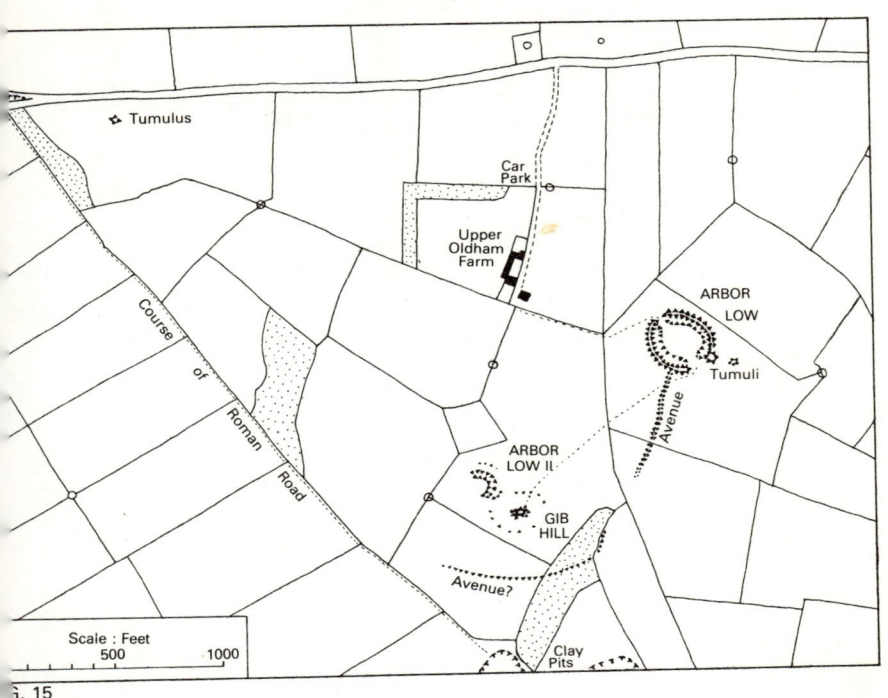

[Map showing Arbor Low area with features including Tumulus, Car Park, Upper Oldham Farm, Arbor Low, Arbor Low II, Gib Hill, Tumuli, Avenue, Course of Roman Road, Clay Pits, and Avenue? Scale: 500, 1000 feet]

have been dug purely to provide material for the bank. In the construction of bank and ditch, two small areas were left to the south-east and north-west, creating entrances which are approximately diametrically opposite (15° out). The north-western one is about 30 feet wide and the other about 20 feet. Another feature in the bank is a large burial mound built on to it W.S.W. This has a diameter of approximately 70 feet and is 7¼ feet high. It has been dug into several times in the eighteenth and nineteenth centuries and as a result now has an irregular top.

Two early Bronze Age 'food vessels' were found in a cist in the centre of the mound, showing that it was built after the completion of the henge. It was probably placed here because of the sacred nature of the site. The mound was higher than the bank and in its construction the rubble needed was taken from the bank, just to the north of the mound and between it and the south-east entrance. This considerably reduced its height here. When the mound was built the henge was still in use as a 'temple' and it must have marred the symmetrical appearance of the site.

The central area has the remains of a ring of standing stones, consisting of 48 to 51 pieces of stone scattered irregularly near the edge of the ditch. All are now fallen, except stone 20 which is leaning inwards, and there are also a few fragmented bases which are still set upright (stones 23, 24, 25, 29, 39, 40, 49). Today only 22 complete stones exist (1 to 22) and even some of these are broken (8/47, 48. 9/49. 14/50. 17/51). Three bases exist with their tops missing (stones 23 to 25) and there are another 21 pieces of stone (26 to 46) which are rather confusing but which are probably to be reconstructed as follows:

stone 26	from stone 24 or possible 23
stones 27-31	four separate stones with stone 31 part of stone 30
stones 32-34	a very confusing group: stone 34 appears to have broken by falling on a buried section of stone 33 but it is not clear if stones 32 and 33 are the same stone or not.
stones 36-37	stone 37 is the top of stone 36
stones 38-39	stone 38 is the top of stone 39
stones 40-44	two stones here originally. Stone 40 is an original base. Stones 43 and 44 are parts of the second stone and stones 41 and 42 could be fragments of either.
stones 35, 45-46	These are probably local outcrops of stone and not significant.

If these conclusions are correct, the ring consisted of stones which were approximately equally spaced, except in six places where there were wider gaps. Those between 6/7 and 8/9 have fragments shown on a plan drawn by Pegge in the late eighteenth century and the gaps between 34/8 and 19/20 probably also had stones which have now disappeared. The last two gaps between 22/1 and 2/3, however, were probably ceremonial gaps through the ring from the north-west entrance. These provisional conclusions make the original number of stones 39.

Controversy has always existed as to whether or not the stones were ever standing, but the evidence points strongly to them being originally set upright in shallow foundations. The main arguments supporting this are: firstly, the existence of stone 20 and the seven upright stumps; secondly, an old man in

The Henges

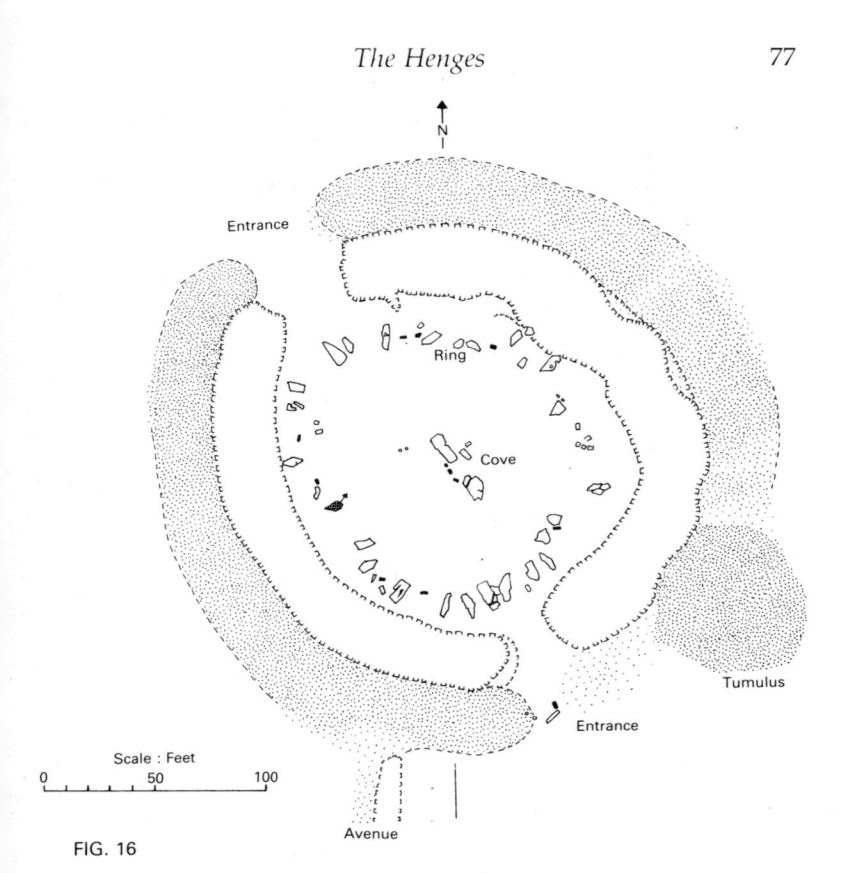

FIG. 16

Scale: Feet 0 50 100

Labels on figure: N, Entrance, Ring, Cove, Tumulus, Entrance, Avenue

the late eighteenth century stated he remembered some stones standing; and thirdly, some of the stones have cracks in them which could only result from falling, particularly stones 8, 14 and 34.

The excavation by Gray failed to answer the question. He concentrated mainly on the ditches in his search for datable material and only investigated stone 7, which did not have much of a pit. This stone, however, has a very flat base and would stand on its own without being sunk deeply into the ground.

It has been suggested that the stones were badly set and the site is exposed to the north wind which has gradually blown down most of the stones, as indicated by the direction of fall of many of them. This is probably partially true but is not the only cause of the present ruined state. There is evidence also suggesting more violent destruction. Firstly, missing stones have been completely removed from the site. A stone with a hole through it, which is obviously from the henge, is now situated next to the path, near the farm. Secondly, the position of other stones, such as 41 and 42, confirm that some have been moved. Lastly, the most convincing evidence is that stone 43 has a hole in it which is probably a borehole for dynamite, indicating a deliberate breaking up of stones perhaps in the seventeenth or eighteenth centuries.

In many cases the direction in which the stones have fallen can be determined. From this the position of the others can be surmised. When this is done it is clear that the stones form a regular, symmetrical ring, an oval elongated to the north-west with a diameter of approximately 120 x 140 feet. The complete stones which still remain are mostly quite large, allowing that approximately a third of each was originally below ground, when standing their heights were between 4 and 9 feet. Most of them being just above head height.

The majority of the stones are very irregular in shape and are badly worn; some even have holes right through them. This is not because it is a long time since they fell, as some people have assumed. The stones were originally erected in this state.

To save quarrying them from solid rock they have been taken from an area of 'limestone pavement' exposed to the weather for many thousands of years. Gray's excavation showed that the limestone in the ditch was a different colour, therefore the stones must have been brought from some other locality, probably nearby. The eroded surface of each stone was predominantly placed facing inwards. This is unusual, as most circles have flat faces inwards to create a more symmetrical appearance from the centre. This arrangement may indicate that the eroded surface had some kind of symbolic significance for the builders.

At the centre of the site is a 'cove' of seven stones, now in ruins. It is difficult to be certain of its original design but it was probably a square with two very large stones (52,53) in the centres of opposite sides facing the entrances. Both of these have now fallen outwards. The excavation of 1901-02 did not find any stone holes in front of these stones, but this is probably because their bases slipped forward when falling, covering the holes. These two stones are the largest in the henge and probably stood about 9 to 10 feet high.

The Henges

The north-east side of the square has two smaller stones. 54 probably stood in the centre of the side while stone 55 was at the corner, or was alternatively part of stone 54. If it was at the corner, this would indicate that there was another stone at the other corner to match it, making this side similar to its opposite which has three small stones set in a line (56-58). These latter may have missing tops but are just as likely always to have been small.

Coves are only found at three other sites in the country: Avebury in Wiltshire, Stanton Drew in Somerset and Cairnapple in West Lothian, all of which are large important sites. The coves were probably built as enclosures for sacred rites. At Arbor Low the two largest stones would obscure the view of the cove centre from the entrances, which could indicate an element of secrecy in the rites celebrated here. There are two other small stones (59,60) in the central area which are not connected with any others. These are probably only natural outcrops and of no significance.

At the centre of the south-east entrance are two stones, one an original base and the other probably its top, although it is difficult to see how they fitted together. Other small stones at the edge of the entrance are probably just exposed bank rubble. The tall pillar was not duplicated in the north-west entrance for two probable reasons: firstly, this entrance has fine views above it to the distant horizon, making a marker unnecessary for alignments; and, secondly, the entrances probably had different functions, as is shown by their dissimilar characteristics. The north-west entrance is wider, has ceremonial gaps through the ring and overlooks the valley below which would have been the logical approach to the site from most of the nearby inhabited areas. The south-east entrance is narrower, with the pillar at the centre, and leads via the avenue described below to other sacred sites nearby. This possibly indicates that the entrance was used for ritual rather than for access.

Outside the bank to the south, a low bank and ditch joins it, which was proved by Gray's excavation to be contemporary. This bank is now only 1½ feet high and the ditch very slight but originally each were about 3 feet and had a total width of 22 feet. This 'avenue' runs S.S.W. and gradually turns westwards in the direction of Gib Hill, a large burial mound 350 yards from the henge centre. Today it becomes too slight to follow well before reaching the mound, if indeed this was its original destination.

Avenues are a relatively common feature of circles and take several forms, the commonest of which is single or double lines of stones, such as those at Avebury. Bank avenues are rare; a double one exists at Stonehenge, and Arbor Low is the only known example with a single bank. They were probably built as processional ways, often connecting sites to water, but this does not appear to be the case at Arbor Low, and a connection with Gib Hill seems likely.

Gib Hill

This large mound was probably built in two phases, a fact that was noted by Radley in 1968. The first is a neolithic oval mound which is 120 x 70 feet in diameter and 4½ feet high, surrounded by a shallow ditch dug to provide earth for the mound. The interesting thing about this mound is that it was not for burial but appears to have a symbolic connection with fertility of the land and its animals. The construction is complex: firstly, it has a central core of red clay formed into four small mounds; covering this are layers of burnt material including bones of oxen, hazel twigs and flints which in turn are covered with stones, and a final thicker layer of earth and stones. An interesting parallel between Gib Hill and Silbury Hill near Avebury is drawn by Dames in his book *The Silbury Treasure*. The second phase of building was the placing of an early Bronze Age burial mound on top of the earlier one. This burial mound has a diameter of 90 feet and makes the total height over 10 feet. Near the surface of this mound a small stone chamber was found, containing a 'food vessel'.

Arbor Low II (SK.1578.6335)

Just to the west of Gib Hill, among small quarry pits, are traces of a bank and ditch which are probably the remains of an early henge. A trial trench proved its ditch was prehistoric, but more digging is needed to prove anything conclusively. The pits have badly disturbed the site and all that remains is the north-eastern half of a 20 to 35 foot wide ditch, traces of a demolished external bank and a possible entrance to the N.N.W. This has an approximate diameter at the external edge of the bank of 140 to 180 feet and at the inner edge of the ditch 80 to 90 feet.

It is not clear if this site was every completed, as there is a suspiciously flat area to the north-west where one would expect to find traces of a ditch. Radley proposed the theory that this site was earlier than the main one and was built in association with Gib Hill, then later replaced by the beaker period henge.

GEOMETRY OF ARBOR LOW I

The geometry of the ring is obviously an egg elongated to the north-west, but an exact reconstruction cannot be effected because of the ruined nature of the stones. There are however a number of clues as to its nature:

a) The egg has a circular arc of approximately 240°, which indicates a hexagon as the basis of the construction.
b) The long axis can be fixed at $311° \pm 4°$, and astronomical indications point to it being about 313°.
c) The centre of the geometric construction can be fixed within a foot near the original position of stone 53 close to its western end.
d) The ring has diameters of approximately 21 x 18 MR, with four hexagon sides of 9 MR and two of 10.5 MR, giving a total of 57 MR (19 x 3) and a circumference of approximately 60 MR, which obviously relates to the hexagon.
e) Stones 25, 16, 15 and 8, 34 possibly indicate a more complicated type of construction with modifications in these sections of the circular portion of the ring.
f) The only stones which deviate significantly from this ring are 23 and 24.

The egg shown on the plan fits with all these facts and is orientated according to astronomical factors discussed below.

The cove is probably a square with sides of approximately 1.5 MR (total 6 MR). Its orientation is offset from the axis of the ring by about 15°, as is indicated by stones 56 to 58. This line goes to the eastern edges of both the entrances. The axis of the ring goes to the west side of stone 53 and the east side of stone 52. Together these create a logical offsetting from the circle's centre.

The entrances fit into the geometric pattern as a logical compromise to fit with astronomical lines. The north-west entrance has edges defined by the main axis of the ring and the central cove line. The south-east entrance is defined by the central cove line and a line which is half way along a hexagon side. The stone in the centre of this entrance is about 19 MR from the ring centre.

The bank and ditch have no exact geometry but were built to follow approximately the ring of stones. They are wider in the west than in the east, offsetting the centre of the bank ring by about 8 feet to the east. There is also an unexplained bulge of the central area to the east.

FIG. 17

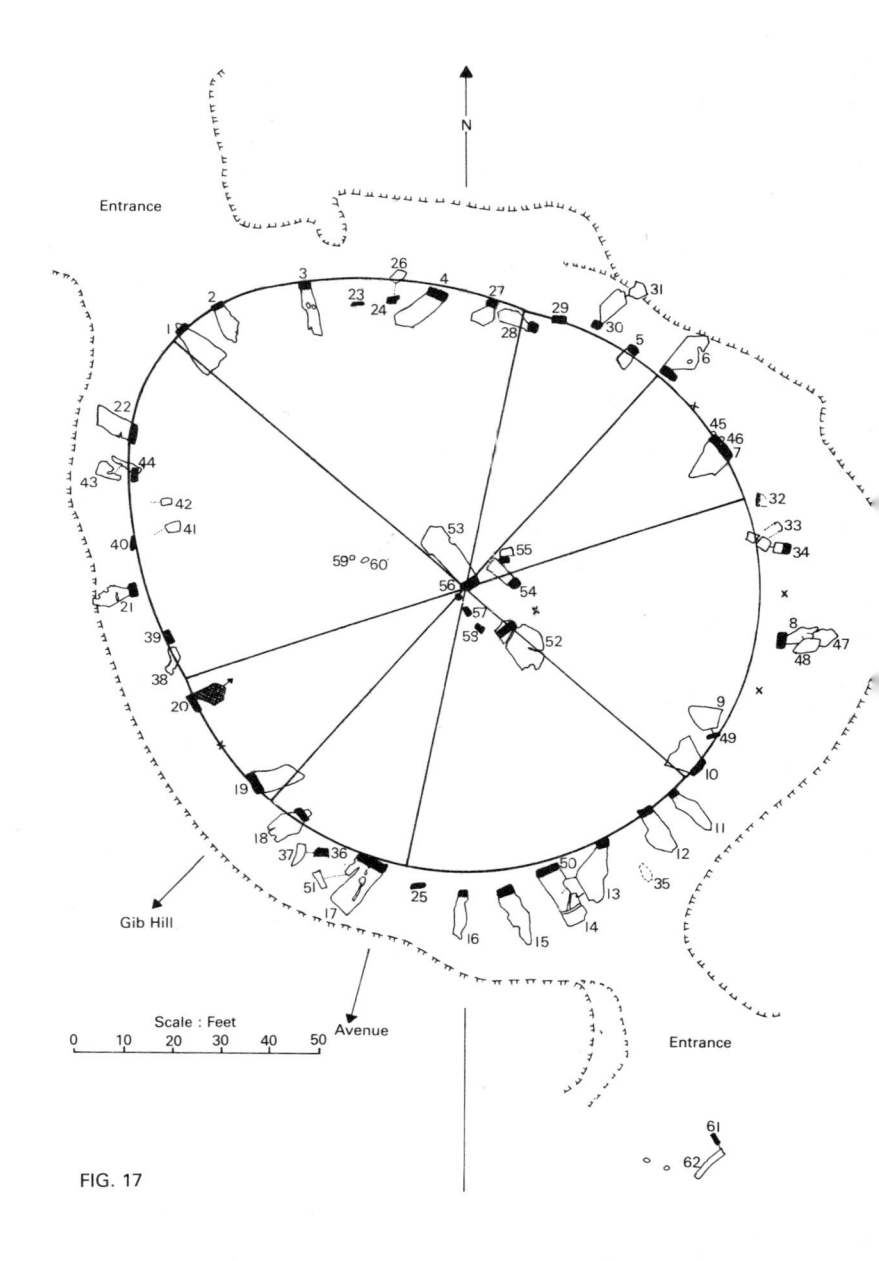

The Henges

BALANCE AND ALIGNMENT

The ring has two types of arrangement of its stones. The first is at both entrances, where they are arranged in pairs with three at each entrance. The second is between the entrances where they are arranged as equally spaced alternating large and small stones. The arrangement of these groups is given below; all the alignments to stones given are accurate even when the maximum tolerances are used in reconstruction.

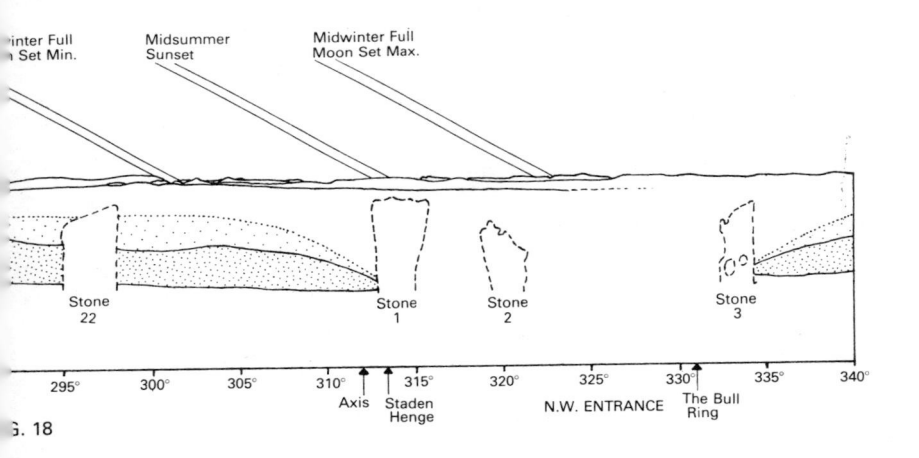

1) The north-west entrance pairs

The central pair, stones 1 and 2, are arranged so that the large flat topped stone 1 marks the left edge of the entrance and the long axis of the ring, the smaller pointed stone 2 is within the entrance. Stone 1 is below Great Low, 4½ miles away where the midsummer sun would set at the centre of the hill above the left half of the stone. The last flash of light was in exactly the direction of the Staden henge which is another 3½ miles beyond Great Low. Because this point is at the elongated end of the ring it indicates that it was the most important alignment of the henge. The whole construction was designed round the midsummer sunset. Stone 2 did not have any alignment and is probably just to create the pair.

Above the centre of the entrance is Black Edge, ten miles away, which was the setting position of the midwinter full moon at its maximum, with the last flash of light in a clearly visible notch. The minimum position of the midwinter full moon was probably intentionally marked, using the horizon to the left of the entrance where there is a distinct junction between Axe Edge and Shining Tor. Stone 1 and 2 are given prominence by isolating them with the two entrance gaps in the ring, and by two flanking pairs of stones. To the left are the large stone 22 and the fragmented stone 43/44 which was probably smaller than 22. To the right are the large stone 3 and stone 23 which was also probably smaller. Stone 3 has two natural holes through it which may have marked it as having special importance. It aligns with the right edge of the entrance and is close to the direction of the Bull Ring henge beyond Taddington Moor. All the alignments in this group were observed from the geometric centre by standing outside the cove at the centre of stone 53.

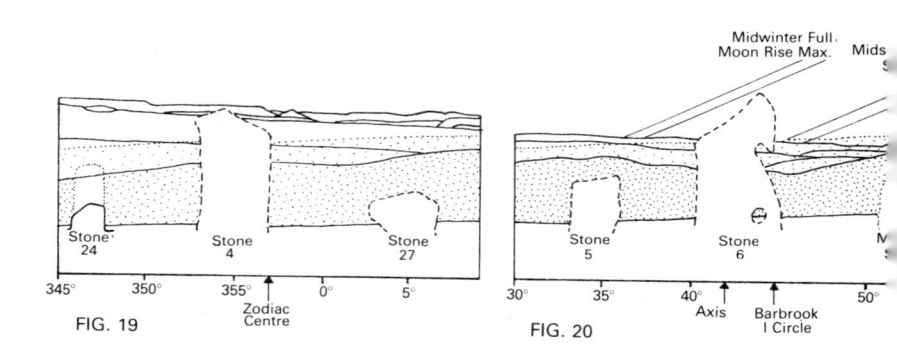

FIG. 19

FIG. 20

2) **The eastern group**
a) Three large stones and four smaller ones are arranged to create a section of the ring with equally spaced stones, as follows:

24 small?, 4 very large, 27 small, 28 large, 29 small?, 30/31 large, 5 small.

The only stone with significance is stone 4 which is exceptionally large, and marks the direction of the zodiac centre described later in the book. This is also marked on the horizon by the dip between Edale Moor and Lose Hill.

b) Stone 6 is another exceptionally large stone and it marks the short axis of the ring; this also has a hole in it, showing its importance. It is at the point where the bank originally obscured the far horizon and it also had various alignments observed by standing by the inside face of stone 53. The rise of the midwinter full moon at its maximum first left the horizon to the east of the stone but must have passed close to its point. The midsummer sunrise must have been very close to the stones right edge and possibly rose from behind it. The stone also marks the direction of the Barbrook I circle which had a midwinter sunset alignment to Arbor Low.

c) In this damaged section the stones again are simply to create a continuous ring, as follows:
   Missing stone small ?, 7 large, 32/33 small ?, 34 large, missing stone small ?, 8 large, missing stone small ?, 9 large, 10 small.
Note that though stone 10 looks as large as 9, a portion must have been below ground, whereas 9 has broken off at ground level.

3) South-east entrance pairs

The central pair stones 13 and 14 stand in front of the entrance with the very large flat topped slab stone 14 marking the western edge, as the similar stone 1 does at the other entrance. Stone 13 is a pointed slab matching stone 2, except that it is much larger. Between the two, the pillar in the entrance is visible, close to stone 13. Flanking these three stones are two more pairs, both with large stones arranged so that they are visually symmetrical. To the left are stone 11, which is a tall thin pillar-like stone, and stone 12, a tall slab with its point away from the entrance. To the right are: stone 15, corresponding to stone 12, also a slab with its point away from the entrance, and stone 16, a tall thin pillar-like stone.

As at the north-west entrance, this group had a solar solstice line at the axis and a lunar solstice line at the entrance. In this case they are observed from outside the cove next to stone 52, a position which is identical to the geometric centre for the solar line. When the henge was first built, the midsummer sunrise was just to the left of stone 11 from where the sun passed behind the stone and reappeared near its point. The first flash of light was offset from the long axis by about 3°, but when the burial mound was built and the bank lowered in the early Bronze Age, it made the sun rise further to the left, with the first flash of light very close to the axis. This correction was possibly coincidental but the fact that the sun now fitted with the arrangement for the rest of the site points to a purposeful improvement.

The rise of midsummer full moon at its maximum first appeared near the right side of stone 12 and crossed the sky behind the entrance, coming into contact with stones until it had passed the right edge, after which it was clear of the stones to the south. The moon completely disappeared behind stone 13, passed near the point of the entrance stone and near the top of stone 14. This complex moon alignment could be observed from stone 52, or alternatively the geometric centre, by standing inside the cove by stone 53. Depending on which was used it would alter the angle slightly. The one shown in the diagram is from the geometric centre. From stone 52 it visually moves the stones slightly to the right making the moon higher in relation to them, but the observations made above still hold true. Stones 15 and 16 do not have any alignments although stone 16 marks south—which could have been intentional.

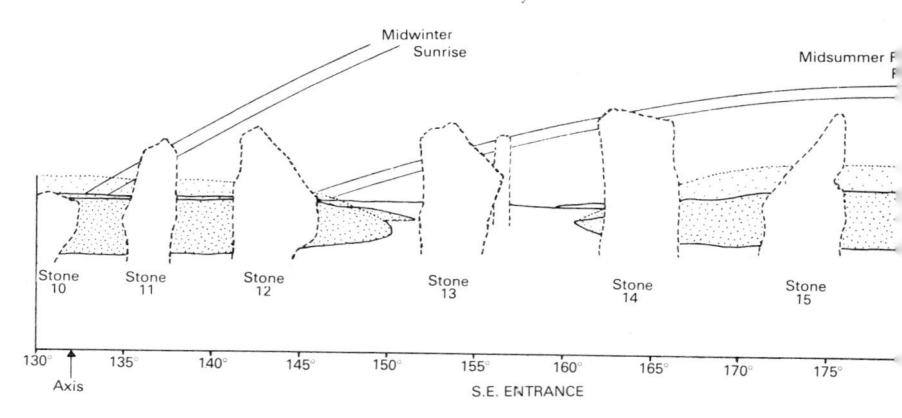

FIG. 21

4) The western group

a) This has the largest stone in the ring, stone 17, flanked by two smaller stones, 25 and 36. This massive slab is deeply eroded; it has a large hole through it and a vertical slit running up virtually the whole height of the visible stone. This stone is important because it marked the setting of the midsummer full moon at its maximum. From the geometric centre, standing at stone 53, the moon disappeared behind the stone close to its top, then passed near the top of the right pillar before continuing across the sky to set above stone 36. The left edge of the stone is also the direction of the beginning of the avenue bank.

b) Stones 18 and 19 are two large stones which disrupt the pattern, as they should have a small stone between them. This was probably done because stone 19 needed to be large to mark an alignment, the position of stone 36 was fixed, marking the moon, and this left a gap between the two which had to be filled and either size of stone would be wrong.

Standing at the geometric centre next to stone 53 makes the pointed left side of stone 19 mark the short axis. This was the position of the midwinter sunset where the sun touched the stone at its point, and passed down its top slope to set above the centre of the stone. The short axis is also the direction of Gib Hill which is a very important arrangement in combination with the sunset. The unusual deposits in Gib Hill indicate a belief connected with midwinter in which it was believed that the sun needed succour to be reborn and so bring another season of warmth and growth.

c) This group is again just to create a continuous ring and is arranged as follows:

Missing stone small ?, 20 large, 39 small ?, 21 large, 40 small ?.

This section has one important line which is the hexagon point between stones 20 and 39. This marks the place where the bank

The Henges

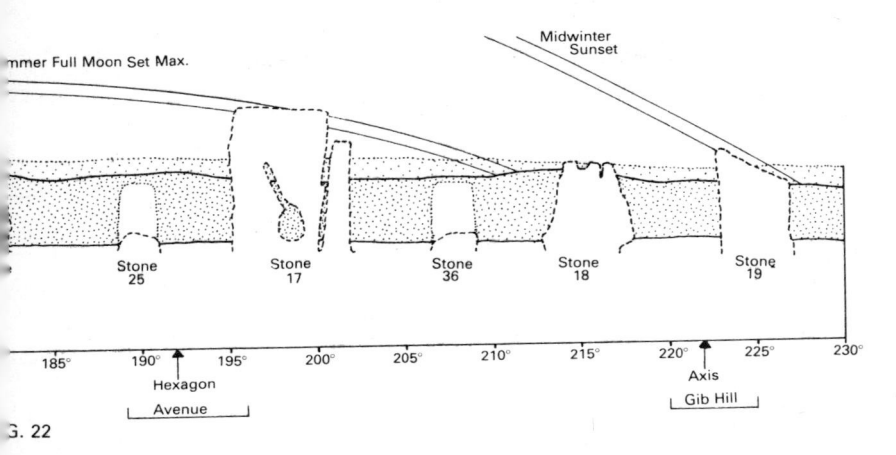

[Figure 22: Horizon profile showing stones 25, 17, 36, 18, 19 with azimuths from 185° to 230°, marked with Summer Full Moon Set Max., Midwinter Sunset, Hexagon, Avenue, Axis, and Gib Hill indicators]

originally obscured the horizon. Together with the point at the other side of the ring this created a planned arrangement where 2½ hexagon sides (150°) have far horizons that are visible and 3½ hexagon sides (210°) are obscured by the bank.

The Cove

The arrangement of the cove is interesting. The two most important groups of alignments in the site at the entrances are obscured from the cove centre by the large stones 52 and 53. This could indicate that the rites connected with the cove include a belief in channelling the power of the sun, moon and landscape through the stones. All the other alignments are observed from the geometric centre by standing at the inner face of stone 53.

Summary

Arbor Low was arranged so that its geometry and entrances aligned with the sun and moon at the solstices, in combination with other important prehistoric sites. The two axes mark the sun at its rising and setting at both solstices; the full moon at its maximum at both solstices is marked by the entrances and the large stones 6 and 17.

The Bull Ring, Doveholes (SK.0784.7823)

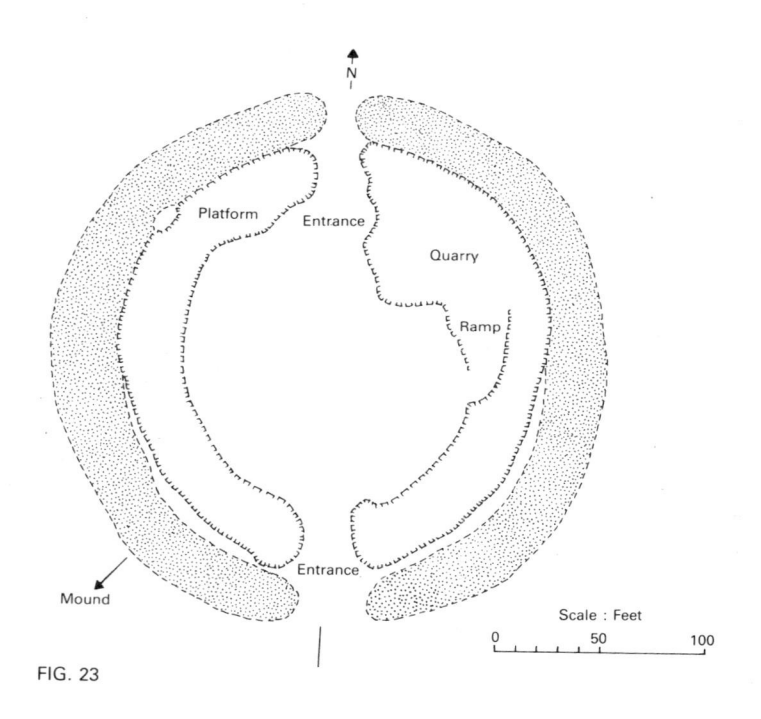

FIG. 23

This monument is situated in a typical position for a henge, in a relatively low-lying spot on flat land near the head of two valleys, Great Rocks Dale to the south-east and Barmoor Clough to the north. Barmoor Clough is the main pass to the north-west from the limestone plateau. Today the views from the site are marred by unattractive houses to the west and extensive quarries to the east, but originally they must have been impressive, with distant views in all directions except to the west, where Black Edge rises high above the site.

The henge is in a grass field and easy to find. It is very similar in size and design to Arbor Low but is not as well preserved. It was partially excavated in 1949 by Alcock who found fragments

The Henges

of neolithic pottery. This shows that it is probably contemporary with Arbor Low, or possibly slightly earlier.

Today the site consists of a bank and ditch with two entrances through them, but no standing stones. The bank is not as impressive as that at Arbor Low, being only 3½ feet high, but it is virtually as large, with an external diameter of 280 x 270 feet, slightly elongated along a north/south line. The ditch is about 2 feet deep, although originally it was between 4 and 7 feet, making the bank originally about 6 feet high. Together, the bank and ditch are 60 feet wide. In the southern half of the site there is a gap between the bank and ditch which is up to 6 feet wide, but this makes no difference to the overall width, as the bank and ditch are narrower here.

There are two entrances, to the north and south, where the ditch was not dug, both originally about 22 feet wide. In the north-east quadrant, there is a small quarry which has disturbed the ditch and central area, making the north entrance narrower.

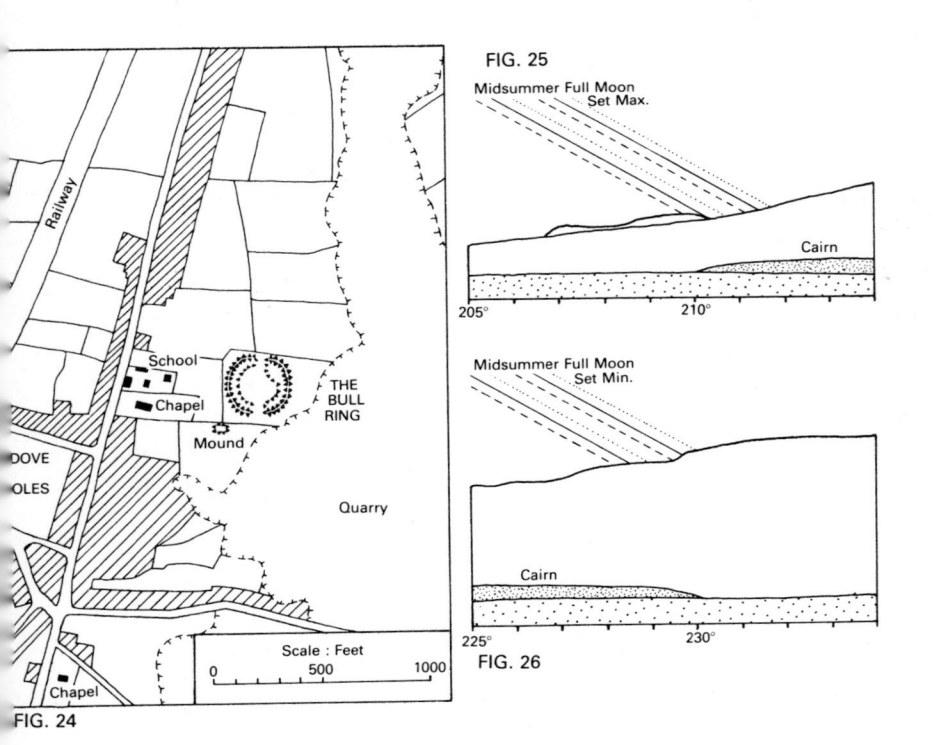

FIG. 24

FIG. 25 Midsummer Full Moon Set Max.

FIG. 26 Midsummer Full Moon Set Min.

In the north-west there is a small platform of unknown age between the bank and ditch. The central area is flat, with no sign of any original feature, it has a diameter of 150 x 140 feet, with the elongation to the north. In 1787 Pilkington stated that one standing stone still remained and this probably indicates that a similar ring to that of Arbor Low once existed. Approximately 100 feet from the outer edge of the bank to the south-west is a large rectangular cairn which is 90 by 70 feet and 8 feet high. This could be of the same age as the henge and is paralleled by Gib Hill, except that this neolithic mound at Arbor Low is further away.

GEOMETRY

As the geometry was probably determined by a ring of stones and the bank only followed it approximately, nothing definite can be reconstructed. However, it looks as though it was elongated to the north as an egg or possibly an ellipse. The bank also has four slight changes of angle: to the south-west in the direction of the cairn, to the north-west at the platform and two more to the north-east and south-east. These changes are reflected in the horizon, the east and west quarters defining Bee Low and Black Edge respectively, while the other two quarters are to more distant moors.

ALIGNMENTS

The horizon was chosen for its alignments with the full moon at midsummer. The rising positions are now obscured by quarries, but were probably marked. The maximum must have been very close to Five Wells chambered tomb on Taddington Moor which would have been visible 5 miles away. The setting positions were well marked, with the full moon at its maximum first touching the horizon at the junction between Axe Edge and Black Edge; the minimum was at a well defined notch on Black Edge. The geometry and stones possibly marked solar lines, as at Arbor Low. This is indicated by the points of changes of angle in the bank which from the centre of the circle were approximately in the direction of the solstices. The centre of the mound to the south-west is below the setting point of the midwinter sun, while its edges are approximately below the midsummer moon lines mentioned above.

The Staden Henge (SK.0693.7211)

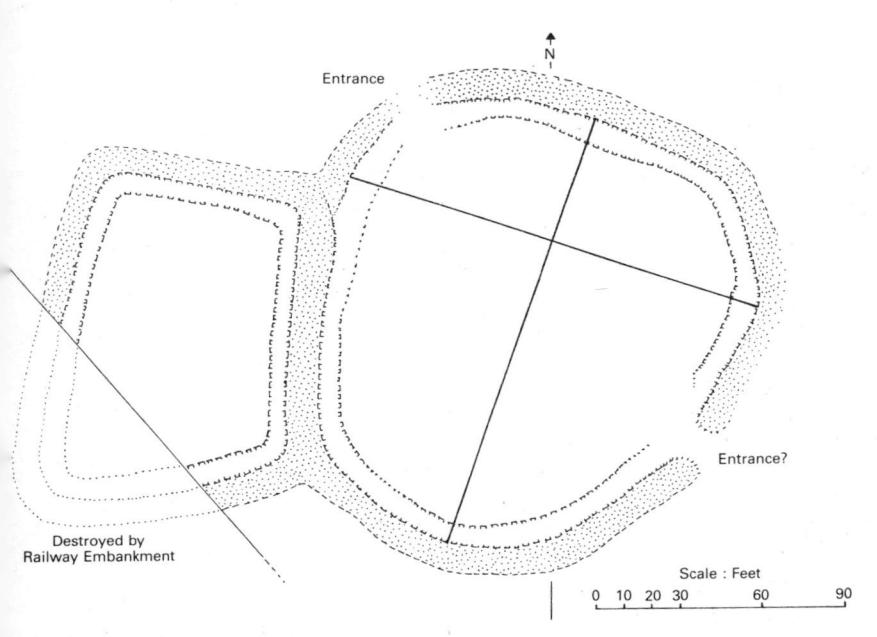

FIG. 27

This henge is also in a low-lying situation, in a hollow on the limestone plateau above the Wye Valley gorge to the north and below the high limestone ridges to the south. There are fine views of gritstone moors to the west and north including Axe, Burbage, Black and Rushup Edges. The nearby Staden Low and Fox Low dominate the horizon to the east and south.

The site is next to the railway line in the third field down from the road. The bank and ditch are very slight and thick grass in summer makes them difficult to see. The henge consists of an oval bank with an outer diameter of 190 x 175 feet. Inside this is a ditch which is very shallow, especially in the north-west. Together the bank and ditch have a width of about 19 feet and a maximum change of height of about 2 feet.

FIG. 28

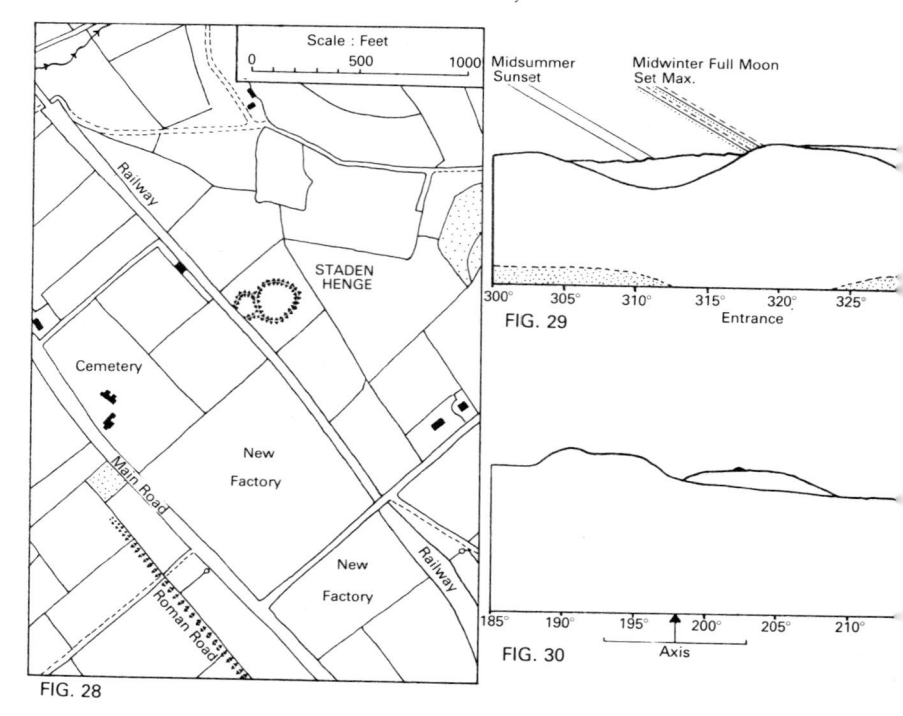

FIG. 29

FIG. 30

The bank is broken in two places by what could be entrances. The one to the north-west is about 15 feet wide with badly defined edges, while the one in the south-east is 14 feet wide with better edges. However, it looks rather like a more recent trench cut through the bank, and is possibly not original. A sketch in the original notes of Hayman Rooke, drawn in the late eighteenth century, does not show this entrance—a further indication that this henge could be an early one-entrance type of the neolithic period.

The central area defined by the bank and ditch has a diameter of 152 x 136 feet and has no features. The most unusual part of the site is an approximately rectangular enclosure attached to the western side of the ring. Unfortunately one corner has been destroyed by the railway embankment, but it appears to have had straight sides with external dimensions of 116 x 96 x 145 x 110 feet. It is similar to the ring in that it has a low bank with an internal ditch defining a central area, with dimensions of 81 x 61 x 110 x 75 feet. This feature has led many people to doubt if this site is a henge, as there are no others in the country with an enclosure like this. It is possible that it is not contemporary with the ring, but even if it is, the ring does not resemble any other form of monument except a henge, although only excavation will prove this beyond doubt.

GEOMETRY

The geometry cannot be reconstructed for the same reason as the Bull Ring. However it is clear that it is a form of egg, elongated to the S.S.W., with three clear changes of angle. The ring balances well round the long axis, except where the rectangular enclosure meets the ring at its southern end. Here there is a bulge in the central area, possibly an indication that the ring is later than the rectangle. Externally, the bank has diameters of 70 x 65 MY, which could be significant. The entrances, both about 5 MY wide, fit with the geometry. The north-western one is at a change of angle and the south-eastern one is half way along a side, possibly an indication that this is an original feature.

ALIGNMENTS

The henge does not have any very convincing astronomical alignments which relate to the geometry or horizon, possibly indicating that this is an early type of henge. These were probably built before celestial bodies were considered to be significant, when the main relationships were purely to the landscape. The elongated end of the ring points to the prominant dip between Fox Low and Harpur Hill, both of which have a burial mound on their summits.

The only astronomical lines with possible significance are connected with the north-west entrance. The midsummer sunset was at the centre of a section of Longhill marked by a slight rise, approximately over the left edge of the entrance. The midwinter full moon set at its maximum was just past the junction between Longhill and Corbar Hill, with the last flash of light in a defined dip. This dip is above the centre of the entrance. These two lines show a similarity with the arrangement of the north-west entrance at Arbor Low, which also has the same astronomical lines.

6

Circles of the Central Area

The Stoke Flat Circle, Froggatt Edge (SK.2497.7679)

This circle is situated on flat moorland on top of the cliffs of Froggatt Edge with impressive views below into the Derwent Valley and beyond to the bleak Eyam Moor; to the south are the limestone moors and to the north a fine view past Win Hill to the high moors and sharp edges of the gritstone in the distance. The circle is just to the left of the footpath when walking from the north and is easily located by its one tall stone, rising from the heather and bracken, looking rather like a gatepost. First impressions of the site are that there is very little to see as it is disturbed and some of its stones are missing but on closer examination it is seen to be a complex monument that is very revealing.

In its present state it consists of a low bank 51 feet across which is 8-10 feet wide and ½-1½ feet high with an internal edge retained by a two-course drystone wall of horizontally laid stones which has a diameter of 38 feet. Breaking this bank are two diametrically opposite entrances, each 6-8 feet wide and flanked by standing stones. The northern one is unusual in that it is blocked with rubble that appears to be original and this is perhaps only a symbolic entrance. The site is untypical in that it has two rings of standing stones one on each edge of the bank. The original number of stones is unknown but they were recorded in 1848 by Bateman as being equally spaced. Today there are only 5-7 on the inner edge, 2-5 on the outer and 2 in the centre of the southern entrance. Only 9 of these are still standing but enough remains to show that the two rings were

Circles of the Central Area

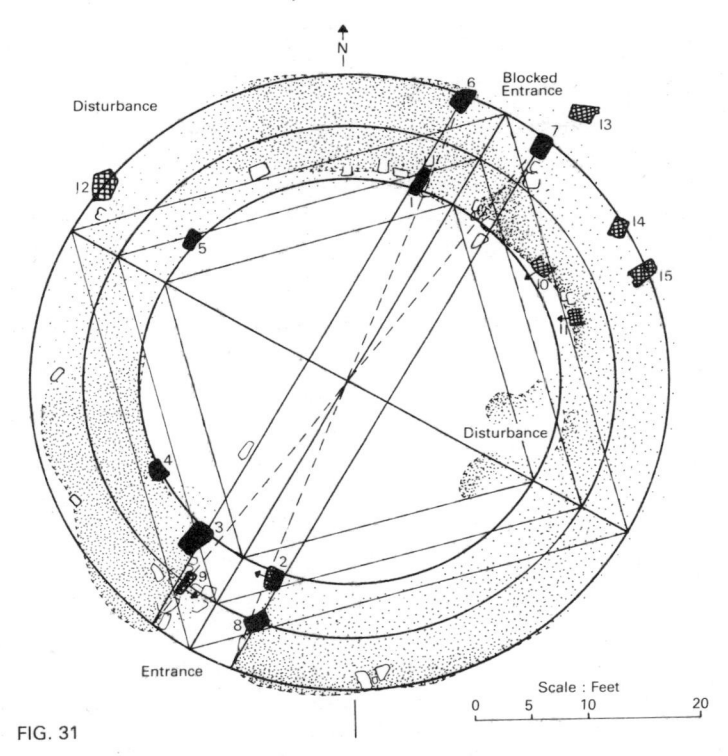

FIG. 31

conceived as having stones in identical directions when viewed from the centre. The entrances are given special emphasis by placing standing stones here with their faces parallel to them. All the surviving stones are of a similar small size except stone 3 in the southern entrance which is significantly larger and pillar-like and had special importance.

Surrounding the circle are many irregular lines and piles of rubble which are remains of prehistoric field clearance which could be contemporary with it.

GEOMETRY

Construction

Despite the disturbance of the site a good reconstruction can be made, which has very convincing results, this is:
Both the edges of the bank and their stones are true circles, and the stones in the southern entrance suggest a third circle can be drawn here at the centre of the bank. The entrance stones are exactly opposite each other forming a long rectangle round the centre of the site and defining an axis.

The dimensions of these in megalithic yards are as follows:

Inner ring	diameter	14
	circumference	44[1]
Central ring	diameter	17½
	circumference	55[2]
Outer ring	diameter	21
	circumference	66[3]
Width of bank		7
Width of entrance		3
Rectangle		3 × 21

The dimensions are all integral because of the use of multiples of 7 for the diameters, which is the only number which gives circumferences with errors so small as to be undetectable. This circle is a convincing and beautiful expression of the builders' knowledge that π is an approximation to $\frac{22}{7}$.

The entrances fit into the construction because the rectangle they form is in the ratio of 1:7. Also if lines are drawn from the centre of the site to the entrance edges at the external edge, it transforms the circumferences as follows:

Outer ring	66	Width of entrance lines 3	Each side of bank 30
(Central ring	55	Width of entrance lines 2½	Each side of bank 25)
(Inner ring	44	Width of entrance lines 2	Each side of bank 20)

Another fact that was probably considered is that if squares are drawn inside each of the circles they have the following perimeters:

> Outer square   60[4]
> Central square   50[5]
> Inner square   40[6]

This obviously relates directly to the measurements given above.

Numbers

When considering all the important numbers of the circle they form a series of basic numbers, as follows:
1. The whole site
2. Two entrances making two sides
3. Three circles, width of entrances 3, one outer side 30
4. Circumference of the inner circle 44, inner square 40
5. Circumference of the central circle 55, central square 50
6. Circumference of the outer circle 66, outer square 60, two outer sides 60
7. Width of bank 7, basis of the diameters, internal × 2, external × 3

The only significant number not included above is the central ring diameter 17.5, MY which is important as it is 7 MR.

Symbolism

The circle can be considered as an expression of the interrelationship of the numbers 1 to 7 which symbolically are: 1 as a whole, 1-3 as the basis of all things, 4 the inner edge, the world, 5 the central ring as the life force at the centre of things, 6 the outer edge, fixing and harmonising the whole structure and 7 the mystical number of initiation which underlies the whole construction.

ALIGNMENTS

Observation of the horizon shows that the exact location for the site of the circle was chosen with great care as is usual with the circles. In this case it was so that three well defined horizon features aligned with the moon. The position with the greatest importance was marked with the axis through the southern entrance, where Middleton Common is visible. This is a very distant flat horizon whose right hand junction is the location of Arbor Low; the full moon at its midsummer maximum would set exactly into the henge. This position could be used as an eclipse predictor because the moon generally would only be partially set when directly over Arbor Low; but if its last flash was here this was the eclipse position.

The rising point for the moon on the same day was also marked where it rose from a small area of Curbar Edge, just visible above the nearby moor. Here the eclipse cycle variation would also be detectable from the bumps on either side of the moon's mean position.

The third moon line is at the midwinter full moon maximum setting, where it would set into the slope of Win Hill, just north of the junction with Eyam Moor; the eclipse variation was also detectable from bumps at either side.

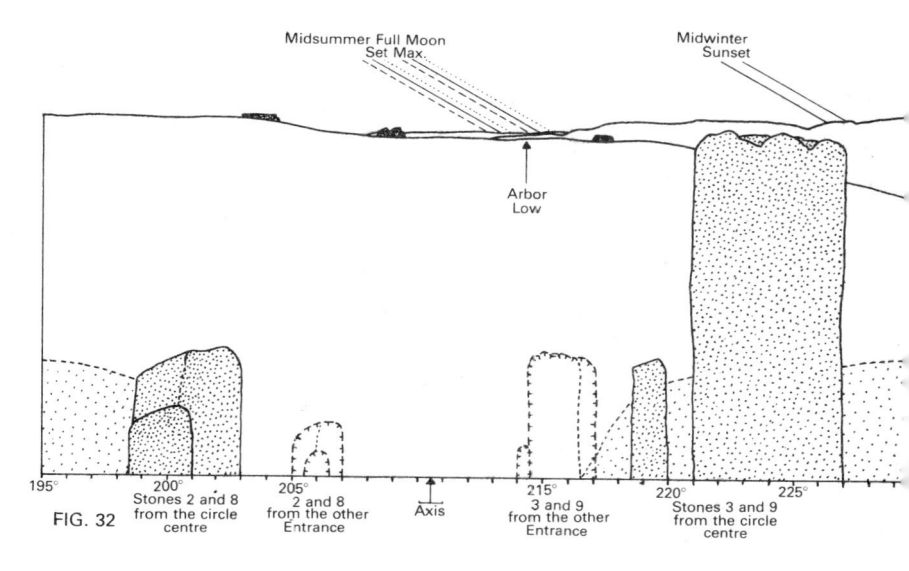

FIG. 32

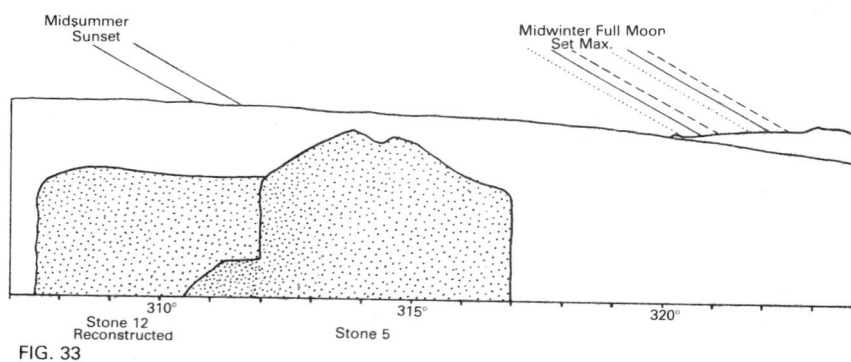

| 195° | 200° Stones 2 and 8 from the circle centre | 205° 2 and 8 from the other Entrance | Axis | 215° 3 and 9 from the other Entrance | 220° Stones 3 and 9 from the circle centre | 225° |

Midsummer Full Moon Set Max.
Arbor Low
Midwinter Sunset

FIG. 33

Midsummer Sunset
Midwinter Full Moon Set Max.
310° Stone 12 Reconstructed
315° Stone 5
320°

FIG. 34

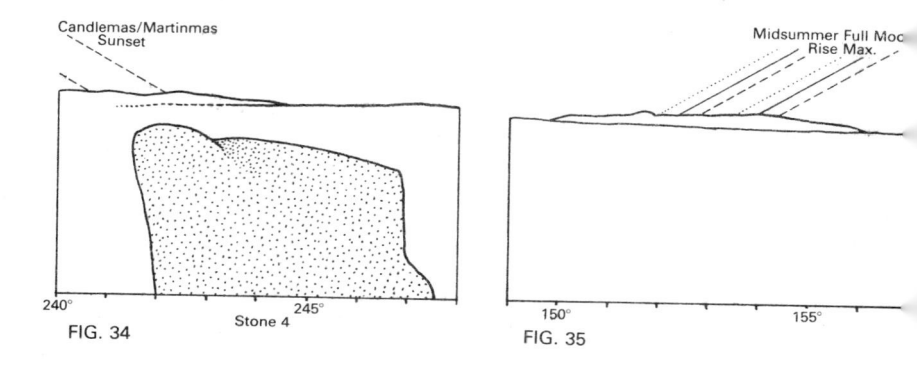

Candlemas/Martinmas Sunset
240°
245° Stone 4

FIG. 35

Midsummer Full Moon Rise Max.
150°
155°

Circles of the Central Area

Once the position for the circle had been determined by the lines above, the builders must have had to decide how to arrange the geometry so that it related to the astronomical lines important to this circle. The solution they chose was to make the geometry align to the moon and the stones to the sun, a procedure which was common in circles of this area. This indicates that they were trying to combine the forces of the sun and moon, and also that the study of the moon was perhaps kept secret.

At this circle a slight compromise had to be accepted. The main axis was orientated to the moon line given above, but slightly offset so that the edges of the entrance flank the dip in the horizon that contained this line. The main reason for this is shown in the careful positioning of the large pillar (stone 3). From the centre of the northern entrance, standing on the outside of the bank stone 3 marked the moon line. Standing at the circle centre, it marked the setting of the midwinter sun. This was on a slight bump on Longstone Edge above the right edge of the stone. However, if one sat down so that the stone top rose above the horizon then the sun would set into the centre of the stone. This main alignment with stone 3 to the sun and moon is emphasised by the entrances and their smaller standing stones (1,6,7,2,8,9).

The ring stones were probably designed to mark the sunsets at all the remaining important times of the year. Stone 4 marked the Candlemas/Martinmas sunset on Longstone Edge with the last flash of light over the point of the stone. This could be determined with some accuracy by using stones 10/14 as backsights, as they are diametrically opposite stone 4.

Stone 5 and 12 marked the midwinter sunset on Eyam Moor, so that the last flash of the sun was between them. There is possibly a missing backsight for this alignment on the other side of the ring.

The other two sunset lines of importance, equinox and May Day/Lammas both on Eyam Moor were approximately in positions where one would expect to find two missing stones between stones 4 and 5.

The only stones not explained by this reconstruction are 11 and 15 which possibly had some geometric balance function that cannot now be ascertained because of the missing stones.

To sum up, the circle was built to relate to the moon at the solstices, especially at its setting into Arbor Low at midsummer. At the same time it symbolically channelled the sunsets throughout the year through the stones to the centre of the ring where they meet the moon lines.

The Barbrook I Circle (SK.2785.7558)

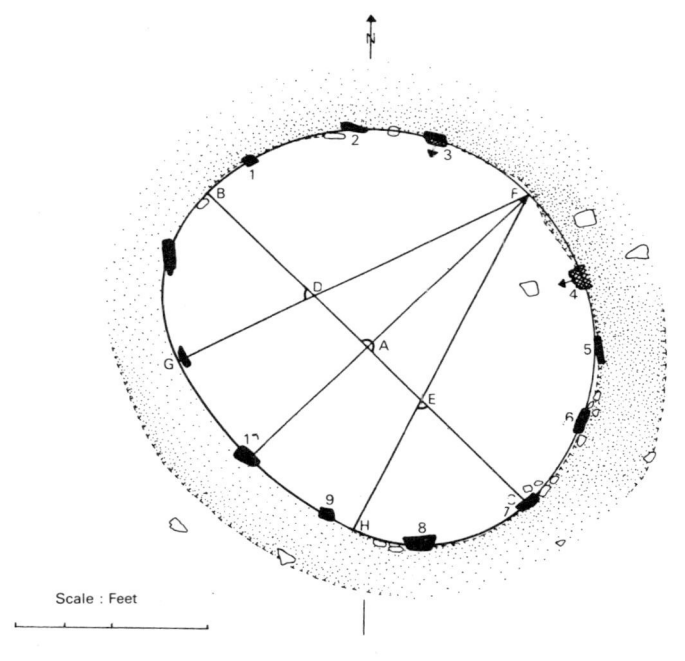

FIG. 36

This circle is in the heart of the bleak gritstone moorlands in a slight hollow above the steepsided upland course of Barbrook. In most directions all that can be seen are the rough heather moors of Big Moor and White Edge. The exception to this is in the south-west where the rolling limestone ridges and plateau can be seen in the far distance over ten miles away. To the left of this are nearer gritstone edges and moors, stretching as far as Stanton Moor, above the stunted trees of the wood lower down the Barbrook Valley. From this spot virtually no traces of modern man are visible and the circle has an atmosphere strangely evocative of the past and the power of nature.

Circles of the Central Area

The circle is clearly visible above the trackway on the right, on a small flat piece of ground covered in heather, bilberry and coarse grass. It is one of the best preserved circles in the Peak District and consists of a ring of twelve standing stones, surrounded by a low bank and several outliers dotted about the moor nearby. The stones are all standing upright (3 and 4 leaning slightly inwards) and are one to two feet high with the exception of stone 10 which is 3½ feet high and clearly visible from quite a distance away. These stones have a diameter of 47½ × 41 feet and are set in the internal edge of the bank. There is evidence that this edge was retained by a drystone wall and the bank appears to be continuous, with no entrance to the central area. This bank is now badly preserved and only one foot high. It is 7-8½ feet wide and has an external diameter of 62-64 feet × 55-57 feet. The central area was originally flat with no features but now has two slight trenches across it, cut earlier this century in an attempt to find burials. Beyond the bank are a series of 9-10 small outliers which are erected in all directions between 130 and 1200 feet away.

GEOMETRY

Construction

Professor Thom surveyed this circle and established the basis of its geometry. It is a classic example of what he calls a 'Flattened type B' circle[7]. This was confirmed by an independent survey. The construction is basically a circle flattened on one side, which in this case has dimensions showing a good case for it being conceived in units of ¼MY, as will become apparent. This geometry is constructed as follows:
1) From A a semi-circle is drawn from B to C forming the long axis of the circle.
2) The diameter BC is divided into three equal parts, points D and E.
3) From F, lines are extended through DG and EH.
4) From D an arc from B to G. From E an arc from C to H.
5) From F an arc to close the ring from G to H. This forms the short axis of the site.
The dimensions in the case of this circle are as follows:
     Long axis 70 × ¼MY
     Short axis 60 × ¼MY[8]
This construction creates a circumference which is an approximation to Diameter × 3 = 210 × ¼MY[9].

The original width of the bank is probably 10 × ¼MY which gives the following external dimensions:

>Long axis   90 × ¼MY
>Short axis   80 × ¼MY

From the basic construction established by Thom a series of mathematical and geometrical relationships have been developed, which due to the dimensions of the ring and arrangement of the standing stones are shown to have been considered by the builders of the circle:

The length of a straight line from G to H is 38 × ¼MY[10]. This length fits virtually exactly five times into the ring (drawn with compasses from G and H), forming a slightly flattened pentagon with equal sides totalling 190 × ¼MY, but with slightly differing internal lengths. This construction is the main factor in the arrangement of the standing stones (as will be shown later) and is probably the simplest method found by the stone circle builders for constructing a close approximation to a perfect pentagon with integral lengths[11].

FKN and FLM are two 3:4:5 triangles which link the construction given above. They have side lengths of 33, 44 and 55 × ⅛MY. The point F is the end of the short axis and a pentagon point. The points K and L are internal pentagon points and the points M and N are justified because the lines AM and AN cut the angles BAF and CAF exactly in half. The lines LM and KN when extended go exactly to B and C with the lengths MB and NC both being 55 × ⅛MY. The lengths FB and FC are 99 × ⅛MY[12].

Balance

Once it is realised that a pentagon is the main factor in the construction it reveals how the stones are arranged: firstly as a series of balanced opposites in relation to the pentagon points and the short axis, which as a line brings in a sixth point.

Short axis	
stone 10	point F, in the centre of the largest gap
Pentagon points	
point H, gap	Point G, stone 11
Pentagon points	
point J, stone 6	Point I, gap.

The sixth point, stone 10 is much larger than any of the other stones and marks the main axis of balance as the basis of the site's stone arrangement.

Circles of the Central Area

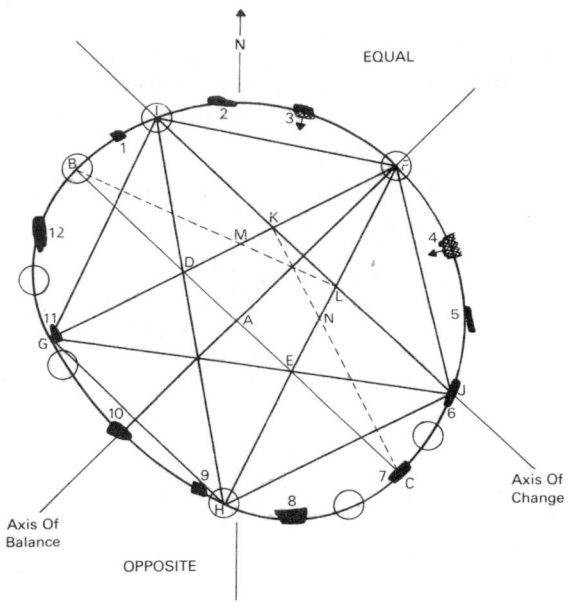

FIG. 37

All the other stones fit with this system of balance as follows:
3 sides of balanced opposites.

Side GH	stone 10 axis	
	stone 9	gap
(Pentagon line)	gap	stone 11
Sides GI/HJ	stone 8	gap
	gap	stone 12
(Long axis)	stone 7	gap
	gap	stone 1
(Pentagon line)	stone 6	gap
2 sides of equal balance.		
Sides IF/JF	stone 5	stone 2
	stone 4	stone 3
	gap	

These two types of balance divide the pentagon across the central area in the only possible way, 2:3 and create 20 fixed points with stones and gaps[13].

Numbers

When considering all the numbers connected with the geometry and measurements it becomes apparent that there was a conscious effort to combine all the basic numbers, as was the case at the Stoke Flat Circle, but in a different way, as follows:

Geometry
1. The whole ring
2,3. Division of the pentagon
4. The four quarters, the four arcs
5. The pentagon
6. The pentagon plus stone 10
7. Six plus the centre of the circle
(12. The number of standing stones)

Measurement
33,44,45. Triangles in units of ⅛MY
6. Short axis (6 MR)
7. Long axis (7 MR)
8,9. External axes (in MR)
99. Length of FC and FB in units of ⅛MY.

The only important numbers not included here are the circumference of 21 MR and the length of the five pentagon sides 19 MR, both of which relate numerically to the 20 marked divisions of the ring.

Symbolism

These numerical relationships create a symbolic temple with the most potent elements : 1 as the whole; 1—3 the basic trinity; 4 as the directions and seasons as shown by alignments to the sun at midwinter, illustrated on the next page; 5 as the life force added to the earth; 6 the balance and fixing of the site and its forces; 7 the centre, the number of initiation; 8 and 9 as the world and finality enclosing the outside of the site.

ALIGNMENTS

The circle was designed to be specifically solar in character, with the geometry and stones both symbolically aligning to the sun at important times of the year. Altogether six alignments were incorporated in this way, the most important ones being at midwinter.

The midwinter sunrise was on the close horizon of Ramsley Moor directly above stone 7 on the long axis of the circle. Stone 7 was obviously chosen carefully with a notch in it from which the sun rose.

The midwinter sunset was on Baslow Edge with the last flash of light just to the left of a prominent natural rock which could have been used to pinpoint midwinters day exactly by observing how many days the sun missed it and dividing the total in half. The sunset was above the right edge of the largest stone (10). Just to the left of this point at the centre of the stone is the short axis which aligns exactly with Arbor

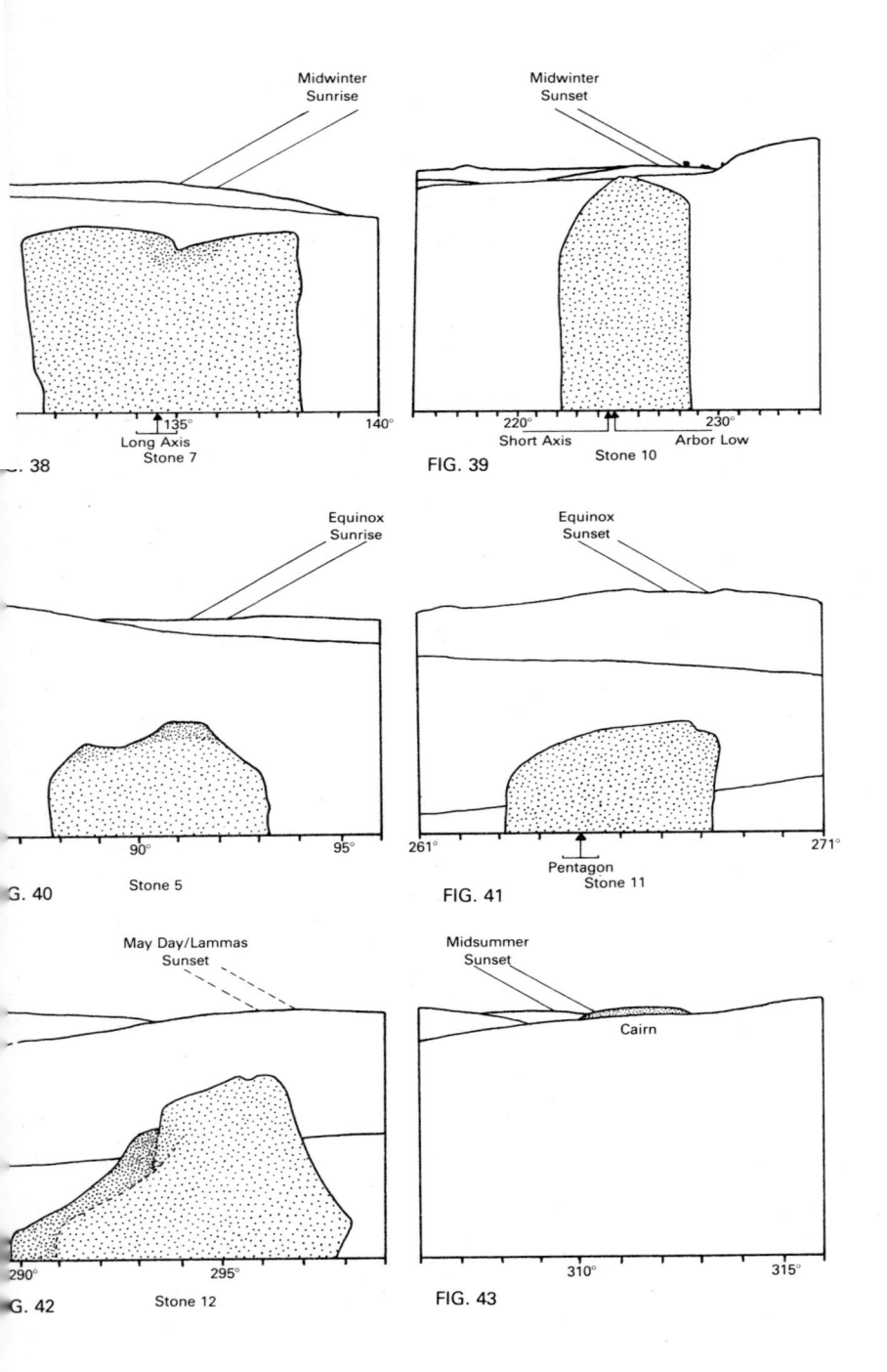

Midwinter Sunrise

135°   140°
Long Axis
Stone 7

FIG. 38

Midwinter Sunset

220°   230°
Short Axis   Arbor Low
Stone 10

FIG. 39

Equinox Sunrise

90°   95°
Stone 5

FIG. 40

Equinox Sunset

261°   271°
Pentagon
Stone 11

FIG. 41

May Day/Lammas Sunset

290°   295°
Stone 12

FIG. 42

Midsummer Sunset

Cairn

310°   315°

FIG. 43

Low on the distant horizon of Middleton Common just where it disappears behind Baslow Edge.

These two alignments show that the circle was primarily designed to be a midwinter solar site, and that the position of the circle had been chosen very carefully so the rise and setting positions virtually formed a right angle corresponding to the axes of the circle. The setting, which is the most important geometrically, was also symbolically into Arbor Low. Both sites were probably connected with magical rites concerned with the belief in the rejuvenation of the sun at midwinter by it being 'captured and restored' in Arbor Low.

Both the Equinox sun lines were marked by the two smallest stones in the ring. The rise was above stone 5 on Ramsley Moor very close to its junction with the close moor. Stone 5 has two points, the highest to the right was to the sunrise and that to the left is to the junction. The Equinox sunset was on White Edge above the flat topped stone 11 near the right edge at the notch. (This stone is also one of the pentagon points.) The remaining two alignments were for different days, firstly the May Day/Lammas sunset on Big Moor directly above the peak of the large stone 12 and secondly midsummer sunset where the sun would set very close to the junction between Big Moor and the nearby moor. At some stage this was improved by building a large cairn so that the last flash of light was at the junction between Big Moor and the cairn. However this alignment was not very accurate because only a small movement on site would throw it out.

These alignments use the following stones: 5,7,10,11,12 which leaves seven more. 1,2 and 6 are needed to balance 5 and 7, 8 and 9 for 11 and 12 which only leaves stones 3 and 4 which are perhaps only for balance to make the stones look approximately equally spaced.

One moon alignment exists to the distant limestone ridges, where at midsummer the full moon at its maximum would set into Aleck Low, moving down its right edge and disappearing in to junction at the base of the slope. This is not marked in the circle and was obviously of no symbolic importance. However, it was probably used in connection with the outliers, as the horizon is so far away that movement in any direction for a few hundred feet would not significantly alter the alignment.

THE OUTLIERS

All the evidence suggests that these outlying stones were gradually erected around the circle after its completion to study the sun and moon at different times of the year.

The first phase of building was the three outliers A,B and C to create two totally new alignments. These were placed so that A and B are both 20 MR from the centre of the circle (36.5 MR apart, possibly

Circles of the Central Area 107

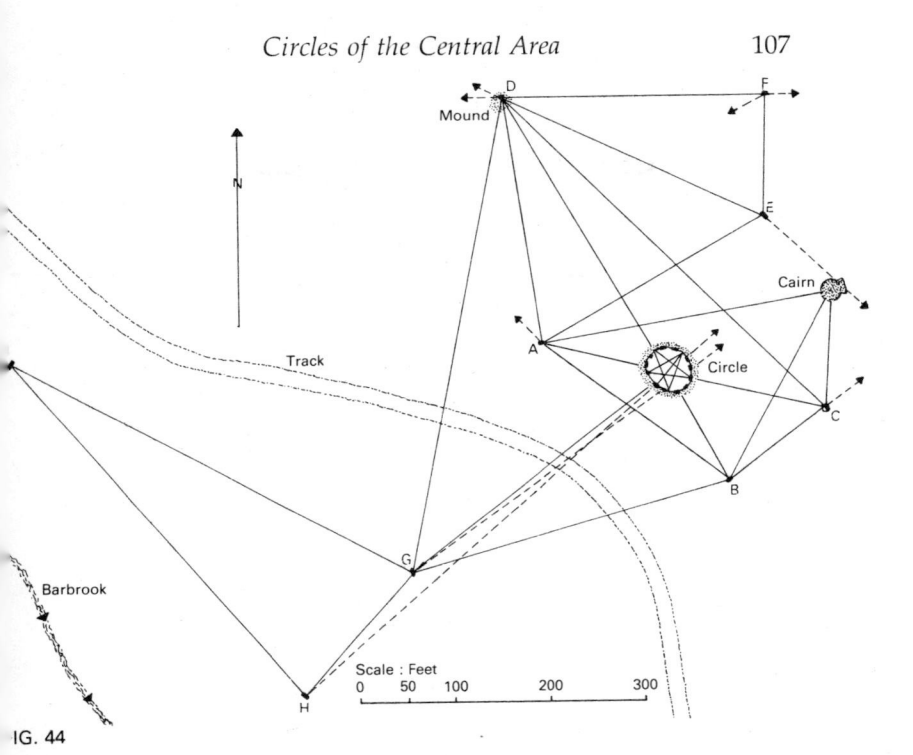

FIG. 44

coincidence or because of 365 days in a year). Then C was built on an extension of the line A—circle—C so that it is 25 MR from the circle centre. (Total line length 45 MR divided in a ratio of 4 + 5 = 9.) A is situated so that the cairn mentioned on the last page now aligned with the full moon at its midwinter maximum set. Standing at B and looking through C (19 MR away) to the close horizon is midsummer sunrise, with the sun directly above C when fully risen.

The next phase of building is to mark lines accurately that were marked symbolically in the circle. The flat moor above the hollow the circle is in was used for this. First, the position of D was fixed by extending the line B—circle—D so that it is exactly the same distance from B and C (71 MR forming isosceles triangle D,B,C, with sides 71,71,19 probably coincidence), also the distance from A to D automatically became 40 MR. Then the position of E was fixed by making it also 40 MR from A and the distance between D and E, 45 MR. (Ratio of 8:8:9 related to ratios 4 + 5 = 9 above.) The line from E to D was exactly the May Day/Lammas sunset corresponding to the stone 12 symbolic line in the circle. At some stage the large reconstructed cairn was built so that to its centre it is 45 MR from A and 19 MY from C (isosceles triangles A—C—Cairn 45:45:19 and C—B—Cairn 19:19:34½). From E,

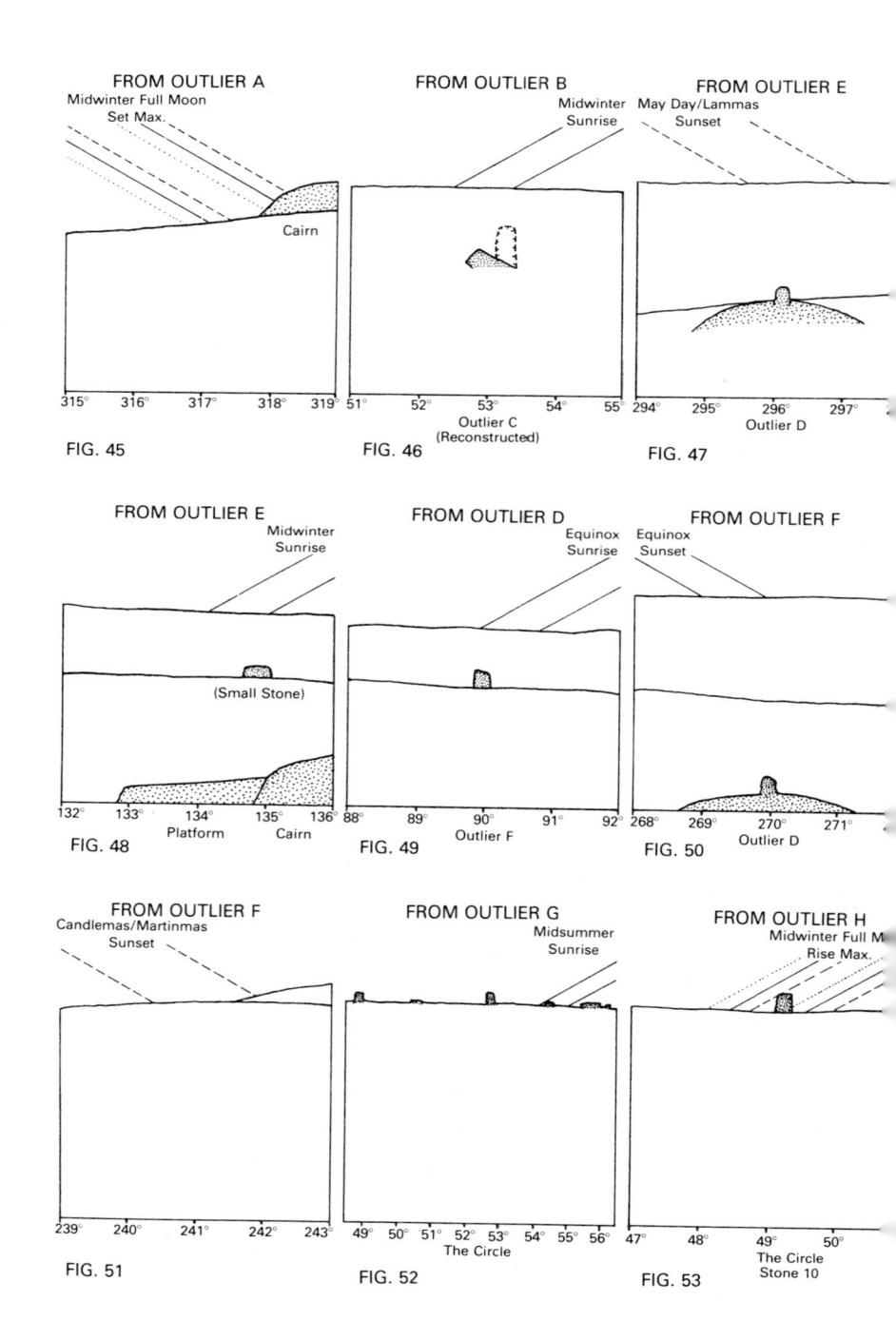

FIG. 45 FROM OUTLIER A — Midwinter Full Moon Set Max. — Cairn — 315° 316° 317° 318° 319°

FIG. 46 FROM OUTLIER B — Midwinter Sunrise — 51° 52° 53° 54° 55° — Outlier C (Reconstructed)

FIG. 47 FROM OUTLIER E — May Day/Lammas Sunset — 294° 295° 296° 297° — Outlier D

FIG. 48 FROM OUTLIER E — Midwinter Sunrise — (Small Stone) — 132° 133° 134° 135° 136° — Platform — Cairn

FIG. 49 FROM OUTLIER D — Equinox Sunrise — 88° 89° 90° 91° 92° — Outlier F

FIG. 50 FROM OUTLIER F — Equinox Sunset — 268° 269° 270° 271° — Outlier D

FIG. 51 FROM OUTLIER F — Candlemas/Martinmas Sunset — 239° 240° 241° 242° 243°

FIG. 52 FROM OUTLIER G — Midsummer Sunrise — 49° 50° 51° 52° 53° 54° 55° 56° — The Circle

FIG. 53 FROM OUTLIER H — Midwinter Full Moon Rise Max. — 47° 48° 49° 50° — The Circle Stone 10

Circles of the Central Area

this cairn's platform was directly below midwinter sunrise, and this could have been accurately marked, corresponding with the symbolic stone 7 circle line.

As a continuance of the last phase or at a later date, outlier F was fixed. This forms a right angle to D and E (sides $19\frac{1}{2}:40\frac{1}{2}:45$, probably coincidence). From D to F was the Equinox sunrise, and reversed from F to D was the Equinox sunset which correspond with the symbolic lines through stone 5 and 11 in the circle. From F to the prominent junction above Barbrook V marked the Candlemas/Martinmas sunset, the only sunset line not already marked in any way.

At some stage after the building of outlier D, building was commenced downhill from the circle. Firstly G, which is visible from the circle on the other side of the track just by the thick bracken. The position of this stone was fixed by basing it on the distance from the circle to D, 51 MR, G to circle, 51 MR and G to B, 51 MR (forming two isosceles triangles, circle:D:G and G:B:circle). This outlier is positioned so that the circle is on the horizon and at midsummer the sun rose out of stone 9. This was much more accurate than the BC line and probably replaced it.

Further down the slope, hidden from the circle by bracken, is outlier H (26 MR from G). From this stone, stone 10 of the circle is on the horizon and was the exact position of the moonrise at the midwinter maximum.

Upstream from H on a steep slope is another possible outlier, stone I which is not visible from the circle but is from H, it is 70 MR from G and H. This stone created a better horizon alignment to the symbolic midsummer sunset.

By the time all these outliers had been constructed the sun and moon could be observed accurately at any time of the year, with every sunset marked, the solstice and equinox sunrises and every lunar solstice maximum position.

The Barbrook II Circle (SK.2775.7582)

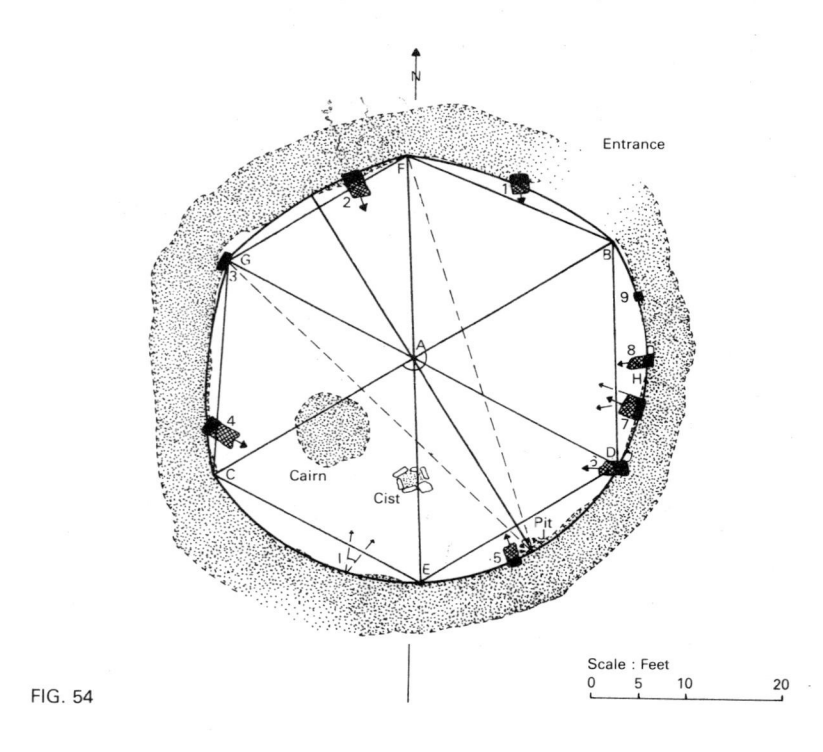

FIG. 54

Scale : Feet
0 5 10 20

This circle is only about 850 feet away from Barbrook I on the flat moor further to the north-west, but because Barbrook I is in a hollow, they are not intervisible.

The excavation by G. D. Lewis in 1966 offers an opportunity to visualise a typical circle in its original state. Unfortunately it has recently been partially restored in a careless way so that the bank looks very rough and two of the standing stones have also disappeared.

The site consists of a rubble bank which is retained externally by a single line of kerb stones with a diameter of approximately 64 × 57 feet, and internally by a drystone wall of 2-3 horizontal courses with a diameter of 49 × 45 feet. The maximum height of this bank was around 1½ feet and a ring of standing stones was set in the internal wall; these are between 1½ and 2 feet high, with the exception of stone 4 which is 3 feet high. The bank has an original entrance to the north-east which is about 10 feet wide. There were 9 stones in the ring of which only one is still standing. The reason for this was discovered by Lewis who found that they were not set into the ground but fixed into the bank by stone wedges. Unfortunately stones 8 and 9 have now disappeared, together with what was probably a vertically set wall stone next to stone 8. An unusual feature of the stones is that they are not evenly spaced. A large gap was left between stones 4 and 5 and stones 6,7,8 and 9 were bunched together. The central area has two features which are well offset from the centre; a small cairn 8 feet in diameter and a small stone cist. They were proved to be of the mid Bronze Age, about 1800 b.c. ± 150 years,* but are not necessarily exactly contemporary with the circle.

GEOMETRY

Construction

The excavated site makes an accurate reconstruction possible. The circle is a unique flattened type of ring based on a hexagon, which is constructed as follows:
1) A semi-circle from A to form the long axis BC, 70 × ¼MY long. Constructed with three equilateral triangles using points D and E with each side being 35 × ¼MY long.
2) Lines DA and EA are entended to G and F.
3) G and F are determined by taking points H and I offset from F and G and drawing arcs from H joining C to G and from I joining B to F. The reason for the two irrational points H and I is to achieve the required flattening of the ring for the short axis. This stage is not essential if stage 4 is drawn first, then an arc is guessed for CG and BF.
4) A closing arc from J joining F to G forming the short axis 65 × ¼MY long.

This construction gives a circumference very close to 210 × ¼MY, the exact measurement being dependent on which way arc 3 was fixed. The hexagon has sides which are as follows:

*b.c. denotes radio-carbon years before 0 AD.

DE, BD, CE	35 × ¼MY	Either	35	or	35
BF, CG	33.73 × ¼MY	Either	33.75	or	32[14]
FG	32.30 × ¼MY	Either	32.50	or	31[15]
Total	204.76 × ¼MY	Either	205	or	200[16]

If the total is meant to be the numerically more desirable 200 then large errors must have had to be accepted.

Balance

The entrance is placed next to the long axis and occupies half of one side. The stones are arranged as balanced opposites round the resultant axis as at Barbrook I.

```
                    Axis J. (Pit)
             Stone 5  │  gap
             gap      │  Stone 6       Points E and D
             gap      │  Stone 7       (Points I and H)
             gap      │  Stone 8
             gap      │  Stone 9
             (gap     │  gap           Long axis)
             Stone 4  │  gap
             gap      │  Stone 1
             Stone 3  │  gap           Points G and F
             gap      │  Stone 2
                    Axis K. gap
```

The confusing area in the circular half could be explained as stone 7 being an extra one to mark point H and stone 8 being misplaced from the other side of the ring. This arrangement has a probable total of 20 balanced points.

The exact geometric centre could be found by intersecting two lines, stones 3 and 6, and stones 4 and 9 (edges). A method which must have been important as the centre was not marked by any kind of feature.

Numbers

The circle has the following important numerical relationships.

    6. The hexagon
    7. The hexagon plus the centre, long axis, (circumference)
    9. Number of stones
(20. Hexagon total, balance points.)

Symbolism

This symbolically can be seen as, 6 harmony combined with 7 the hidden number of initiation, with 9 finality.

ALIGNMENTS

All the astronomical lines were to the relatively flat horizons of Ramsley Moor and White Edge, except for the midsummer full moon rise and set at its maximum at both edges of the far horizon to the south. The rise was marked by the short axis J, and the set was at the exact junction between the far horizon and White Edge. As this should be the position of stone 8, it might be further evidence of the secrecy of moon alignments. The only two hexagon points with standing stones symbolically marking sun lines, are stone 6 the Candlemas/Martinmas sunrise and stone 3 the May Day/Lammas sunset. The movement of stone 8 made it mark the equinox sunrise. This circle therefore is identical to Barbrook I in that the horizon is lunar and the stones solar. The other stones, except for 7, are needed to balance stones 3, 6 and 8. Stone 4 is significantly larger than the others; the reason for this is obscure unless it is just that it is approximately opposite the entrance.

The Barbrook III Circle (SK.2834.7728)

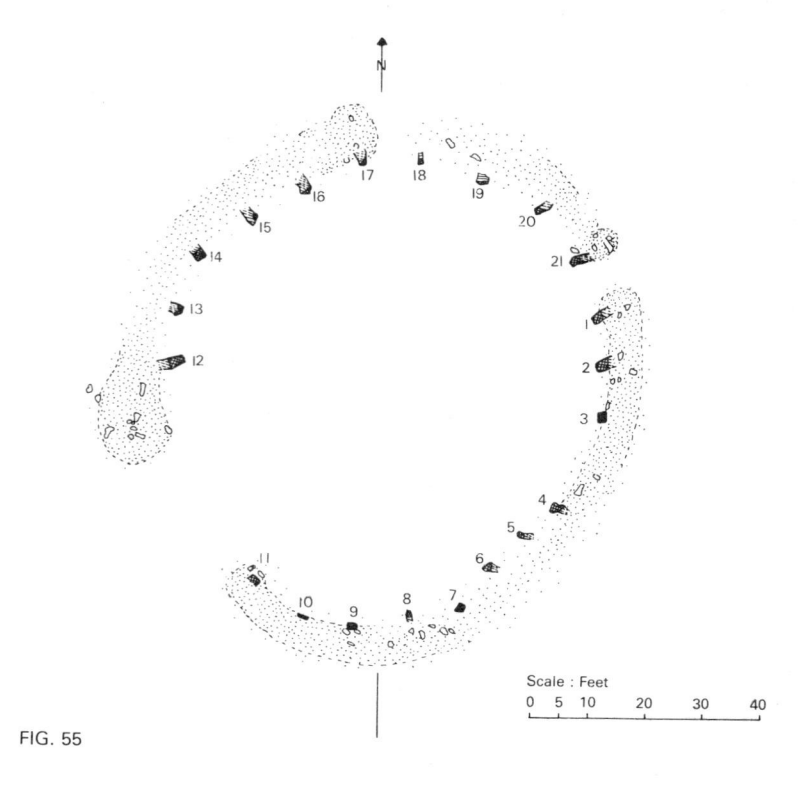

FIG. 55

This circle is just over a mile north of Barbrook I and II on a flat-topped ridge below Flask Edge, overlooking the Barbrook stream valley and reservoir well below. From this spot there are commanding views in most directions, to the east the foothills between Sheffield and Chesterfield, to the south the gritstone moors and to the west White Edge.

The site is unusual in that it is covered in coarse grass with a thick soil cover which has buried many features of the circle. This area of land is completely featureless and the site is best found by going southwest from the nearest junction of tracks (see itineraries map). The circle consists of a ring of 21 standing stones with a diameter of 86 × 77 feet. These are evenly spaced except for a large gap to the W.S.W.; the original number of stones may have been as many as 25. Only four are still standing, five are leaning badly and the rest have fallen inwards. Probing the ground has shown that in most cases over half of each stone is completely buried and they now look deceptively small. Surrounding the stones is a low poorly preserved bank. This is about six feet wide and has an approximate external diameter of 97 × 88 feet. There appears to be three gaps which are probably disturbances, two of them are about 6 feet wide and are situated in the north and the E.N.E., the third to the W.S.W. is about 26 feet wide. The bank at the sides of these is wider than usual, and it looks as if material from the disturbed bank has been piled here, although it is possible these are original features to accentuate entrances.

Professor Thom came to the conclusion that the circle is a 'Flattened type B', but when the buried portions of the stones are taken into account this no longer fits. Because of the uncertain original positions of the stones, any kind of definite reconstruction is impossible; only excavation will determine the original shape. The ring is an oval which is approximately 31 × 28 MY in diameter, the most likely solution is a 'Flattened type A' but this seems to miss a few stones. Another alternative is an 'Egg type' ring but this also misses stones.

It is hard to relate the astronomical alignments to the geometry because of its uncertain nature. The most likely line of significance is the midsummer full moon maximum set by the main junction between the distant limestone hills and White Edge. This is the approximate line of the long axis at stone 11. Despite the ruined nature of the circle, it is still worth visiting because of its large size and unusual number of stones.

Near the three Barbrook circles already described are three other circles which are not as well preserved and not worth visiting except by the real enthusiast.

The Barbrook IV Circle (SK.2896.7561)

This circle is to the east of Barbrook I at the edge of Ramsley Moor on a slight rise with large expanses of very marshy land between the two. The circle is covered with thick heather which makes the site very difficult to find and also hides many of its details. The circle consists of a rubble bank with no well defined edges, and diameters of approximately, outer edge 77 × 70 feet and inner edge 62 × 53 feet. There are no other distinguishable features, but it is quite possible that there are some fallen standing stones which are now buried. The site was surveyed by plotting a series of maximum and minimum points for each edge of the bank, this showed that without doubt the only standard geometric shape that fits the circle is a 'Flattened type B', orientated to the south-east. This has the following dimensions in ¼MY units, long axis 90, short axis 80, pentagon side 50, circumference 270, pentagon total 250, width of bank 10. This solution is not geometrically exact and errors of about 10 inches had to be accepted.

The Barbrook V Circle (SK.2695.7515)

This circle is to the west of Barbrook I on the flat moor at the other side of the stream. It is best found by crossing the stream by Barbrook I and climbing to the top of the steep edge at the other side. From here follow the edge westwards until a point is reached where the moor starts to rise steeply again onto White Edge, immediately before this is the remains of the circle next to where an old trackway starts to drop down from the edge. This site is very badly damaged by the track which cuts across it and all that survives is half of the bank to the east of the track. It is 6—7 feet wide, retained internally by a ring of kerb stones, with diameters of inside 49 feet, outside 62 feet. The section of bank that has survived fits exactly onto a circle of 18 MY diameter but the original geometry could be any shape because of possible deviations in the missing half. The circle has very good views to the south and west which have astronomical potential which has not yet been investigated.

The Brown Edge Circle (SK.2883.7898)

This site is over the top of Flask Edge about a mile north of Barbrook III. It is on the eastern ridge of these moors overlooking the small valley running northwards that separates this ridge from the main moor to the west, about a hundred yards north of the wall that crosses the moor. This small circle, excavated by Radley in 1963, has an unusually wide bank in relation to the size of the central area. It was built on the site of an earlier Bronze Age dwelling. The bank is very low and today is hardly recognisable, it is 10 feet wide and has diameters of, outside 44 × 41 feet and inside 24 × 20 feet. On the internal edge are two standing stones, now fallen, and the central area has a small cairn which contained burials dated at 1530 b.c. ± 150, 1250 b.c. ± 150 and 1050 b.c. ± 150. If these dates also relate to the building of the circle, they indicate a late date for its construction. The bank was damaged in parts, but enough remains of the retaining rings to say that the geometry was almost certainly a 'Flattened type B' orientated to the west; this has the following dimensions in ¼MY: long axis 35, short axis 30, pentagon side 19, circumference 105, pentagon total 95, width of bank 15, outer long axis 65, outer short axis 60. The circle has fine views to the east over Sheffield which have astronomical potential.

Barbrook Circles' Relationship

The Barbrook circles form an integrated complex with extra-ordinary relationships on macro- and microcosmic scales, associated with geometry, number and the landscape.

On the macrocosmic scale a group of geometric constructions can be drawn:
a) An isosceles triangle with its apex at circle III to circles I and IV on the flat moor below. This has an angle at circle III which is identical to that at the basis of a 'Flattened type B' pentagon construction, relating to circles I and IV, both of which are of this shape.
b) If the line from circle I to circle III is extended, it goes exactly to the Brown Edge circle which is also a 'Flattened type B'. This is arranged so that circle III is half way between the other two.
c) The position of the Brown Edge circle also creates a triangle to circles I and IV with a right angle at circle IV.

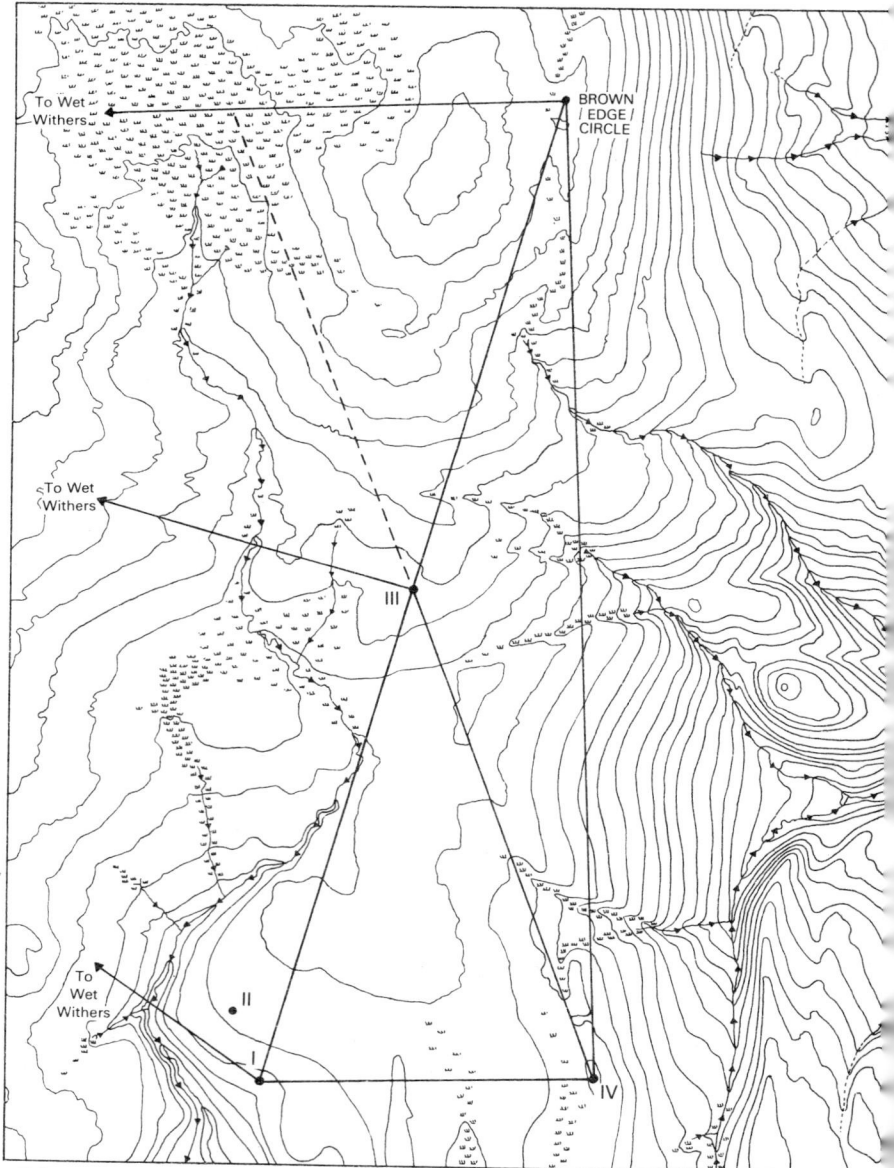

FIG. 56

Circles of the Central Area

These three constructions relate to the landscape in a strange way as if they underlie the formation of this area of the moors. The first construction defines the relatively flat northern half of Ramsley Moor. If the second is extended to form an identical triangle this defines the southern half of Flask Edge. Circle III at the centre of these two is on a shelf of land half way between the high and low moors. The most curious thing about these triangles is they contain no streams, which in many cases take distinct changes of angle to avoid them. The only water within the triangles is in areas of marshy land where it is stagnant. The line from the Brown Edge circle to circle IV defines the approximate eastern edge of the moors, where they begin to drop into the valleys around Sheffield.

d) The integrated relationships above probably connect geometrically to Wet Withers beyond White Edge on Eyam Moor. A line from this circle to circle III forms right angles to circle I and the Brown Edge circle, creating two 90° triangles. Also a line from Wet Withers to the Brown Edge circle is at right angles to a line to circle IV. Other geometric constructions which may be significant are that circle I is part of an isosceles triangle from Arbor Low to Wet Withers, and of an equilateral triangle from Arbor Low to the Bull Ring. These relate to the 'Great Triangle' discussed later in the book and are an extension of that pattern. It is interesting to note that a line from circle I to Arbor Low is also the direction of the midwinter sunset.

Circles II and V do not relate geometrically but perhaps they can be seen as part of the circle I complex. Between the three circles is a group of over 100 burial cairns of different sizes. Also on the flat moor between circles I and V are intricate arrangements of Bronze age field enclosures and at least one hut site (recently excavated).

On the microcosmic level the circles also relate to each other with circles I, IV and Brown Edge all being 'Flattened type B pentagons' arranged so that they fit inside each other as follows:

	Brown Edge Circle	Circle I	Circle IV
Internal diameter	35 × 30	→70 × 60	→90 × 80
External diameter	65 × 60	90 × 80	110 × 100

The unusually wide bank at the Brown Edge circle is probably designed so that its internal edge is exactly half that of circle I.

Circle II also relates to this group as it is flattened with a diameter of 70 × 65 but this time based on a hexagon, perhaps to complement circle I. Circle III at the centre of the macrocosmic geometry and circle V unfortunately cannot be reconstructed so the whole picture cannot be determined.

The circles are orientated so that the patterns are emphasised. Circle I aligns to Arbor Low and the sun; circle IV has two of its pentagon sides aligning to circles I and III; and the Brown Edge circle has its short axis aligned to Wet Withers and its long axis to circle IV.

Wet Withers, Eyam Moor (SK.2255.7900)

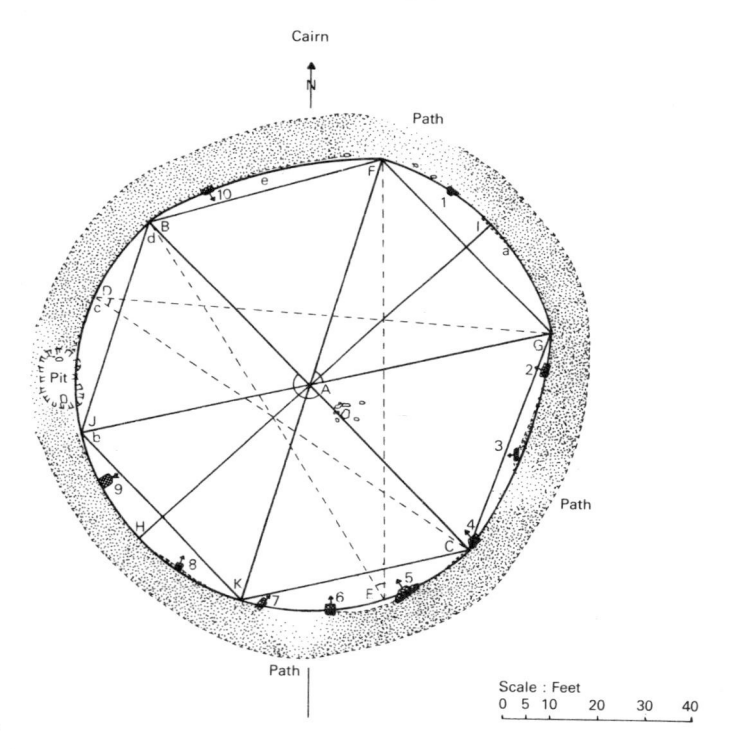

FIG. 57

This circle on Eyam Moor is located in an impressive spot cut off from the modern world by thick heather moorland, far from any well used footpaths. The site is on flat land near the northern edge of the moor, and a walk of a few hundred yards in this direction reveals a fine view down to Highlow Brook five hundred feet below, dividing Eyam Moor from Offerton Moor. From the circle itself there is a very extensive view of much of the high gritstone moors covering the northern half of the skyline. These views alone make the walk to the circle well worthwhile.

Circles of the Central Area

Because of the thick heather the circle is rather difficult to find, but this is made considerably easier if you follow the trackway suggested in the itinerary to the flat area of moor just before the Highlow Brook Valley. Then look to the right of the track for a small head-height metal signpost erected by the Department of the Environment next to the circle.

The circle is the largest of the gritstone sites in the Peak District and like most rings it is a circle of standing stones surrounded by a low bank. This bank has an external diameter of 116 × 119 feet, is 9 feet wide, 1 to 3 feet high and has an internal diameter of 98 × 101 feet. It is very low in three places and also has a small pit dug into it; but all these are probably relatively recent disturbances to an originally continuous bank with no entrance. The ring of stones is set in the internal edge of the bank. Today there are only 10 standing stones remaining, though Wood recorded 16 in 1842. The original number was probably between 16 and 18, making them approximately equally spaced. Of the remaining stones, 7 are standing, 3 fallen and they are all 1½ to 2 feet high. The central area is flat and a scatter of small stones and a pit near the centre could be the site of a large standing stone reported by Wood, but it is doubtful if this ever existed as he was only going on heresay.

140 feet to the north of the site (centre to centre) is a large mutilated cairn in which mid Bronze Age artifacts were found in 1759 by stone robbers. It is at present oval with diameters of 90 × 50 feet, although originally it could have been circular as it was called 'the Round Hillock' in the eighteenth century.

GEOMETRY

Construction

Professor Thom surveyed the standing stones and concluded that the site was circular. When the shape of the bank is taken into account where the stones are missing, the shape is found to be not quite circular; due to its large size the geometry can be determined accurately. It is an egg shaped ring which is a modification of Thom's basic types of eggs, and is constructed as follows:
1) From A a semi-circle from B to C, with a diameter of 36 MY.
2) Two arcs from points D and E which are placed 7.5 MY along the semi-circle, from C to G and B to F. These arcs have a length of 35.21 MY. This is probably not integral because this length was necessary to create more important lengths given below. The positions of G and F are fixed at 60° to the axis BC from A.

3) From A again, an arc of 60° to close the ring from F to G. The length of this arc is exactly 19 MY and creates a long axis HI of 37 MY. This ring has a circumference of 113.87 MY which is a close approximation to 45.5 MR[17].

The division of the arcs from A into a semi-circle and three 60° arcs suggests that this site is based on a 6 sided figure, with points J and K as extensions from GA and FK, creating an elongated hexagon with the six outer straight sides of the following lengths:

BJ, JK, KC	18 MY	half of short axis
BF, CG	18.5 MY	half of long axis
FG	19 MY	arc 3 radius

The sum of these six sides is 110 MY (or 44 MR).
The lengths from the centre A to these six points are:

Arc 1	AB, AC, AJ, AK	18 MY
Arc 3	AF, AG	19 MY

This again gives a total of 110 MY[18]. All these exact numbers were made possible by making arc 2 irrational.

Numbers

Of all the numbers used in this site, the most important are probably:

6	Hexagon
7	Hexagon plus the centre
110	Hexagon total
36	Short axis (6^2)
37	Long axis

The other numbers are probably only constructional to achieve those above. Some of the important numbers are harder to interpret than those in most circles.

Symbolism

The hexagon (six) symbolises wisdom and perfection, and is ideal as the shape of a temple. This is also to be considered as 7 the centred 6, the number of initiation and rebirth, a very appropriate symbol for a hexagon within an egg. The return from 6 to 7 as an expression of the unity of 1, which also is perhaps represented by the length 110.

The axes lengths of 36 and 37 are interesting as being numerically the basis of nearly all the numbers proposed by John Michell in his book *'City of Revelation'*. Their significance to ancient societies in their system of numbers (geometria) is well shown by Michell. Though his case that they were consciously aware of these numbers is less convincing.

Circles of the Central Area

ALIGNMENTS

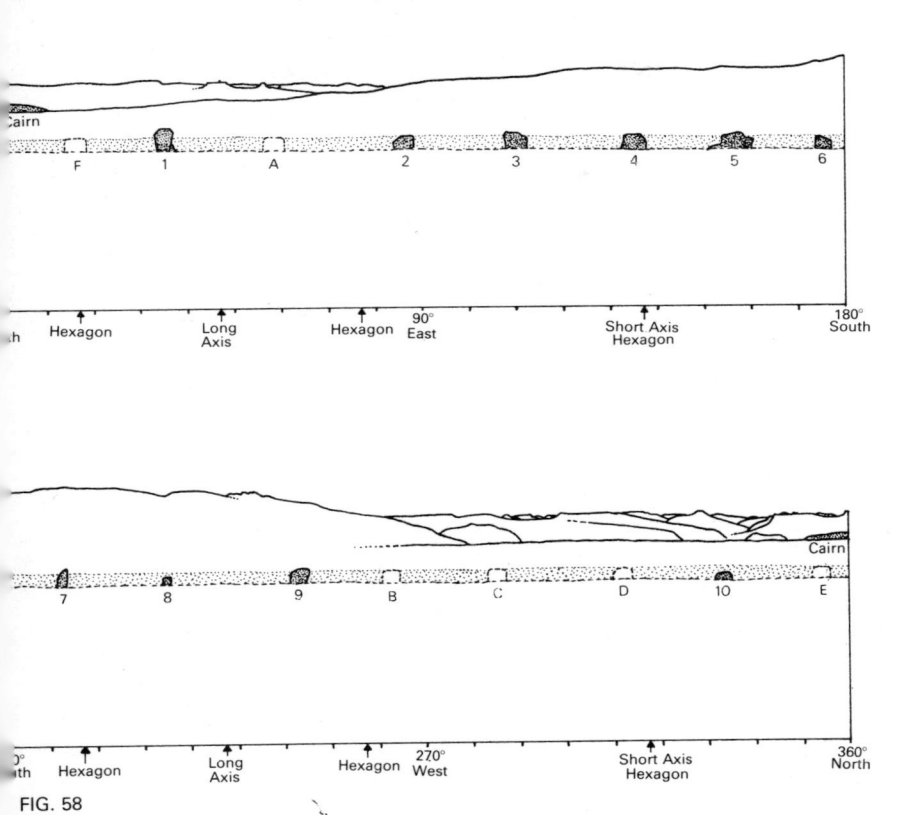

FIG. 58

This circle has a large number of good astronomical lines marked by the horizon. To find such a spot in the landscape must have taken a considerable amount of time; the large size of the circle would reflect the importance given to this achievement. All these lines are to distant horizons, and it looks as if the builders purposely chose the site so that it is only the northern half of the skyline which has distant views. This makes good sense for the study of the sun, using accurate distant points in summer when there is a good chance of fine weather, and closer points in winter when the weather was less predictable.

There are five of these horizon lines which appear to have been considered important:

Midsummer sunrise. This is one of the most visually impressive astronomical alignments found to date in the Peak District. It was to

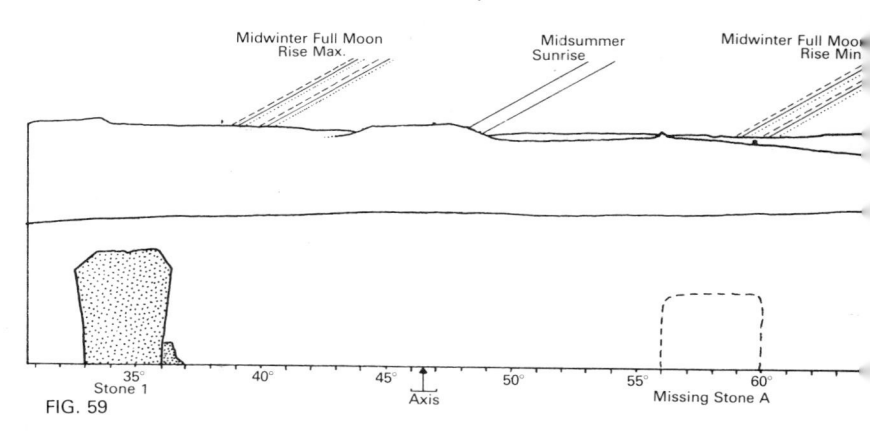

```
              Midwinter Full Moon              Midsummer         Midwinter Full Moon
              Rise Max.                        Sunrise           Rise Min
```

FIG. 59

Labels along horizon: 35° Stone 1, 40°, 45° Axis, 50°, 55°, 60° Missing Stone A

the flat topped Higgar Tor which rises with steep sides from the surrounding moors. The right edge of the Tor was used with the first flash of light near the top between two prominent natural outcrops of rock. When half risen the sun covered most of the slope and when it finally left the horizon, it touched another prominant rock further down the slope. The central group of rocks used with the first flash of light could have been a day counter to find midsummer's day exactly.

Midsummer sunset. This was just to the right of the junction between Offerton Moor and Edale Moor with the sun first touching the horizon at an indistinct junction $1\frac{1}{4}°$ from the main junction. This line was improved, as will be shown below.

Midwinter full moon maximum, set. This was to a small flat section of Bleaklow which is visible between Edale Moor and Win Hill. This is $3\frac{1}{2}°$ across and the moon would set into its centre, which was made into a very accurate eclipse predictor as is shown below.

Midwinter full moon minimum, set. This was at the left end of Offerton Moor, arranged so that when the moon first touched the horizon it was at the exact peak of the moor at the mean position of the eclipse variation; the fluctuations of this make the first touch vary slightly to either side of this point.

Midwinter full moon minimum, rise. This rose from a flat area of Burbage Moor where just below the horizon the Mother's Cap is clearly visible. This is an impressive natural pillar of stone which stands about twenty feet high and has vertical wind-eroded sides. The Peak District has a number of these freaks of nature. The frequency with which they are used as alignment foresights indicates they were given magical significance by prehistoric man, perhaps because the earth forces are particularly strong here. If a large fire was lit behind the stone this would have created an alignment of particularly strong

Circles of the Central Area 125

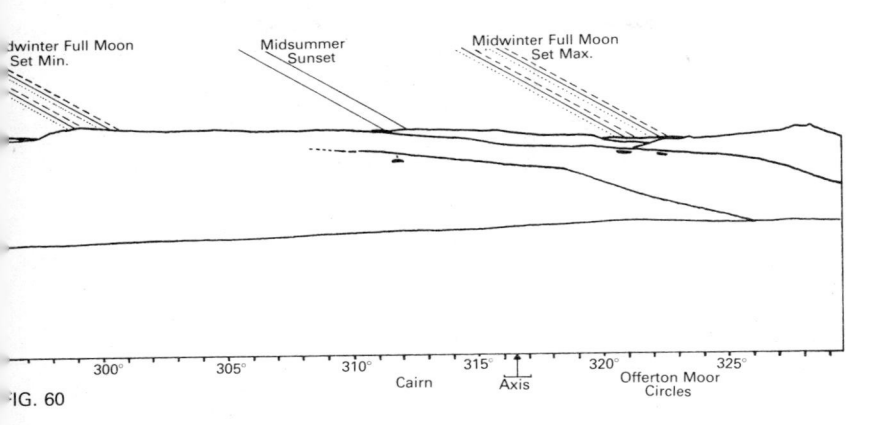

FIG. 60

Horizon diagram labels: dwinter Full Moon Set Min. / Midsummer Sunset / Midwinter Full Moon Set Max. / 300° / 305° / 310° Cairn / 315° Axis / 320° / 325° Offerton Moor Circles

symbolism and beauty, with the maximum impact when the moon was half risen.

Once the spot for the circle had been determined, the next stage was to orientate the geometry to the alignments. This site is a classic example of the compromise that often had to be accepted to include all the desired lines.

The main direction in the circle is the long axis towards the elongated egg end of the ring. This was orientated towards the midsummer sunrise; but instead of aligning it exactly to the sun, a position in the centre of Higgar Tor was chosen. There are various possible reasons for this, perhaps it is simply that symbolically the whole of Higgar Tor was regarded as the place of the sunrise. Another reason is that the axis aligns with a prominent rock on the horizon which is of a similar nature to Mother's Cap. This rock is a rather remarkable pile of wind-eroded stone, nearly fifteen feet high, which has a crack up the centre that can be climbed to the top where there is a natural pothole. It is just the right size to sit in so that only one's head is out of the hole. From here there is one of the best panoramic views in the Peak District. Perhaps a third reason for the misplacement of the axis was that it placed it between the sunrise and the midwinter full moon rise at its maximum.

The short axis through stone 4 to the south-east goes to the close horizon and the first flash of light from the midwinter sunrise was less than 1° from this point. If this line is not coincidence, it could be that the builders purposely found a spot in the landscape where an approximate right angle was formed between the sunrise positions of both solstices (1° out).

The short axis to the north-west was midway between the midsummer sunset and the midwinter full moon set at its maximum, both

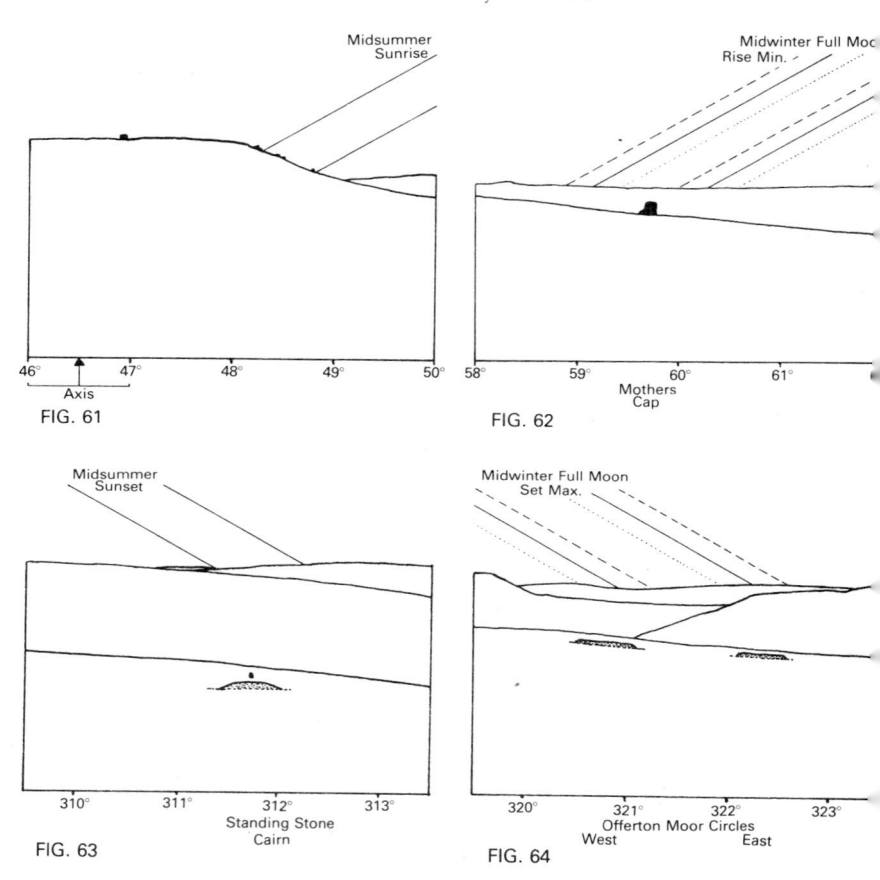

FIG. 61 — Midsummer Sunrise; 46°–50°; Axis at 47°

FIG. 62 — Midwinter Full Moon Rise Min.; 58°–61°; Mothers Cap at 60°

FIG. 63 — Midsummer Sunset; 310°–313°; Standing Stone Cairn at 312°

FIG. 64 — Midwinter Full Moon Set Max.; 320°–323°; Offerton Moor Circles West 321°, East 322°

of which were marked by the horizon. This is very similar to the Higgar Tor line. Both moon positions are in sections of flat horizon flanked by higher land, and it could be that the axes are meant symbolically to unite the sun and moon.

Once these relationships had been established the stones were positioned as follows:

Stone 1 and the missing stone A flank the long axis and the Higgar Tor sunrise line, with 1 marking the southern end of Stanage Edge, A marking Over Owler Tor and the Mother's Cap moon line, creating a beautiful visual alignment with the horizon emphasised in the circle by the stones.

Stone 10 and the missing stone D flank the midwinter maximum moon line. Stone 4 marks the short axis and the midwinter sunrise

Circles of the Central Area

line, stone 5 and the missing stone C mark arc 2 positions, and most of the other stones are used to balance the ones mentioned above and to make them evenly spaced.

Unlike many circles, Wet Withers seems not to use the stones directly for the sun or moon but relies on the horizon and geometry for its lines with the stones only emphasising these.

At some stage after the completion of Wet Withers two of its main alignments were improved by the building of other monuments on Offerton Moor about a mile away.

The major improvement was to make the midwinter full moon set maximum into an eclipse predictor by the building of two circles, Offerton West and East. These are visible from Wet Withers, two-thirds of a degree below the horizon. Today they are not very clear because of their thick cover of heather and bracken, but in their original state with standing stones were probably clearly visible, and could easily have been made more so with the aid of bonfires.

The way these circles were used to detect the eclipse variation is as follows:

At the minimum of the cycle the moon first touched the horizon over the left edge of Offerton West. By the time it was half set it was over the right edge of the same circle, and its final flash of light was between the circles.

At the mean position in the cycle, the moon first touched the horizon near the right edge of Offerton West. When it was half set it was half way along the flat far horizon, and also midway between the two circles filling the gap between them. The final flash of light was over the left edge of Offerton East.

At the maximum of the cycle the moon first touched the horizon just to the right of Offerton West, was half set near the left edge of Offerton East, and the last flash of light was over this circle's right edge.

This alignment is a good example of the magnificent building concepts put into practice by Bronze Age man in Britain, where structures were planned on a vast scale while still retaining their harmony with the landscape by keeping the marks minimal.

The other alignment which was improved was the midsummer sunset, which had the only large cairn on Offerton Moor placed directly below the line to Wet Withers. Behind this cairn is also a standing stone which was probably erected at the same time. These two monuments also relate to the Offerton Moor circles and are discussed further under these.

The Offerton Moor Circles:
West (SK.2127.8055), East (SK.2132.8057)

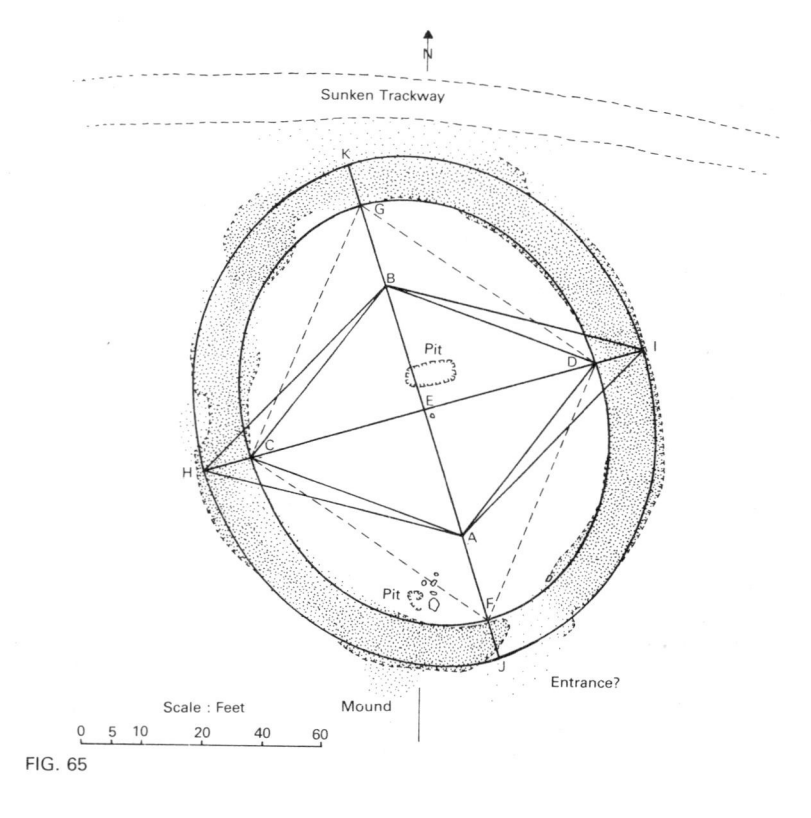

FIG. 65

These two circles are close together on relatively flat ground sloping down to the south, with a good view to the east of the rugged stone-covered landscape of Stanage, Higgar Tor, Over Owler Tor and White Edge. The rest of the horizon is much closer with Eyam Moor to the south, where Wet Withers can be picked out, and Abney Moor and Shatton Moor to the west. The circles overlook a small wooded valley which separate them from Smelting Hill, where there are further prehistoric sites.

Circles of the Central Area

If the circles are approached from the direction suggested in the intineraries, they are found by looking out for the East circle which looks like a large two-foot high bracken-covered mound. If you pass the wood in the small valley, you have gone too far.

The western circle is covered with heather, but its outline is easily traced. Today this site consists of only an oval bank of earth with no standing stones, but in the eighteenth century Rooke and Pegge refer to it as having stones. They are however very vague; only excavation would settle this question. The bank shows no evidence of retaining rings above ground, but internally it has a defined edge for most of its course. To the south there is a gap in the bank which could have been an entrance, but it is more likely to be recent levelling, perhaps to remove the standing stones. Just to the west of this is a mound attached to the bank's outer edge. In the northern section a sunken trackway passes very close to the site, making the bank appear much wider here than it really is. Internally the bank is 75 × 60 feet, externally approximately 88 × 76 feet and it is about 1½ feet high. The only features in the central area are a shallow pit near the centre of unknown age and another small pit with a scatter of rubble which looks recent near the bank.

The eastern circle is covered in bracken, making its features hard to pick out. It is 170 feet from the western circle (centre to centre) and consists of a bank badly disturbed by a shooting butt dug into one side and other areas which are badly eroded. Its diameters are approximately—inside 39 feet, outside 53 feet and a gap to the east looks as if it could have been an entrance.

Uphill from the circles are various small low tumuli, and across the valley on Smelting Hill is a very large disturbed cairn. To the west of this is a 4 foot high standing stone built into the junction of two walls. On both its faces are crosses, probably carved in the mediaeval period when it was used as a boundary stone. To the east of the large cairn are numerous small cairns which could also be prehistoric.

GEOMETRY: WEST CIRCLE

Construction

Although there are no standing stones, an accurate reconstruction can be made due to the large size of the circle and its distinctive shape. This site is so oval that the only simple geometric shape that will fit it is an ellipse. There is only one which has integral lengths which will fit the inside edge of the bank with any accuracy, this is constructed as follows:

1) Place two stakes firmly in the ground 66 × ¼MY apart at points A and B.
2) Take a continuous loop of rope 176 × ¼MY long. Stretch it taut round A and B so that it forms two identical right-angled triangles AEC and BEC. These have dimensions of: BE, AE 33 × ¼MY. EC, (ED) 44 × ¼MY and AC, (AD), BC, (BD) 55 × ¼MY creating a short axis CD of 88 × ¼MY.
3) If the rope is held at C and is moved round the ring keeping it taut at all times and running freely round A and B, then when the full circle had been made, a perfect ellipse will have been marked out. This creates a long axis FG of 110 × ¼MY (twice triangle hypotenuse 55 × ¼MY) and a circumference of 311.97 × ¼MY[19].
4) A possible part of the conception is that a diamond C,G,D,F has sides which are each approximately 70 × ¼MY long[20], giving a total of 280 × ¼MY.

The external edge of the bank is harder to define but the only triangle which fits it tolerably well with integral lengths and using the same stakes A and B is as follows:
Triangle AE, BE 33 × ¼MY. EH, EI 56 × ¼MY. AH, AI, BH, BI 65 × ¼MY.
Length of Rope 196 × ¼MY. Short axis 112 × ¼MY. Long axis 130 × ¼MY.
Circumference 380.85 × ¼MY probably meant to be 380.
Width of bank: Short axis 12 × ¼MY, Long axis 10 × ¼MY.

GEOMETRY: EAST CIRCLE

Construction

This site is circular and has an internal diameter of 56 × ¼MY and a circumference of 176 × ¼MY. The entrance indicates an axis and a square can be drawn inside the circle which has sides of 40 × ¼MY. Each[21] giving a total of 160 × ¼MY (in MY: diameter 14, circumference 44, square total 40).

Circles of the Central Area

RELATIONSHIPS BETWEEN THE TWO CIRCLES

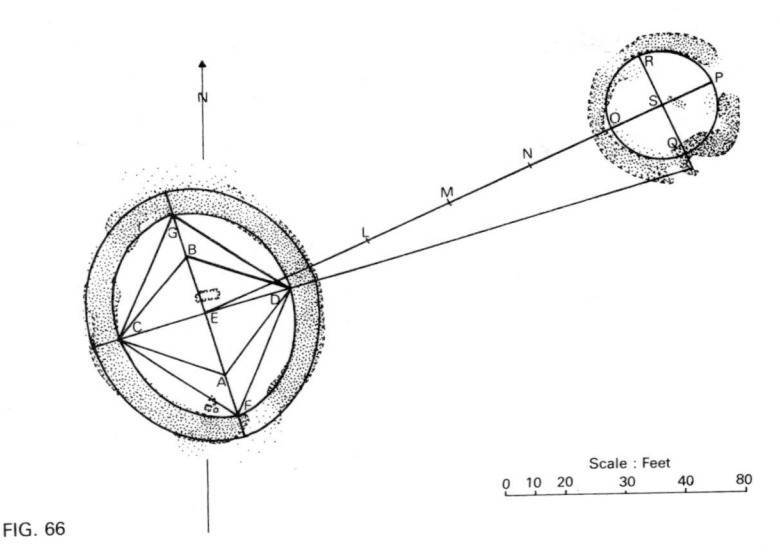

FIG. 66

Construction

These two circles are without doubt built at the same time as is revealed by the following relationships:
A) The short axis of the western site when extended passes approximately through the original outer edge of the eastern site, creating a line which is 250 × ¼MY long from E to Q^{22}.
B) A line from the centre E to the centre S halves the entrance at P and indicates this line is important. The reason the eastern site is in its exact position is determined by two factors. Firstly the misplacement from the line EQ is to fit horizon considerations illustrated later. Secondly the distance from the western circle is governed by the distance DO as follows:

    CD   88 × ¼MY short axis of western circle (slightly displaced)
    DO   176 × ¼MY (88 × 2)
    ORPQ 176 × ¼MY circumference of eastern circle

This was probably seen as 10 lengths of 44 × ¼MY each, the total length of all these is 440 × ¼MY which is four times the length of the long axis of the western circle. Another length which is 176 × ¼MY long is the rope used for the construction of the western circle's ellipse and this could indicate this was used in fixing the others given above.

These relationships indicate that the western circle is the main part of the complex and the eastern one is only a secondary feature attached to the other.

Numbers

Examining the measurements of both sites they have the following numerical relationships:

33, 44, 55	Triangles
66	A to B
88	Short axis
110	Long axis
70	Diamond sides
176	(66 + 55 + 55) Rope length for the ellipse (88 × 2 or 44 × 4) Distance between sites circumference of East circle
440	(44 × 10 or 110 × 4) Total line 10 = 2 + 4 + 4 or 1 + 2 + 2 = 5
40	Square sides in the East circle

Basically these sites are a combination of the basic numbers 3, 4, 5, 6, 8, 10 all as multiples of 11. Also 1, 2, 3, 4, in the relationship between the two sites and perhaps 7 as a hidden number in the West circle.

Symbolism

These sites consist symbolically of most of the basic numbers but perhaps the most important are:

West circle. The diameters 8 × 10, the material universe combined with the absolute whole. All the other numbers are the real and symbolic stages of construction to achieve these finished products. The diamond 4 with sides of 7 could be said to represent the physical world and man (the centred 4) combined with initiation.

East circle. The square within the circle. The physical combined with the whole on a more basic level than the West circle.

ALIGNMENTS

These circles together with the cairn and standing stone on Smelting Hill were all important foresights for alignments from Wet Withers. This close link is strengthened considerably by various facts revealed at Offerton Moor.

The cairn and standing stone form an isosceles triangle with the centre of the main circle at its apex showing they were all part of the same concept.

The main alignment at Wet Withers is to Higgar Tor and at the

Circles of the Central Area   133

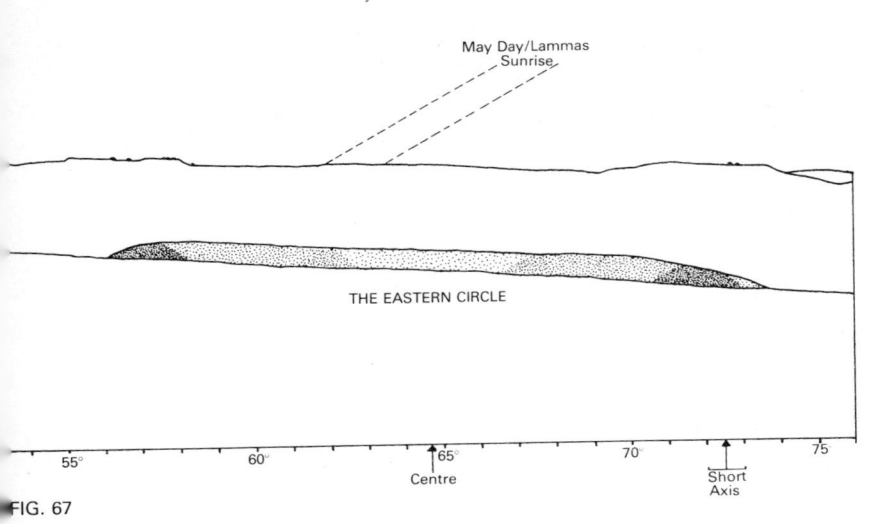

FIG. 67

Diagram showing horizon profile with markings: May Day/Lammas Sunrise indicated above; "THE EASTERN CIRCLE" labeled on the profile; horizontal scale from 55° to 75°, with "Centre" at 65° and "Short Axis" near 73°.

Offerton circles this is also the case, arranged as follows:

The short axis of the western circle goes through the outer edge of the eastern one, to the same stones on top of Higgar Tor. The offsetting of the eastern circle from this line is explained by its relationship to the horizon. Looking through the eastern circle above its southern end you see Higgar Tor, and above its northern end Stanage Edge, with a lower flat horizon between. Seen from the centre of the western circle this forms a beautiful example of visual balance with the shape of the eastern circle being a mirror image of the horizon, while if the sections of the bank are imagined together with the circles flat central area between, they are exactly the same shape as the horizon. The centre of this flat area of horizon was the position of the midwinter full moon rise at its maximum from Wet Withers; but from here it was the May Day/Lammas sunrise. This is not marked on the horizon, but could easily have been pinpointed by standing stones or by a person standing at the northern edge of the entrance in the eastern circle. Lammas is the time of the harvest festival, and this fits perfectly with the symbolic interpretation of the numbers of these circles with their earthy emphasis.

Perhaps another relationship to Wet Withers is that the short axis of the western circle in the opposite direction goes to the centre of the zodiac explained later in the book, for which Wet Withers is one of the main points.

There are also two astronomical lines to the horizon which complement those at Wet Withers, chosen so that the three main positions for

134   Stone Circles of the Peak

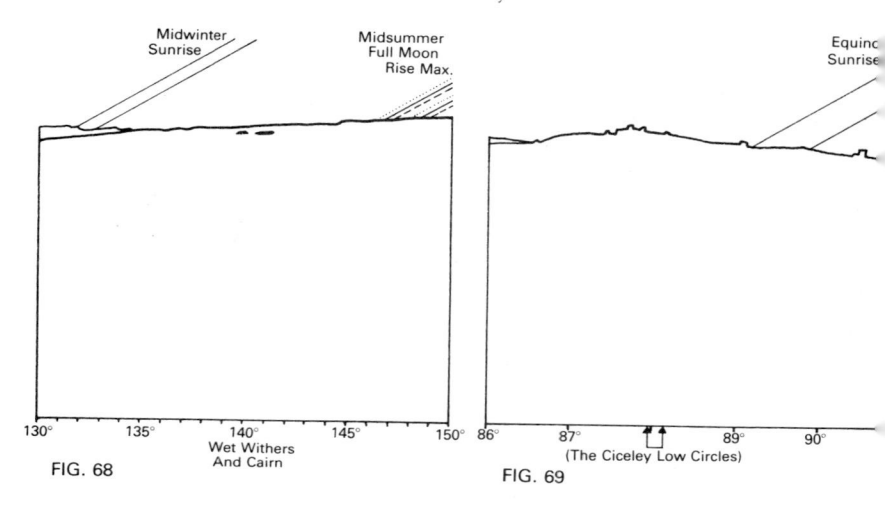

FIG. 68 — labels: Midwinter Sunrise, Midsummer Full Moon Rise Max.; horizontal axis 130°, 135°, 140° (Wet Withers And Cairn), 145°, 150°

FIG. 69 — labels: Equinox Sunrise; horizontal axis 86°, 87°, (The Ciceley Low Circles), 89°, 90°

the solar year are marked, midsummer solstice at Wet Withers and Equinox and midwinter solstice here.

The equinox sunrise was from the small area on the horizon around Over Owler Tor. Three prominent outcrops of stone rise above the flat moor, Over Owler Tor to the left, Mother's Cap to the right and a smaller stone in the centre. The first flash of light of the sun was just to the right of this central stone, although it did not actually touch it this was the only day when it was anywhere near this point. Over Owler Tor marks the direction of the Ciceley Low circles which are a little over a mile further away just below the horizon, these are possibly also connected with Wet Withers.

The midwinter sunrise was from a prominent dip in White Edge with the first flash of light on a short slope which is very steep. To the right on Eyam Moor was the position of the midsummer full moon rise at its maximum, today not marked by any prehistoric feature. What makes this position interesting is that Wet Withers is half way between it and the sunrise line. This arrangement is identical with the axes at Wet Withers which were also midway between sun and moon.

The Ciceley Low Circles, Burbage Moor (North SK.2752.8079 South SK.2752.8077)

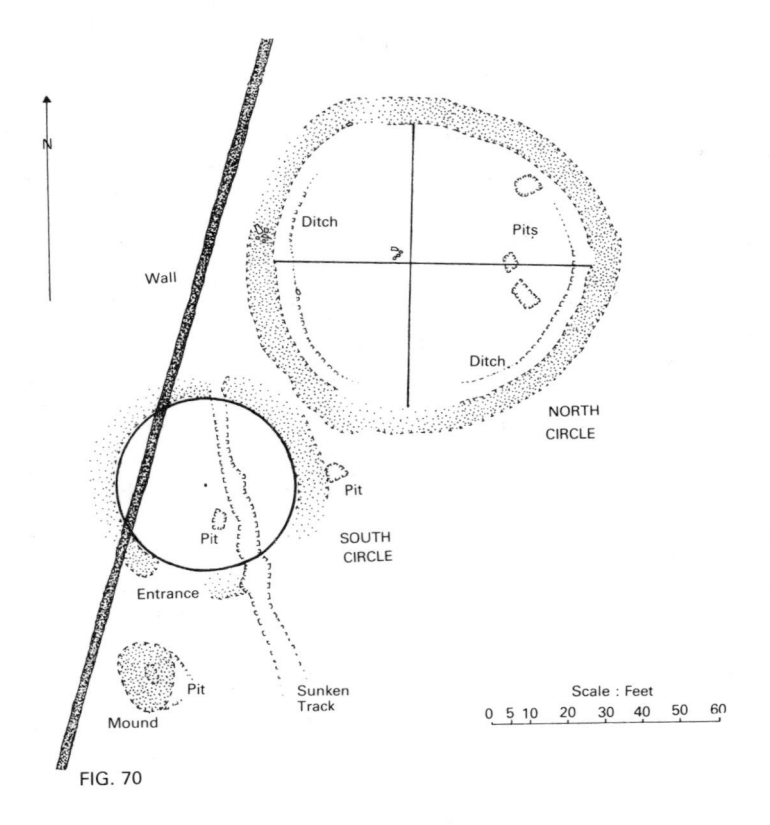

FIG. 70

These two circles are next to each other on a gently sloping heather moor above the top of a dip in the main gritstone moors on its northern side. They have distant views to the east and west, to the east is a flat horizon many miles away. In contrast, to the west are many moors of the limestone plateau and the western gritstone area beyond. The circles are easily found by walking two-thirds of the way up the wall next to the ruined house by the main road on its heather covered side.

These sites are similar to the Offerton circles in the fact that they consist of a main circle with a secondary one nearby. The main circle (north) consists of a low continuous bank with no sign of retaining rings although some sections of the internal edge are well defined. It has diameters of, outside 98 × 93 feet and inside 84 × 79 feet. This site possibly has an unusual feature, an internal ditch but this could just as easily have been formed by water erosion. Next to this circle with their banks virtually touching is the second smaller one. It is much more damaged with a trackway crossing through the centre and the wall cutting off a section which is much lower, probably due to ploughing. This ring has a bank which has diameters of, outside 64 feet and inside 49 feet. To the S.S.W. there is a gap which could have been an entrance and further down the slope is a 2½ feet high mound which is possibly a prehistoric cairn.

Neither of the circles are well enough preserved to reconstruct their geometry exactly, but indications are that the main circle is some kind of modified egg elongated east/west and the secondary one is probably circular with a diameter of 72 × ¼MY and a circumference of 225 × ¼MY[23]. This possibly contains a square with each side of 50 × ¼MY[24], total 200 × ¼MY.

The major alignment was probably from the centre of the main circle through the other which covered the whole range of settings for the full moon at midsummer and is also the direction of Arbor Low. The long axis to the west possibly aligns with the Offerton circles and the equinox and midwinter sunsets were marked by the horizon completing the solar lines missing from the previous two circles.

7

The Southern Circles

The Nine Ladies Circle, Stanton Moor (SK.2491.6349)

This small well known circle is on the top of Stanton Moor surrounded by relics left by prehistoric man, including four other circles and numerous Bronze Age cairns. It is situated in a sheltered hollow near the northern end of the moor which is covered by small silver birch trees that have grown in the last twenty years, obscuring most of the view from the site.

The name 'Nine Ladies' together with that of the nearby outlier 'the King Stone' are interesting indications of folk legends similar to many others throughout the country. These are connected with ancient dancing rites of the old religion which were frowned upon by Christians; the dancers were 'turned to stone' for these practices, hence the circle of maidens together with the presiding priest. This is the only surviving circle in the Peak District with a name of this type but its associated legends have not lasted. A circle called the 'Seven Brides', a similar name, was documented on Matlock Moor in the eighteenth century but there is no longer any trace of it.

This circle is situated to the left of the path amongst the trees. It is surrounded by an ugly modern circular wall which stands out making this site easy to find. The circle still contains its complete ring of nine standing stones (2 now leaning badly). These are between 1½ and 3 feet high and form a ring which is 35.5 × 38 feet in diameter. The stones are set at the inner edge of a bank which is now very low and badly disturbed with two gaps which were possibly entrances. In the central area is a mound only 6 inches high with a diameter of 16 feet; this has been badly disturbed by the diggings of Bateman and others and could have been higher originally. 130 feet away from the circle to W.S.W. there is a single outlier 'the King Stone', a three foot high slab set upright with its narrow side facing the site, today leaning badly and surrounded by another modern wall.

GEOMETRY

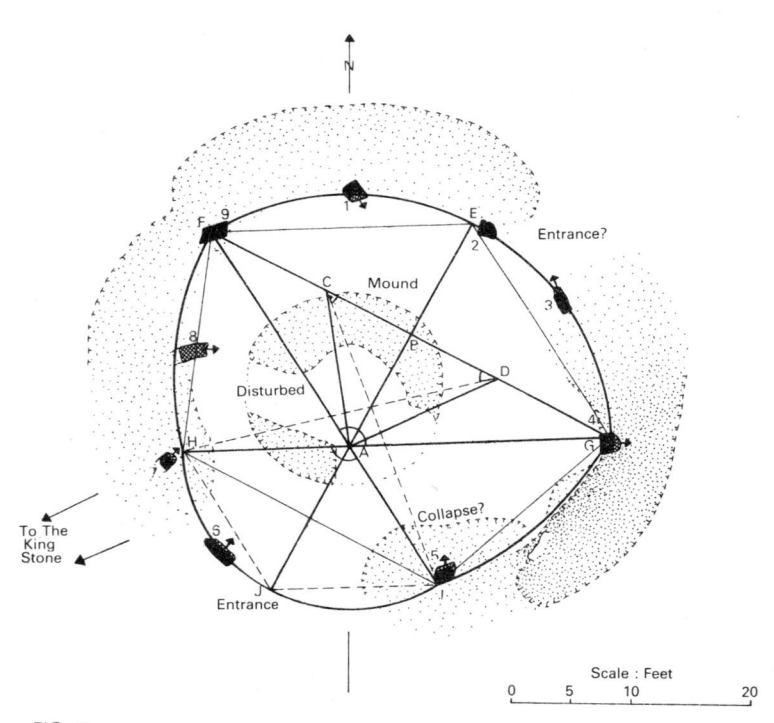

FIG. 71

Construction

The reconstruction of this circle is a problem because the bank is badly disturbed and only seven stones are in their original positions. Professor Thom states that it is circular, but this solouution does not fit particularly well. I suggest an alternative—a modified egg—which is justified by its very good geometric properties, but nothing can be proved because only seven fixed points exist, and this shape has no geometric precedents. It fits to the stones more closely than a circle and only misses stone 7 slightly. This is constructed as follows:

1) Two 3:4:5 triangles ABC and ABD are constructed with 4 as the common side; these have lengths of 3, 4 and 5 MY.
2) The line CD is extended in both directions and an arc from A going from F to G on the CB line is drawn, creating two angles of 60° FAE and GAE and lengths of AF, AG 8 MY. BE 4 MY. BF, BG 7 MY[1]. This makes the long axis, FG 14 MY[2].
3) From C an arc is drawn from G to an extension of the line FA at I, creating an angle of 60° GAI, a corresponding arc is also drawn from F to H. The length of both these is 10 MY[3].
4) A second arc using A is drawn from I to H to close the ring. This has a length of approximately 5 MY[4], and an angle of 120°, creating a short axis EJ of 13 MY[5] and a circumference of 42 MY[6]. This length of 42 MY is the long axis × 3, a better approximation to $\pi = 3$ than either of Thom's flattened types A or B.

There are two possibilities for an internal geometric shape, the first one, a pentagon, is the most likely. This has sides as follows:

EF, EG	8 MY
FH, GI	7 MY[7]
HI	9 MY[8]

The total length of 39 MY is the short axis × 3, fitting well with the circumference relating to the long axis.

The second possibility is a distorted hexagon suggested by the 60° angles from A; this has the lengths JH and JI replacing HI and these are both 5 MY[9], giving a total sum of 40 MY. Visually this does not seem as convincing as the pentagon.

The King Stone is approximately 50 MY from the central area. It is directly along an extension of the line DA and from B aligns with stone 7.

The other feature of the site, the central mound, is circular and offset from the geometric centres, making one suspect it is an addition to the site rather than part of the original concept.

Balance

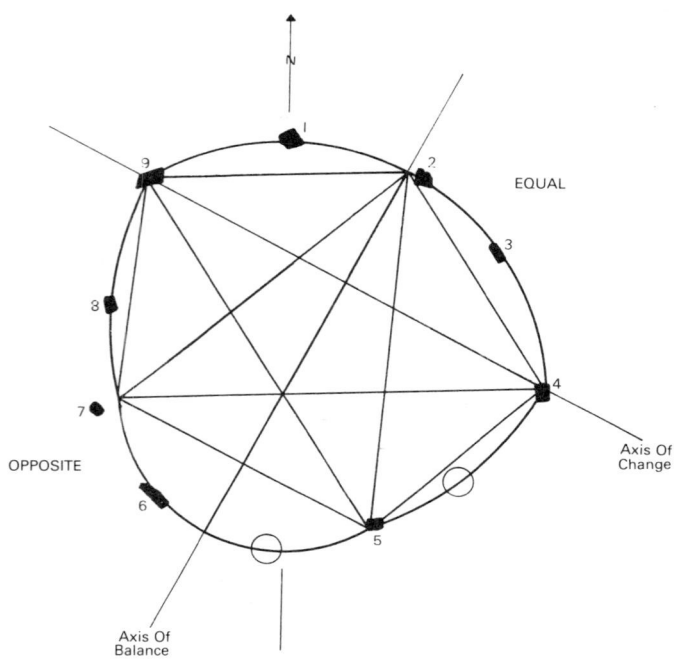

FIG. 72

(Diagram labels: N; EQUAL; Axis Of Change; OPPOSITE; Axis Of Balance; stones numbered 1–9)

At Nine Ladies the stones are arranged in a similar way to those at Barbrook I, balanced round the resulting axis EJ, and probably with two sides of equal balance and three of opposite. They differ in having all five pentagon points marked with stones, making the balances less obvious. The arrangement is as follows:

Axis, pentagon Point		stone 2	
		stone 1	stone 3
Pentagon Points		stone 9	stone 4
		stone 8	gap
Pentagon Points		stone 7	stone 5
		stone 6	gap
		gap	

The Southern Circles

This is not as perfect as that of Barbrook I, as stones 7 and 5 are both offset slightly for some unknown reason, and stones 6 and 8 are both on the same side. The resulting 12 points of balance perhaps relate to the axes' lengths of 13/14; the peculiarities of this arrangement could indicate that there are two missing stones, balancing stones 6 and 8, which must have been removed in the distant past. This would make the pattern more logical, with 11 stones and 12 points.

The stones are so positioned that they function as foresights and backsights through the centre A. They could thus have been used to make alignments more accurate. This is arranged as follows:

Foresight	Backsight
stone 1	(missing stone ?)
stone 2	(twelfth balance point)
stone 3	right edge of stone 6
stone 4	1 foot from the right edge of stone 7
stone 5	1 foot from the left edge of stone 9
stone 6	1 foot from the left edge of stone 3
stone 7	1 foot from the left edge of stone 4
stone 8	(missing stone ?)
stone 9	1 foot from the right edge of stone 6

The offsetting of backsights is based on the geometry. In the first arc you stand just to the left of the stones and in the other arcs just to the right. Another use of this arrangement is to find the exact geometric centre of the circle by intersecting two lines. Both uses perhaps indicate an element of secrecy in how to use the circle.

Numbers

This circle has many integral numerical relationships which when brought together are:

Geometry
1. The whole circle, the egg
2. The two axes, two identical halves
3. The central triangles
4. The four arcs
5. The pentagon
6. The pentagon plus the balance point or centre. (The hexagon?)
7. The pentagon plus the balance point and the centre. (The hexagon plus the centre?)
9? The number of stones?
(11? Possible original number of stones?)
12. Balance points

Measurement	3 MY	Triangle sides BC, BD
	4 MY	Triangle side AB
		Length BE
		Length CF, DG[10]
	5 MY	Triangle sides AC, AD
		Arc lengths AJ, AH, AI[11]
		(JH, JI of hexagon)
	(6 MY	Length CD)
	7 MY	Axis lengths BF, BG[13]
		Pentagon lengths FH, GI [14]
	8 MY	Arc length AE, AF, AG
		Pentagon length EF, EG
	9 MY	Pentagon length HI[15]
		Length BJ[16]
	10 MY	Arc lengths CG, CI, DF, DH[17]
	13 MY	Axis EJ[18]
		Pentagon total
	14 MY	Axis FG[19]
		Circumference (42 = 6 × 7)
	(40 MY	Hexagon total)

Placed together they include every number from 1 to 14.

Symbolism

The circle contains all the aspects of the basic numbers, combining together to form a unified whole. Perhaps the most important numerical meanings are:

Geometry 1. As the whole and the beginning
             5. As man and the life force
             6. The fixing and balancing of the forces in the circle
             7. The hidden point of initiation
Stones   9. Finality
          12. The complete world, the zodiac

The perfection of this circle represents a truly amazing expression of the builders belief in harmony and is a remarkable achievement.

It is a great pity that the astronomical alignments cannot be studied because of the trees; these would undoubtedly reveal further information on the circle as there are potentially good marked lines, especially to the east.

The Central Circle, Stanton Moor (SK.2480.6327)

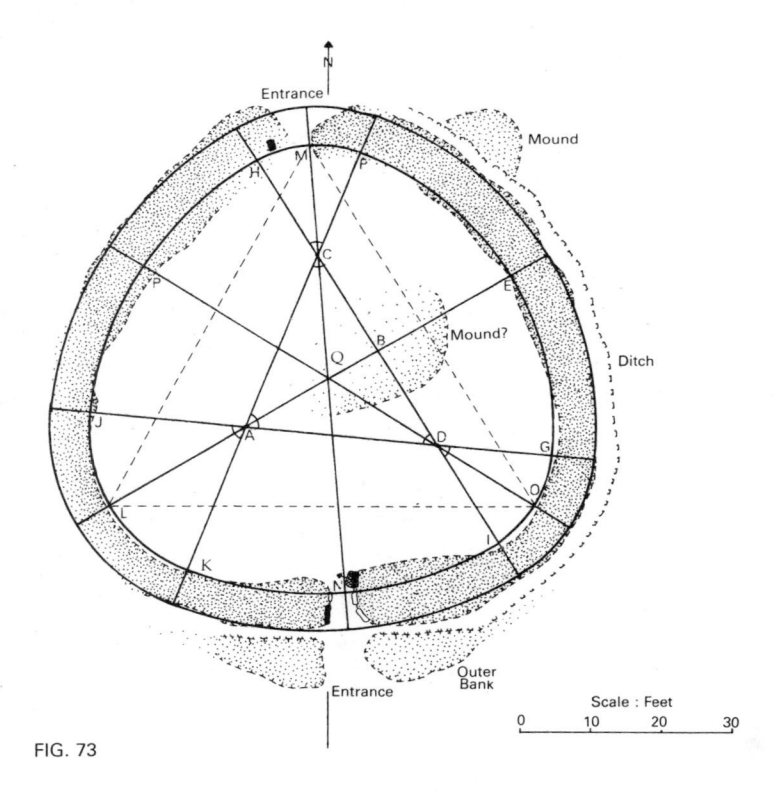

FIG. 73

This circle is about 270 yards south of Nine Ladies on slightly higher ground; it also has many small trees round it, except in the east where the main eastern moors can be seen across the Derwent Valley. If the circle is being visited on the way to Nine Ladies, one should go to the left at right angles to the path just before it starts dropping more steeply, as it enters an area more thickly covered in trees. The site is only 50 yards from the path but cannot be seen easily, it is in the last clear area before the trees meet the path.

This circle is the largest on the moor and was possibly the most important, but today is not as well preserved as the Nine Ladies. It consists of a well preserved bank which is 2 feet high, has maximum diameters of, outside 78 feet, inside 64 feet and is somewhat triangular in shape. It is retained on both edges by drystone walls, traces of which appear above ground. The bank is broken by two opposite entrances to the north and south which are about 4 feet wide. These are flanked by small standing stones as at the Stoke Flat circle, but only three now survive: one in the northern entrance and two in the southern one, which is the better preserved and which has traces of paving flags on the floor. At either side of the entrances the bank is wider than usual, and reaches a maximum of 10 feet. Outside the bank is a further complexity not usually found in the Peak District circles, on the downhill side of the circle are the remains of a slight external ditch 1-2 feet wide, and outside this, next to the southern entrance, are two low mounds forming an outer bank, each 6 feet wide and 15 feet long. A low mound to the east of the north entrance is possibly a similar feature. The area within the bank is relatively flat, although irregular ground near the centre could be a disturbed mound.

It is unfortunate that most of the important views from the site are obscured by trees, making astronomical reconstruction impossible.

GEOMETRY
Construction

The very pronounced triangular shape of the ring makes it obvious that none of the standard geometric shapes fit this circle. Because of its large size, it has been possible to reconstruct its geometry (which is unique, being based on a triangle):

1) Two pythagorean triangles are placed at the centre, ABC and ABD; these have lengths of BC, BD 6 MY. AB 8 MY. AC, AD 10 MY.
2) Line AB is extended to twice its length 16 MY to E. AC is extended to F and AD to G and an arc drawn from F to G creating lengths AE, AF, AG 16 MY.
3) Line BC is extended to H and BD to I, and then arcs are drawn from C to F, H and from D to GI. These have lengths of 6 MY. BI and BH are double this length (12 MY) in the same way as AB and AE.
4) Line CA is extended to K and DA to J. Then arcs are drawn from C to IK and from D to HJ with lengths of 18 MY.
5) A closing arc is drawn from A to join J and K this again has a length of 8 MY (as have AB and BE).

The Southern Circles

6) If each of the arcs is divided in half by the lines LE, MN, OP then various important relationships are created. LE is the balancing axis and MN marks the entrances. The points L, M, O create a triangle with sides which are approximately 22 MY long[20]. All the lines intersect at point Q which is the geometric centre of the circle and is exactly 5 MY from A and 3 MY from B.

7) This construction creates all diameters which are identical although it is far from circular: EL, HI, JG, FK, OP, MN are all 24 MY. Also a circumference of 75 MY or 30 MR[21]. The arcs between HJ and IK do not fit very well with the bank and it is probably that they have been flattened here to make the circumference almost exactly the required length.

8) The bank is 9 × ¼MY wide and creates axis lengths of 28.5 MY and more importantly a circumference of 33 MR.

It is interesting that this circle's shape is very similar to the Staden Henge. The entrances are possibly arranged in the same way, one at an angle change and the other at the centre of a triangle side. These are probably placed on the line MN rather than EL so that they are orientated to the north/south line. The mounds outside the southern entrance approximately cover the arc IK but this is perhaps coincidence.

Numbers

The circle has a very interesting series of numbers which are:

Geometry	1	The whole side
	2	Identical halves, entrances
	3	Triangles
	6	Arcs, triangles divided by the centre lines
	7	Geometry plus the centre
Measurement	6	Triangle BC, BD
		Arcs CF, CH, CM, DG, DI, DO
	8	Triangle AB, BE
		Arcs AL, AJ, AK
	10	Triangle AC, AD
	12	DC, BH, BI
	16	Arc AE, AF, AG (+ BL)
	18	Arcs CI, CK, CN, DH, DJ, DP
	22	Triangle sides LM, LO, MO
	24	Axes EL = 8 + 8 + 8, HI = 6 + 6 + 6 + 6, FK, GJ = 6 + 10 + 8, MN, OP = 6 + 18
		Triangles ABC, ABD
	66	Triangle total (22 × 3)
	75	Circumference (25 × 3)
	(30,33 Circumference in MR)	

A good case can be put forward for the original construction to have been conceived in 2 MY units giving the following series 3, 4, 5, 6, –, 8, 9, –, 11, 12, 33.

Symbolism

This site is another classic example of the use of basic numbers, with 6 and 7 being the most important elements, harmony and initiation. Here these are emphasised with 3 as harmony and energy on a more basic level, together with 12 as the ultimate harmony of everything.

The South Circle, Stanton Moor (SK.2471.6289)

This circle is just over 400 yards south from the central circle and is on a more open area of the moor with a good view of the main gritstone moors to the east and Bonsall Moor to the south.

This site is easily found as it is right next to the path and clearly visible. It consists of a bank which is retained on both edges by drystone walls, is 2 feet high, has diameters of outside 57 × 51 feet and inside 44 × 39 feet and is rather triangular. The bank is broken by one original entrance to the south which is only 3 feet wide and possibly originally lined with vertical stones. On the internal edge of the bank are remains of a ring of small standing stones, with 3 to 6 still surviving, two are still standing, there is also a larger fallen stone and three small fallen stones which could just as easily be wall stones. The central area is badly disturbed with a pit at the centre and a mound around it although it is not clear if this is an original mound or just material from the pit.

GEOMETRY

Construction

This circle is also triangular in shape and its well defined edges have enabled a good reconstruction. This is similar to the central circle but not as complex, also based on a triangle as follows:

The Southern Circles

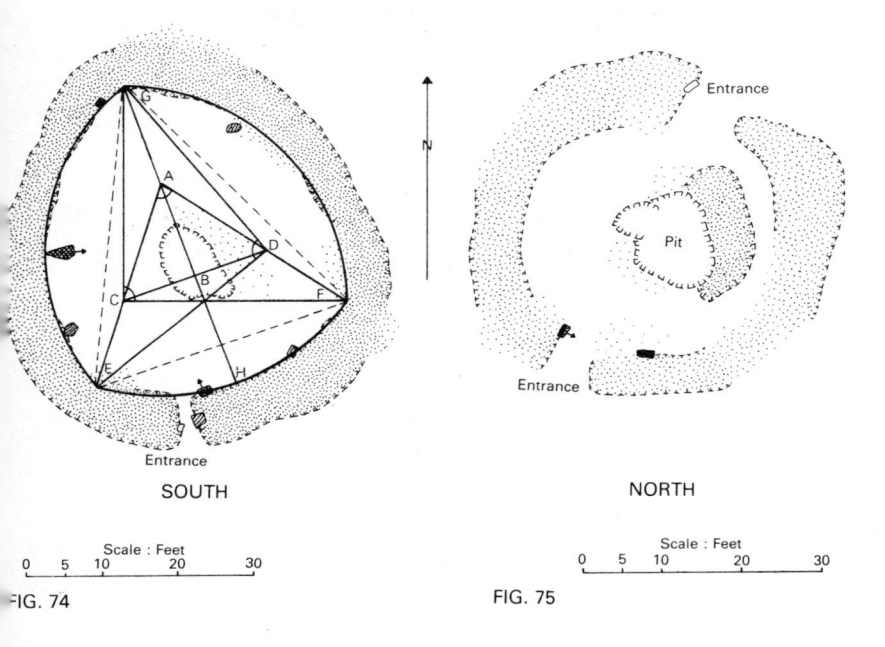

FIG. 74 — SOUTH

FIG. 75 — NORTH

Scale : Feet 0 5 10 20 30

1) Two 3, 4, 5 triangles are placed in the centre, ABC and ABD, with Sides of BC, BD 15 × ¼MY. AB 20 × ¼MY and AC, AD 25 × ¼MY (sum of ABC or ABD is 60 × ½MY and ACD is 90 × ¼MY).
2) AC and AD are extended to the points E and F and an arc drawn from A to join E to F. This arc is 44 × ¼MY long, (creating lengths CE, DF of 19 × ¼MY and BH 24 × ¼MY).
3) A unique property of this construction is that the lines DE and CF also have a length of 44 × ¼MY[22]. The ring is completed with two arcs from C to join F to G and from D joining E to G. Thus the circle is defined by three arcs all 44 × ¼MY long. Another unique property is that the angles FCG and EDG resulting from the last two arcs are 90°[23].

The construction has a long axis GH which is 65 × ¼MY long [24] and a circumference of 195 × ¼MY[25]. This is a better approximation to 'diameter × 3' than the flattened type circles. The outer edge is obviously determined from the same points with the result that the bank gets narrower towards the apex. One would expect a large triangle in the circle EFG, but this does not have very convincing measurements, these are EF 52.8 × ¼MY and EG, FG 62.51 × ¼MY. Possibly they were meant to be 54[26] and 63[27] which gives a total of 180 × ¼MY (60 × 3).

Balance

Not enough remains of the standing stones to establish their relationship to the geometry but it seems that they might be balanced as opposites round the axis GH. The entrance is probably offset from the geometry to mark south.

Numbers

The circle has the following significant numbers:

Geometry	1	The whole site
	2	Two halves
	3	Triangles, 3 arcs
	4	Triangle plus the centre
Measurement	44	Arcs
	60	= 20 × 3 ABC, ABD
	90	= 30 × 3 ACD (180 = 60 × 3 EFG)
	65	Long axis GH. 195 = 65 × 3 circumference

Note: 65 is 5 more than ABC, ABD and 195 is 15 more than EFG and 15 is 5 × 3 which relates to the 3:4:5 triangle × 5.

Symbolism

An interesting set of numbers based on the relationships between 3 and 4 with 3 as basic harmony and energy, and 4 as its synthesis into the world. This is an arrangement which underlies many circles, but this is the only site found to date to express it so clearly.

The North Circle, Stanton Moor (SK.2495.6367)

This circle is 200 yards to the north of Nine Ladies with trees growing on the site itself. It is found by following the path north from Nine Ladies, until a wall is reached that runs to the east which should be followed for 70 yards; the circle is very near here just in from the wall.

This small site is badly damaged, but enough remains to show it was similar to the other circles on Stanton Moor. It has a bank which is between 6 and 9 feet wide, with the widest parts in the north; this has diameters of, outside 48 × 44 feet and inside 33 × 30 feet. There are two entrances, to the N.N.E. and S.S.W., with

The Southern Circles

a flanking stone in the southern one indicating they were similar to the central circle. The bank has collapsed near the entrances, so it is difficult to say how wide they are; probably between 6 and 8 feet. Near the southern entrance is a standing stone set in the internal edge of the bank, indicating a ring of stones as in the southern circle. The central area is very badly disturbed by a large pit with its rubble thrown to the east. There are also fragments of what looks like an original mound around the other edges of the pit, indicating it was dug to find the contents of the mound.

GEOMETRY

The circle is too small and badly damaged to reconstruct its geometry. It looks as if it could be elongated to the west with a similar shape to the other Stanton Moor circles with an internal diameter of approximately 12×11 MY. If this is the case it makes the northern entrance at a change of arc and the southern one at an arc centre, which is identical to the central circle.

The Doll Tor Circle, Stanton Moor (SK.2383.6287)

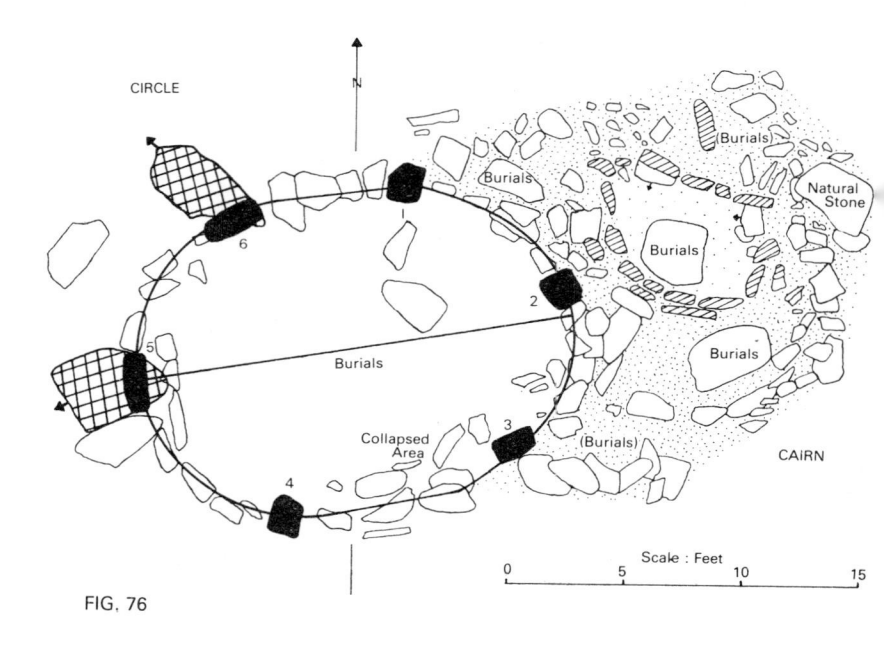

FIG. 76

This small unusual circle is on the other side of Stanton Moor on a gentle slope below the Andle Stone, just above where the hill falls sharply away to the valley below. It is in a small conifer plantation which obscures most of the views. Originally it would have had a fine view to the west over the valleys below and the limestone plateau beyond.

This site is reached by firstly going to the Andle Stone, a large natural stone surrounded by a circular wall visible from the road. In the field below near the north-east corner is an enigmatic standing stone possibly connected with the Andle Stone. In the south-west corner of this field is a gate which is the way on to Doll Tor. From here follow the trackway down the north side of the plantation until just before it bends sharply to the right. The circle is visible just inside the wood, covered in thick grass and bracken.

This circle was dug into by Bateman in 1852 and excavated in 1931 by Heathcote who left it uncovered. It has a ring of six standing stones all about 3 feet high with no apparent bank; this has a diameter of 19 × 14 feet. Unfortunately the two largest stones are fallen. A peculiar thing happened during the excavation — when returning to the site one day, the excavators found that stones 1 and 4 were smashed into fragments (now reconstructed with concrete). This was put down to unknown vandals, but one wonders who would take a large sledge hammer up onto the moors for this purpose. Should they have considered a paranormal explanation?

At some stage in the construction of the site the stones were joined together by a continuous ring of small flat stones, but it is not clear whether they are contemporary with the standing stones. If this is the case, they could have been a retaining ring for a low turf bank with no external stones which had completely eroded away by the time of the excavation. The fact that it was not found under the cairn to the east points against this theory. Alternatively they could be regarded as a degenerate form of bank.

At some time after the completion of the circle a cairn was added to the eastern end of the ring enclosing a third of it, but not encroaching on the central area, indicating the circle was still in use. Near the cairn's centre is a roughly rectangular enclosure of small vertically set stones containing a large slab which had burials under it. Four other areas, two at either side, are stone free and at least two of these also contained burials. The edge of the cairn is not circular, but appears to be a series of short straight sides totalling five or six, which are far from being geometric in character. The central area of the circle also had burials placed in it at some stage. The grave goods found with the burials included some faience beads which point to a late date no earlier than the fifteenth century BC and support the theory that the circle is a degenerate form.

GEOMETRY

The circle is too small to reconstruct its geometry with certainty. It is obviously far from circular and is probably an egg type elongated to the east, but an ellipse also fits reasonably well. The long axis can be fixed accurately and the dimensions are approximately 7 × 5.5 MY. The arrangement of the stones is interesting and points to how the circle could have been used for symbolic alignments by using them as foresights and backsights. Firstly if you take the three stones in the western half of the ring, stones 4, 5 and 6, and sit by the left edge of each, then by looking through the centre of their opposite stone, a point at the centre of the circle is defined. This same point is marked by doing the same thing with stones 1, 2 and 3 but this time sitting by their right sides.

ALIGNMENTS

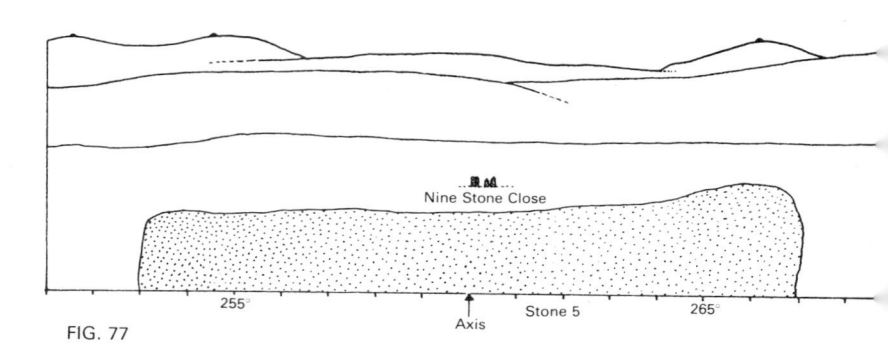

FIG. 77

The orientation of the long axis is accurately fixed and aligns to the west through stone 5 to Nine Stone Close, 0.8 miles away, which if it wasn't for the trees would be clearly visible because of its large stones, on Harthill Moor across the valley below. When you sit next to stone 2 and look through stone 5, it defines approximately 7° with Nine Stone Close at its centre. This is flanked above the edges of the stone by two prominent hills, End Low and Lean Low, both of which have early Bronze Age barrows on their summits. This main alignment of the Doll Tor circle does not have any astronomical significance; it must have been chosen for its relationship to the other circle and its visual perfection, as is shown by the reconstructed horizon in the diagram.

Stanton Moor

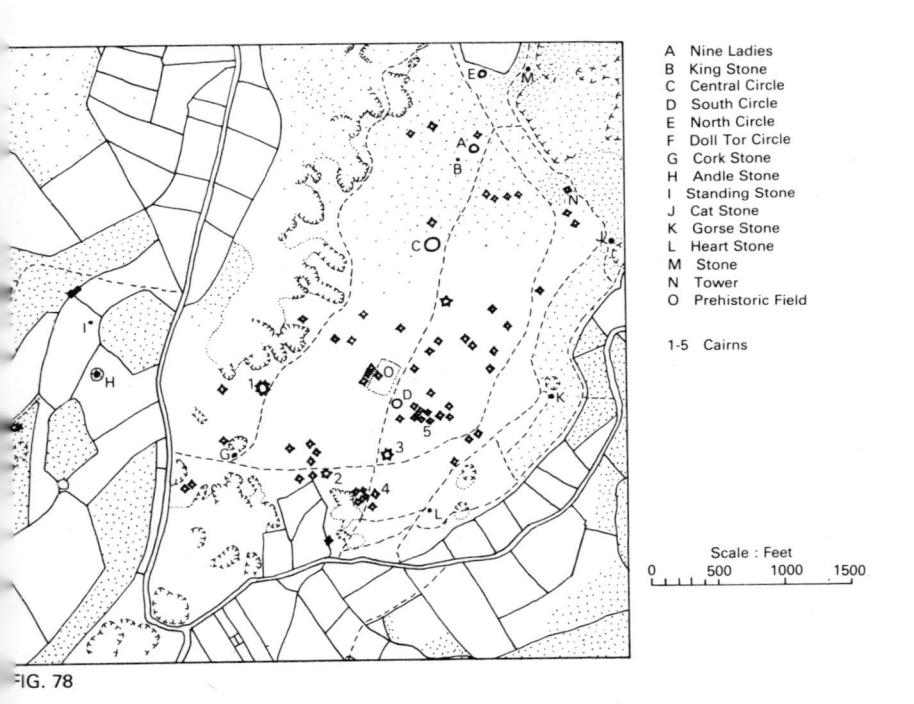

A   Nine Ladies
B   King Stone
C   Central Circle
D   South Circle
E   North Circle
F   Doll Tor Circle
G   Cork Stone
H   Andle Stone
I   Standing Stone
J   Cat Stone
K   Gorse Stone
L   Heart Stone
M   Stone
N   Tower
O   Prehistoric Field

1-5   Cairns

Scale : Feet
0   500   1000   1500

FIG. 78

Stanton Moor is an insular block of gritstone detached from the main moors by the River Derwent. Its top is covered in prehistoric sites and they form a well defined sacred complex, offering an opportunity to see a variety of monuments in a small area. This moor was probably chosen as a focal point because it is in an elevated central position, surrounded by valleys and shelves which would have supported a relatively high population. The main sites are the five circles already described. Surrounding these are over 70 burial mounds, many of which have been excavated and found to contain cremations of the mid Bronze Age which are roughly contemporary with the circles.

Among the mounds worth looking at are the following:
1) This mound is very unusual as it is rectangular rather than

circular. It is 40 × 22 feet in size and 3 feet high orientated approximately north/south. It is also unusual because it was used for 13 separate burials rather than the single burial more usual in the mid Bronze Age.

2) This circular mound has a diameter of 30 feet, is 2½ feet high and is built of earth with no supporting ring. It contained a burial in a rock cut pit under the mound.

3) This rubble mound is the largest on the moor with a diameter of 54 feet and a height of 5 feet. It is badly disturbed which enables the internal features to be seen, at the outer edge is a ring of large horizontal stones with a smaller ring 3 feet within this, at the centre is a stone cist which contained the main burial of the site although 12 others have been found.

4) This rubble mound is oval, diameter 28 × 20 feet; it is 2 feet high and is retained by a ring of curb stones. This contained a central pit with a cremated woman and a bronze knife.

5) This area just to the east of the southern circle has a scatter of more typical mounds which are smaller with diameters no greater than 15 feet, they are low and retained by stone rings.

As well as the mounds, the moor also has several prominent natural pillar-like rocks of a similar nature to 'the Mother's Cap' and others already described. These were possibly another reason for using this moor for a centre as they were probably regarded as sacred. The most impressive is the Cork Stone in the centre of the moor which looks at first glance to be erected and shaped, but is completely natural. It stands over 10 feet high with vertical sides and can be climbed with the aid of metal hand-holds placed in the stone over a hundred years ago. At the top is a symmetrical pothole which usually contains water. In 1789 Rooke described the stone as having 4 standing stones placed round it with a diameter of 25 feet, but no sign of these remains today. The stone is surrounded by quarries and it is probable the quarrymen removed these sometime last century (Rooke calls the stone the Andle Stone which is obviously a mistake as his drawings show). On the west of the moor is the true Andle Stone (dialect for Anvil Stone) a massive block of stone which is surrounded by thick shrubbery and a circular wall. This is clearly visible from the valleys below and has a standing stone in the field below it, which is possibly connected with this. On the eastern edge of the moor are three more smaller pillars, the Cat, Gorse and Heart Stones which were also possibly important as they are visible from the Derwent Valley below.

The Southern Circles

The circles on Stanton Moor are harder to interpret on a macrocosmic scale than those around Barbrook; there are however some clues. A line from Nine Ladies through the King Stone goes to the Andle Stone and then on to the Doll Tor Circle. This line was probably the direction of the Candlemas/Martinmas sunset but this cannot be checked because of trees covering the moor. Another line is between the northern and central circles with the King Stone midway between. All four circles on the eastern half of the moor are in an approximate line which runs N.N.E./S.S.W. They all have similar geometries based on modified eggs showing they were built by the same group of people. Nine Ladies does not have the flanked entrances which could indicate a slightly different date from the others. These three are very similar in construction, are approximately equally spaced and were probably parts of a single building project. The Doll Tor circle is probably a very late addition to the complex, away from the others and closely linked to Nine Stone Close on Harthill Moor.

Nine Stone Close, Harthill Moor (SK.2254.6264)

This is the only circle in the Peak District which has large standing stones and it is a great tragedy that so little has survived here. The site is in a large flat area of relatively fertile grass fields, at a lower altitude that any other circle in the Peak District. Dominating the horizon is Robin Hood's Stride a few hundred yards to the south, which is a massive natural outcrop of gritstone with cliffs on all sides and two pillar-like stones on the top. This impressive freak of nature was probably regarded as being particularly sacred to prehistoric man as the name indicates, for Robin Hood is nothing to do with the mediaeval hero but is an alternative name for 'the Green Man', the old god of fertility.

The circle is clearly visible from the road and should be approached from the gate opposite the track to Harthill Moor Farm, as the drystone walls are rather unstable and should not be climbed. Today the circle consists of only 4 free standing stones each over 6½ feet high placed on half an arc of between 40 and 45 feet diameter. Originally there were 9 stones; one of the missing ones has been moved across the field to the south, to act as a gatepost. Old drawings show that most of the missing stones were slightly smaller than those which have survived.

GEOMETRY

There is not enough left of the circle to reconstruct its geometry and all that can be said is that 9 stones would be equally spaced on a ring of about the right size.

ALIGNMENTS

The horizon from the site was obviously chosen with great care, for it creates a beautiful symbolic arrangement which combined the sun, moon and landscapes as follows:

Stone 1: Carlton Pasture which is relatively close just across the Wye Valley.

The Southern Circles

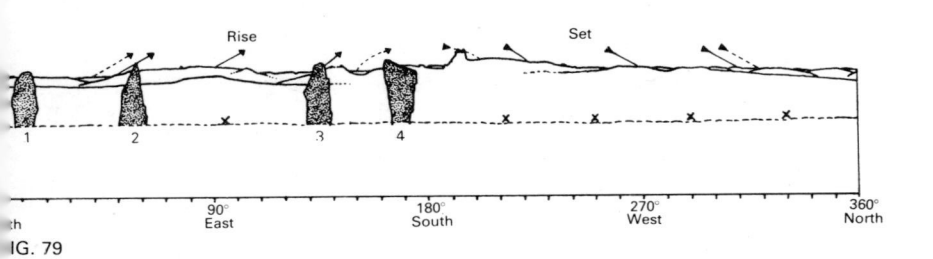

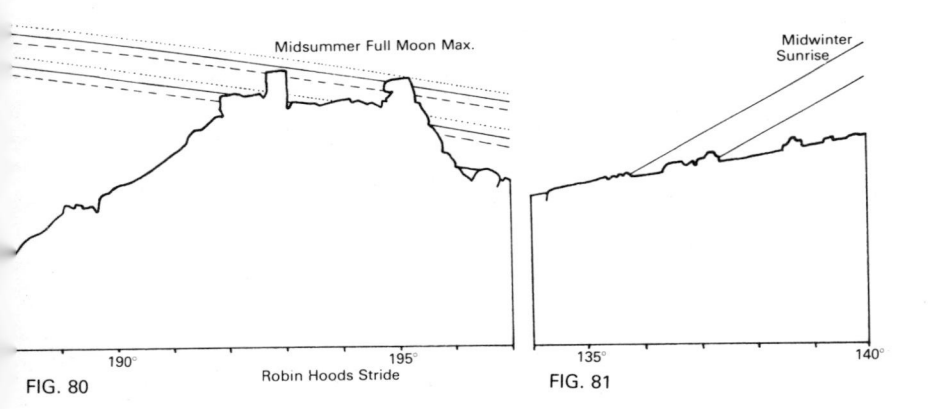

FIG. 79

FIG. 80

FIG. 81

gap: Just offset from the centre is a distant view, Beeley Moor, the centre of which was the rising point of the midwinter full moon maximum.
Stone 2: This marks the northern end of Stanton Moor, a relatively close horizon. Offset from the point of the stone was the rising position of the midsummer sun, which would have passed through the stone soon afterwards.
(gap: Stanton Moor)
Missing stone: The equinox sunrise from Stanton Moor
gap: An horizon which is relatively far away.
Stone 3: Cratcliffe Rocks, a close horizon which was the position of the midwinter sunrise. This alignment was also marked on the horizon by rocks, it rose so that the first flash of light was in a notch and before leaving the horizon it was cut by a prominent stone.
gap: A small section of the distant Bonsall Moor is visible, the centre of which was the rise position of the midsummer full moon maximum.
Stone 4: Close horizon

gap: A small section of Elton Common is visible but more important than this is Robin Hood's Stride in the centre of the gap. This is the main alignment of the circle and was to the midsummer full moon maximum. The circle was obviously very carefully positioned so that the Stride could be used to study the moon's eclipse variation. At the minimum of the wobble the moon first touched the Stride at the left pillar then crossed to the right one so that its upper edge just went behind the top. At the maximum the moon first touched the Stride at its left edge then went completely below the top of the left pillar, crossed the central area so only half the moon was visible and then went behind the right pillar so that it completely disappeared for a few seconds. After leaving the Stride the moon crossed the sky finally setting 5° further north.

Missing stone: Close horizon of Dudwood Hill.

(**gap:** Area of same moor slightly further away.)

Missing stone: Offset close horizon of Harthill Moor.

gap: Offset small section of the distant Middleton Common.

Missing stone: Close horizon of Castle Ring.

gap: Distant horizon of Taddington Moor and the midwinter full moon set maximum (obscured by trees).

Missing stone: Relatively close area of the Bole Hill.

gap: Distant view of Longstone Edge (obscured by trees).

To summarise, the three main rising positions of the sun are symbolically marked by the stones which also mark areas of close horizon and the maximum positions of the moon are marked by the gaps where there are usually more distant horizons. Because the circle is lower than most, it is possible that some lines were obscured by trees: but Robin Hood's Stride rises so high that this line at least would have been easy to keep clear. The problems with trees could also explain why the circle has such large stones.

The Park Gate Circle, Beeley Moor (SK.2804.6851)

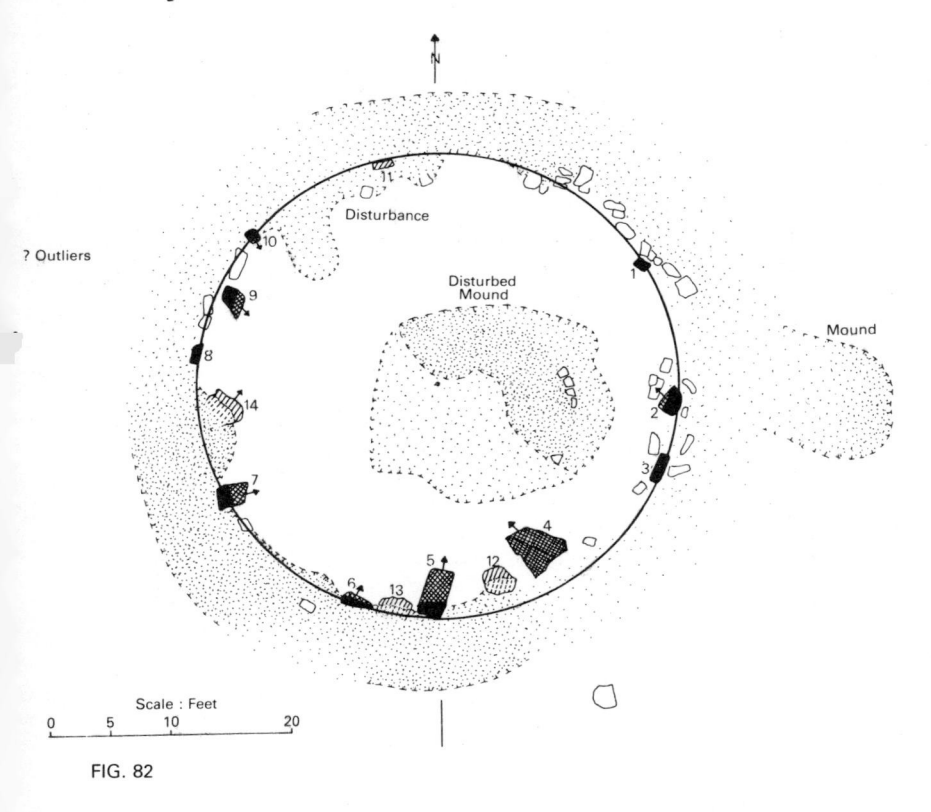

FIG. 82

This circle is situated on flat moorland covered in coarse grass and heather, with the high Harland Edge rising to the east, and a fine view over much of the Peak District to the west, some of the moors up to twenty miles away.

The site is found by following the track from the high gate, past where it levels out, until just before it begins to turn to the north-west. Leave the track to the right through the gap that goes through the thick areas of bracken. The circle is not visible from the track because of the bracken, and it is on clear land just to the other side of this.

The circle is badly damaged but enough remains to visualise its original state. It consists of a continuous low bank with badly defined edges, often collapsed inwards. It has diameters, outside 50 to 52 feet and inside 36 to 40 feet. On the internal edge of the bank is a ring of 10 to 14 standing stones of varying sizes, some of which are possibly large walling stones. Only 6 or 7 are still standing and the others are leaning badly or fallen inwards. The remaining stones are very unevenly spaced and it is possible that others have now disappeared. In the centre of the circle is a large scatter of rubble which originally was a cairn, and traces of its retaining ring remain; this had a diameter of between 16 and 18 feet. Adjoining the bank to the outside in the east is a low mound of unknown age and to the W.N.W. are two small vertically set stones a few feet outside the bank. These are too small to be useful outliers and remain a mystery.

Near this circle are other prehistoric sites including two which are worth looking at while visiting Park Gate. The first is the Beeley Moor Central Circle which is a bank covered in bracken with no standing stones. It has diameters of, outside 60 × 65 feet and inside 41 × 48 feet with an entrance to the south-east. This is an egg shaped ring similar in shape to the Nine Ladies Circle, based on a pentagon.

The second is a large Bronze Age cairn 285 feet to the south of the central circle. It is 36 × 42 feet in diameter, 3 feet high and surrounding this is a low bank which is 8 feet wide with diameters of, inside 60 feet and outside 76 feet.

There are three other small circles on Beeley Moor which are badly preserved and not worth visiting.

GEOMETRY

Construction

The site appears to be a true circle with a diameter of $60 \times \frac{1}{4}MY$ and a circumference of $190 \times \frac{1}{4}MY$[28]. This circle fits to the inner edge of the bank and the stones are set inside it. This is rather unusual but appears to be correct, as a smaller circle has very poor number relationships (one with a diameter of 14 MY is too small). Inside the circle a square can be drawn with sides of $42.5 \times \frac{1}{4}MY$[29] which has a total of $170 \times \frac{1}{4}MY$. However, because of the ruined stones, its orientation cannot be determined.

The Southern Circles

Numbers

The numbers of the circle are a combination of 4, 5, and 6:

Geometry	1	Circle
	4	Square
	5	Square plus its centre
Measurement	60	Diameter
	190	Circumference, 170 square, midway is
		$180 = 60 \times 3$

ALIGNMENTS

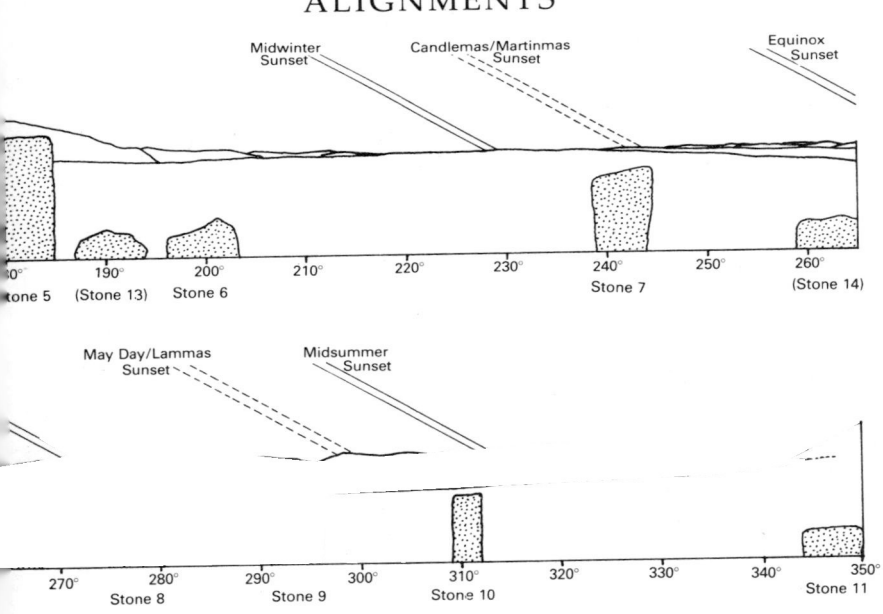

FIG. 83

The horizon was chosen for its solar setting positions which are:

Midsummer sunset This first touched the horizon at the junction between Rushup Edge and Kinder Scout.
May Day/Lammas sunset First touched the horizon at the exact southern end of Longstone Edge.
Equinox sunset Would set into the short steep slope of Axe Edge.
Candlemas/Martinmas sunset Would set at the southern end of Calton Pasture.
Midwinter sunset Now obscured by bracken but must have been near the prominent End Low.

8

The Northern Circles

The South Circle, Bamford Moor (SK.2211.8453)

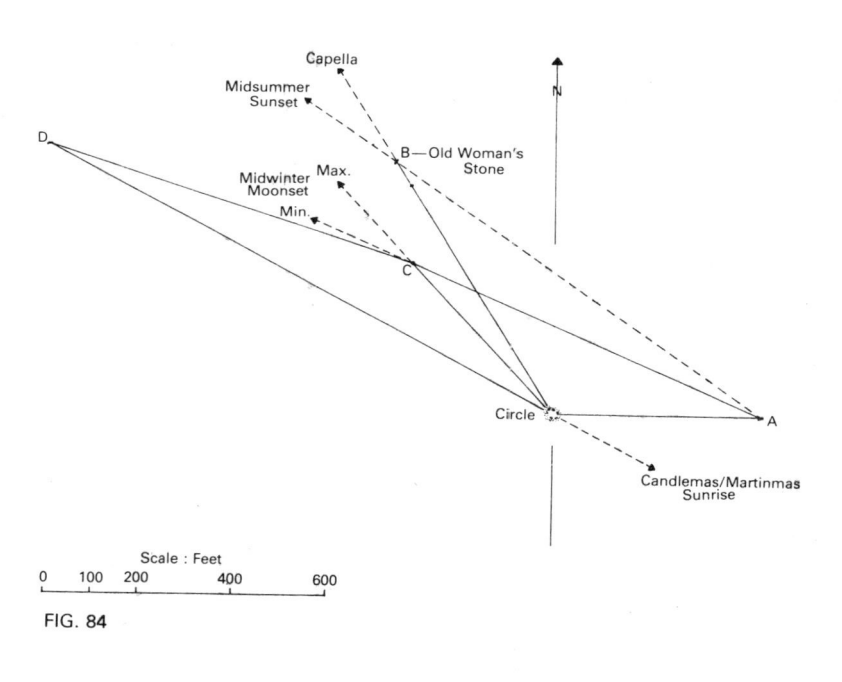

FIG. 84

This small circle is on the south-east slope of the bleak featureless Bamford Moor with Stanage high above, half a mile to the east. Near at hand to the west is a ridge which causes the land

The Northern Circles

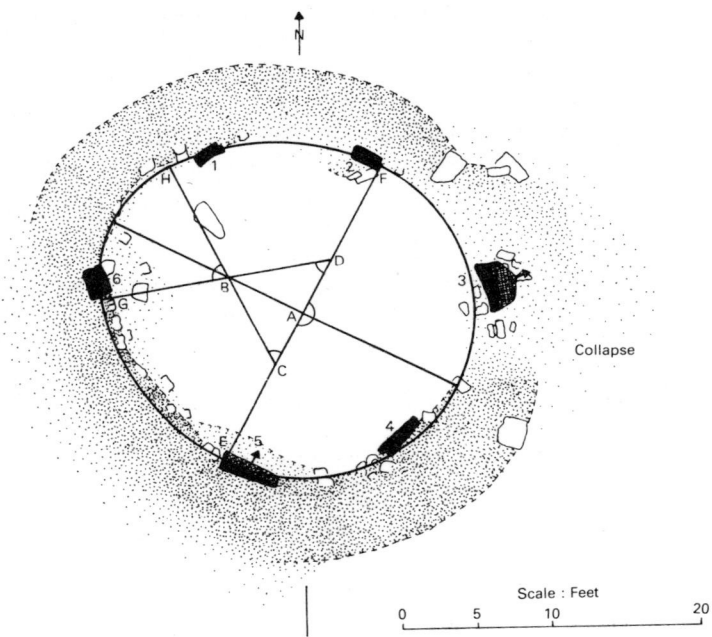

FIG. 85

the circle is actually on to slope to the north-east. The only distant views are to the moors flanking the Derwent Valley in the south.

The site is difficult to find because the whole moor is covered in thick heather with no footpaths, and the circle only becomes clearly visible when one is close to it. The best way to find it is to set off from the corner of the wood towards the near end of the wall that can be seen running down the horizon. When about three-quarters of the way to this the circle should be slightly to the right (provided you went in a straight line).

This is a very small but well preserved circle which consists of a continous bank which has diameters of, outside 33 × 36 feet and inside 23 × 26 feet. Because the site is on a slope, at one side the outer edge is very low and the inner high and at the other side the situation is reversed. The internal edge of the bank contains a complete ring of 6 standing stones which are between 1½ and 2 feet high, surrounding a small flat central area. Around the circle are a number of outliers in different directions, placed as follows:

A. A small vertical slab nearly two feet high, 447 feet downhill on flatter ground to the east.
B. 'The Old Woman's Stone'. This pointed slab once stood nearly eight feet high, 642 feet to the N.N.W. of the circle. Early this century it was split near the base and pulled down to stop walkers using it as a guide stone. The base is still vertical in its original position with the rest of the stone lying next to it. 65 feet from the stone in a direct line to the circle is a smaller stone which may mark this direction.
C. A pillar-like stone 2½ feet high now leaning to one side, 440 feet to the north-west of the circle slightly to the west of the line to the Old Woman's Stone.
D. A pointed slab 2½ feet high, 1220 feet away uphill to the W.N.W., which is positioned so that the point of the stone touches the horizon. This is not always clearly visible as it blends into the background on dull days.

GEOMETRY

Construction

This circle is too small to reconstruct its exact geometry but it is definitely an egg elongated to the W.N.W. The simplest solution found fits reasonably well, but does not have particularly convincing numbers which could indicate this is not quite correct:
1) Two triangles are placed in the centre, ABC, ABD with sides of AC, AD 6 × ¼MY. AB 8 × ¼MY. BC, BD 10 × ¼MY.
2) A semi-circle from A is drawn from E to F with a length of 17 × ¼MY creating a short axis of 34 × ¼MY.
3) An arc from C is drawn to join F to H and a corresponding one from D joining E to G (23 × ¼MY long).
4) A closing arc from B is drawn from H to G (13 × ¼MY long). This creates a long axis of 38 × ¼MY and a circumference of 110.72 × ¼MY which is probably meant to be 111 or 110[1].

Balance

The stones are approximately arranged so that they flank the long axis: 1 and 6 the smallest, at the egg end, 2 and 5 medium stones in the centre; and 3 and 4 the largest stones at the semi-circle's main alignment.
 The stones are also arranged so that the geometric centre can be found by intersecting lines, from stone 1 to stone 4 and from stone 2 to stone 5 (from point to point). This could explain why stone 1 is offset

from the balance mentioned above. Another reason is that it marks the direction of the Old Woman's Stone. The egg end of the long axis marks outlier D.

ALIGNMENTS

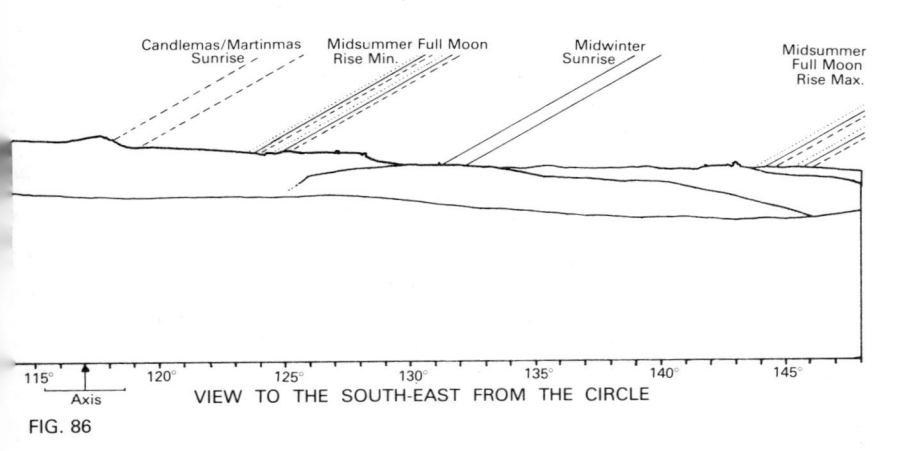

FIG. 86

VIEW TO THE SOUTH-EAST FROM THE CIRCLE

Labels on horizon diagram: Candlemas/Martinmas Sunrise; Midsummer Full Moon Rise Min.; Midwinter Sunrise; Midsummer Full Moon Rise Max. Axis at 115°.

When the astronomical alignments of this circle and its outliers are studied, phases of building are revealed as at Barbrook I. The circle itself has an horizon which marked the following lines:

Candlemas/Martinmas Sunrise. The first flash of light was close to the prominent change of angle at the base of Stanage Edge. The semi-circular end of the long axis goes in this direction and was probably to the exact sun position.

May Day/Lammas Sunrise. The first flash of light was from a prominent distinctive stone on Stanage Edge.

Midwinter Sunrise. The sun rose from Carhead Rocks Hill so that the first flash of light was just past a rock which could act as a day counter.

Midsummer Full Moon Maximum Rise. This rose just to the right of Over Owler Tor, the only year of the moon's cycle where this would happen.

Midsummer Full Moon Minimum Rise. This rose from the left edge of Higgar Tor in a well defined dip, where the eclipse variation could possibly be detected.

After the circle's site had been determined by the alignments above, the outliers were constructed to create further lines (see figs. 87-92):
1) Outlier A was placed 65 MR from the circle. This location produced a better position for observing the midwinter sunrise which rose from the right junction between Carhead Rocks Hill and the moor behind.

FIG. 87 FROM THE CIRCLE
May Day/Lammas Sunrise — 63° 64° 65° 66° 67°

FIG. 88 FROM THE CIRCLE
Setting Of Capella — 1780, 1800, 1820 — B — 327° 328° 329° 330°

FIG. 89 FROM OUTLIER A
Midsummer Sunset — B — 303° 304° 305° 306°

FIG: 90 FROM OUTLIER D
Candlemas/Martinmas Sunrise — Circle — 116° 117° 118° 119° 120°

FIG. 91 FROM THE CIRCLE
Midwinter Full Moon Set Max. — C — 315° 316° 317° 318° 319°

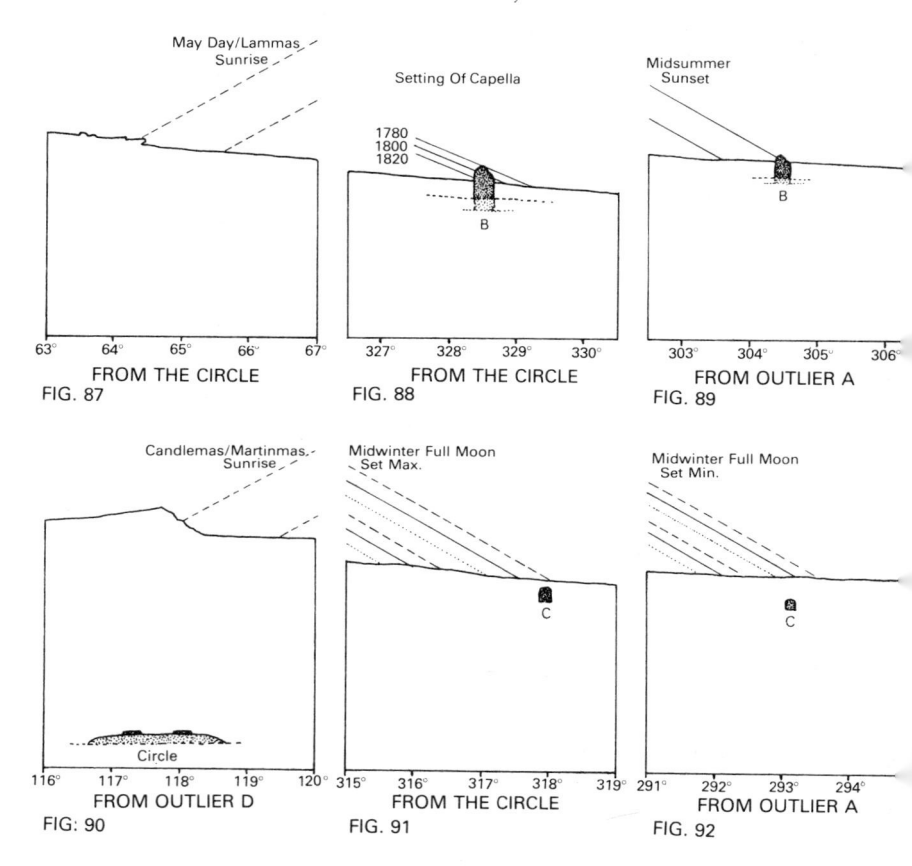

FIG. 92 FROM OUTLIER A
Midwinter Full Moon Set Min. — C — 291° 292° 293° 294°

2) Outlier B 'The Old Woman's Stone' was placed 95 MR from the circle (and approximately 140 MR from A creating a triangle with a total length of 300 MR, possibly coincidence). Standing at A, stone B rose above the horizon so that the last flash of light of the midsummer sunset was behind the stone.

Another possible alignment to this stone was from the centre of the circle, from where the stone marked the setting of the first magnitude star Capella in 1800 BC ± 20 years, which may be coincidental.

3) Outlier C was placed 65 MR from the circle so that it formed an isosceles triangle with outlier A, with a distance of AC 120 MR giving a total of 65 + 65 + 120 = 250 MR. The positioning of this stone is remarkable, for not only does it have a geometric position, but it also

marked two moon alignments, creating perfect conditions for studying the moonset at midwinter. Firstly from the centre of the circle the stone top was just below the horizon at the maximum of the moon's cycle, positioned so accurately as to mark the last flash of light at the maximum of the eclipse variation. Secondly from outlier A the stone marked the last flash of light at the minimum of the moon's cycle.

4) Outlier D is 120 MR from C although this could be coincidence. This stone is along the long axis line of the circle but does not align to anything in this direction. From D to the circle creates a line to the southern end of Stanage where the sun rose at Candlemas/Martinmas slightly further to the right than from the circle so that the first flash of light was more accurately marked at the base of the cliff.

It is not clear if there was any time lapse or not between each of these phases and it is also possible that stage 2 came after 3 and 4.

By the time all the outliers were erected the builders had marked all the main solar positions except for the equinox, either by their rise or set. Also the moon is marked at both the solstices with a particularly good arrangement for midwinter. If the alignment to Capella is not coincidence, it could be a good indication of the age of the circle.

North Circle, Bamford Moor (SK.2088.8525)

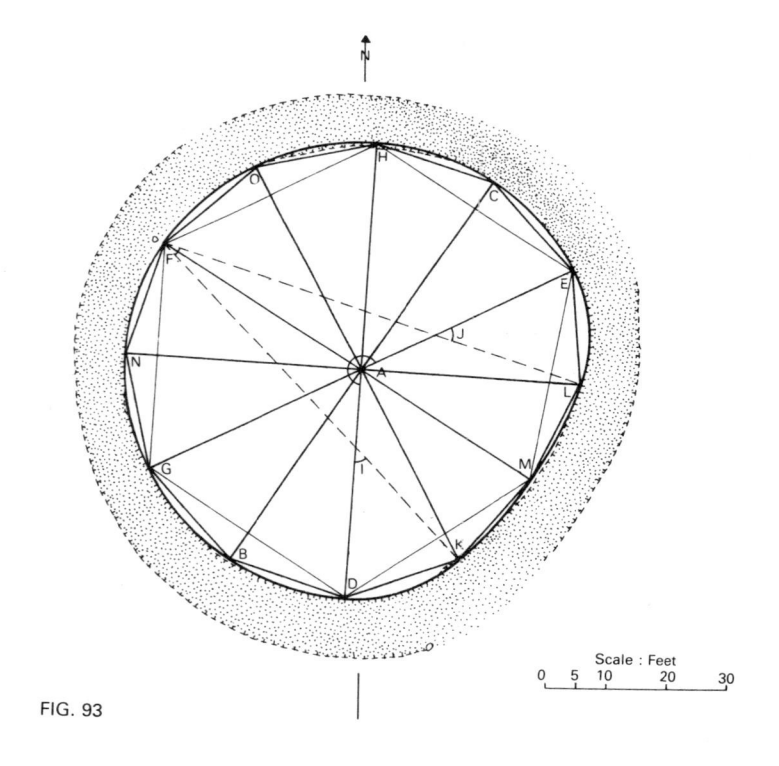

FIG. 93

Scale : Feet
0 5 10 20 30

This circle is on a gentle slope near the western edge of the bleak heather-covered moor. The site is one of the highest circle locations in the area, and is in an exposed position, open to the north wind. From this spot are some of the finest views in the Peak District over its most imposing landmarks. The dominant feature is Win Hill across the Derwent Valley, flanked by Mam Tor and Lose Hill. South of this is the limestone plateau of Bradwell Moor and moors beyond. To the north the Kinder

The Northern Circles

Scout, Bleaklow and the Derwent moors, the highest area in Derbyshire, with their near vertical edges and flat windswept tops.

The walk along Bamford Edge to reach the circle also has views which are just as impressive, and these make the long walk well worth the trouble despite the circle's unimpressive nature. The site is rather hard to find because it barely stands out from the surrounding landscape. The best way is to find the wall to the north of the moor's summit, (marked on itineraries map); follow it down for about 170 yards then look for the site 80 yards out from the wall. This circle is another which has no standing stones but only a low earth bank. The site was not known about by eighteenth century antiquarians, so no records exist of it before the building of a nearby nineteenth century wall; it is therefore possible the site had stones before this was built. At the present time the circle is visible because the heather has been burnt off, but in a few years it will be scarcely visible again. The bank is relatively well defined but with no signs of retaining rings. It is less than one foot high in many places, with an external diameter of 93 × 98 feet and an internal diameter of 74 × 80 feet. The central area within the bank is flat and has no features.

GEOMETRY

Construction

Because of the large size of the circle, and the fact that very accurate measurements were possible as the vegetation had been burnt off just before the survey was made, a good reconstruction of the geometry was possible. This has convincing measurements in ¼MY and is a 'Flattened type D'[2] which is constructed as follows:

1) An arc from A of 240° from D to E which has a radius of 58 × ¼MY. The positions of D and E being defined by constructing four equilateral triangles AFG, AFH, AGD, AHE. This gives a long axis BC of 116 × ¼MY (29 MY).

2) The lengths of AE and AD are divided into thirds, defining points I and J. The lines FI and FJ are then extended to K and L and arcs constructed from I and J to link D to K and E to L, with lengths of 38.66 × ¼MY.

3) The ring is completed with an arc from F joining K to L, this is 108 × ¼MY long (27 MY). The arc is also the short axis FM[3]. This circle has a circumference of approximately 360 × ¼MY or 90 MY[4].

This construction gives the following angular divisions of arcs from A:

60° FG, FH, MD, ME
30° CH, CE, BG, BD

These divisions can be developed further if lines are drawn from A to L and K, the only points in the construction not directly connected to A. Then if these lines are produced to N and O, the whole ring is divided into twelve 30° parts from A. It is obvious from the lengths given below that the builders knew about this and it is unique to this basic construction. The lengths from A to the points are integral as follows:

58 × ¼MY D, B, G, N, F, O, H, C, E
54 × ¼MY L, K[5]
50 × ¼MY M[6]

These numbers form a good series on the flattened half of the ring, with four units difference between each.

What makes these divisions more significant is the circumference of 360 × ¼MY which would give 12 curved divisions of 30 × ¼MY if this were a circle, but this is impossible because of the flattened nature of the site. (It is impossible to construct a true circle of 360 circumference with an integral diameter). What the builders tried to achieve was a clever compromise between curved and straight lines. In the first arc of 240° the eight straight lines are all 30 × ¼MY long[7]. The remaining lines are shorter so that the curved perimeter is still 360. They are EL, DK 29.27 × ¼MY and KM, LM 27.32 × ¼MY (29 and 27 are quarters of the two axes). The twelve straight lines have a total length of 353.36 × ¼MY.

Numbers

Summarising all the measurements of the site, they are:

116	Maximum diameter
108	Minimum diameter[8]
360	Circumference[9]
30	Twelve divisions—eight parts
(29.27 two parts 27.32 two parts)	
353.36	Total sum
(58,54,50	Distance from A)

These lengths show that the prime factor for the circle was the division into 12 and its relation to 36 and 3 MR. The other numbers are secondary but kept integral wherever possible. These include the interesting groups 116:58:29 and 108:54:27. The total straight line perimeter 353.36 is very close to 354, an approximate lunar year.

Symbolism

This circle is unusual as its main numbers probably relate to the zodiac 12 in combination with an approximate solar year of 360 days. This figure was often considered by ancient societies as the year and five days were added as extras. The combination with the lunar year is also possible if this relationship is not coincidence.

ALIGNMENTS

This circle shows the remarkable achievements of prehistoric man in a choice of site where between five and seven astronomical lines were marked by the horizon:

Midwinter Full Moon Maximum Rise. This was very close to the junction between the distant horizon and the close moor. At the maximum of the eclipse variation, the first flash of light would have been at the junction. The line was only of symbolic value however, because a slight movement on site would have changed the angle to the junction.

Midsummer Full Moon Maximum Set. This was in the junction between Taddington Moor and Brier Low, arranged so that the last flash of light at the maximum of the eclipse variation was in the junction, while at the minimum the first touch was near the junction.

The most interesting fact about the choice of site is the view to the south-west where a series of distant hills have just their summits visible above Bradwell Moor creating a series of well defined points. These combined with other points further north fit together to form an ideal horizon for a solar setting calendar.

Midwinter Sunset. A perfect alignment to Axe Edge of which $1\frac{1}{2}°$ is visible. The first touch was by the left junction with Bradwell Moor and the last flash of light near the summit. This is flanked by two peaks which are only just visible; these are: another part of Axe Edge to the right and Leap Edge to the left.

Candlemas/Martinmas Sunset. This would set into another small distant section of horizon, Black Edge. $4\frac{1}{2}°$ are visible and the sun first touched this at the peak in its centre.

Equinox Sunset. This would set into the centre of a 4° section of the flat ridge Brown Knoll, between the peaks of Win and Lose Hills. This line was not as well defined but it could not be mistaken for any other day as the sun was moving quickly along the horizon at this time of year.

May Day/Lammas Sunset. Again this would set into a section of flat horizon, between Edale Moor and Rowlee Pasture. This $5\frac{1}{2}°$ portion of Featherbed Moss does not fit as well as the others, the first touch of the sun was near the left junction and this only defines the point within a couple of days.

Midsummer Sunset. This was only marked by a slight rise on the top of Bleaklow and could be coincidence.

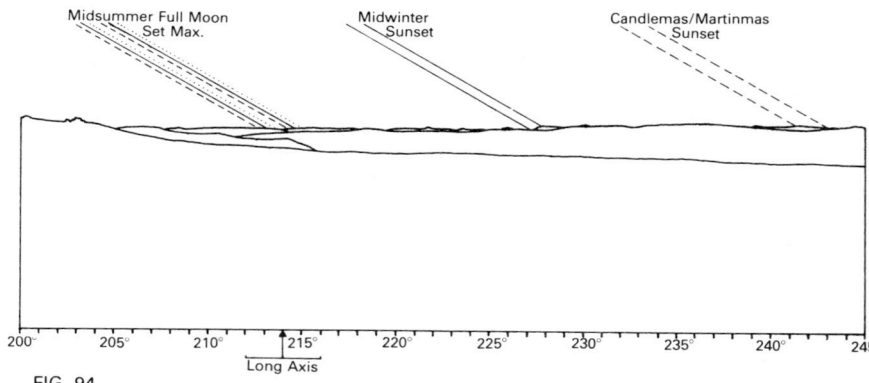

FIG. 94 — Midsummer Full Moon Set Max.; Midwinter Sunset; Candlemas/Martinmas Sunset; Long Axis at 215°

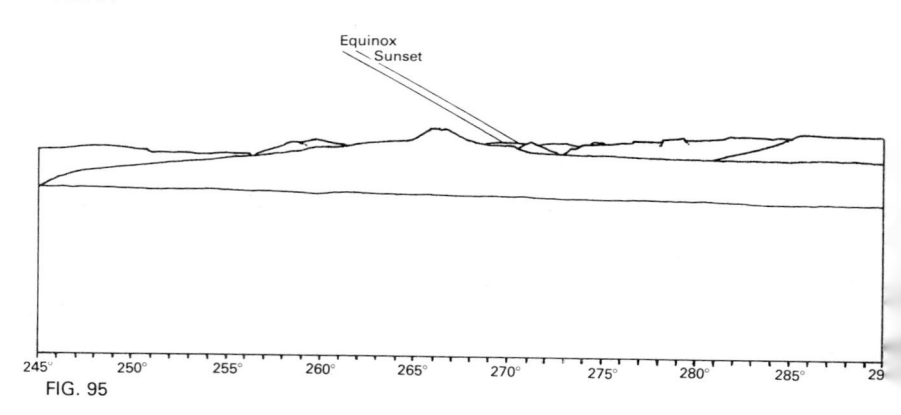

FIG. 95 — Equinox Sunset

FIG. 96 — May Day/Lammas Sunset; Midsummer Sunset; Short Axis at 295°

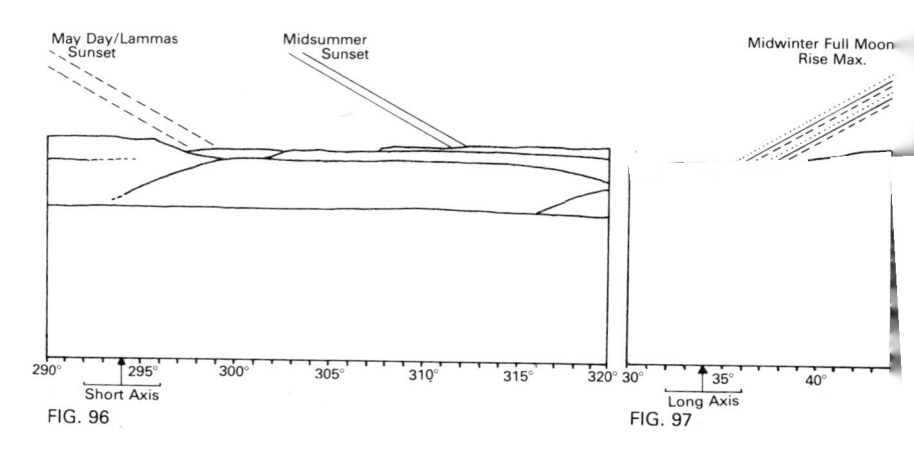

FIG. 97 — Midwinter Full Moon Rise Max.; Long Axis at 35°

The Northern Circles

The geometry of the circle appears to combine the lines of the sun and moon. The long axis aligned exactly to the midsummer moonset line and in the other direction, it was within 1° of the second moon line. The short axis at its flattened end goes to the close horizon formed by the nearby moor. All the astronomical rising lines were on this close horizon, and the geometry of the ring was aligned to these, rather than the marked horizon solar lines which were ignored. These lines were:

Short axis	Candlemas/Martinmas sunrise
Point L from A	Equinox sunrise
Point E from A	May Day/Lammas sunrise

These three points were the best that could be hoped for as this was the maximum number out of twelve that could fall within the range of solar rising positions. The short axis is also the exact direction of the Ciceley Low circles about 5 miles away (not visible), which have a large circle of a similar type to this one.

The Hordron Edge Circle (SK.2152.8685)

This small circle on the flat top of Hordron Edge is in one of the wildest and most evocative sites in the Peak District. It overlooks the Derwent Valley to the west 400 feet below, with Ladybower Reservoir at the bottom and Win Hill and Kinder Scout beyond. To the east the cliffs of Stanage rise up, half a mile away.

The site is found by walking along Hordron Edge from the north following sheep tracks above the steep edge until the first area of bracken which goes well back from the edge is reached. The circle is in this, often completely hidden in summer, about 50 yards from the track.

This circle is unusual in that it has no bank but only a ring of 10 standing stones, between 1½ and 3 feet high with a diameter of 53 × 50 feet. These stones are not equally spaced but placed in three groups, four to the north, three to the south-east and three to the W.S.W. Between these groups are 14 small loose stones which are possibly original although they could easily have been moved. It is possible that there were more standing stones originally, as Bateman described the circle in 1848 as being 'a very complete cirque', but this is the only evidence and the ring does not look disturbed.

GEOMETRY

Construction

Professor Thom surveyed the circle and concluded it was a 'Flattened type A' but this is not a good solution when the movement of stones 2 and 3 is taken into account. All the stones except 9 and 10 fit onto a true circle, and these two stones indicate that the geometry is probably a type of egg, but not enough remains to reconstruct it. All that can be said is that it is approximately 18.5 × 19.5 MY in diameter elongated to the west, with a circumference of roughly 60 MY.

FIG. 98

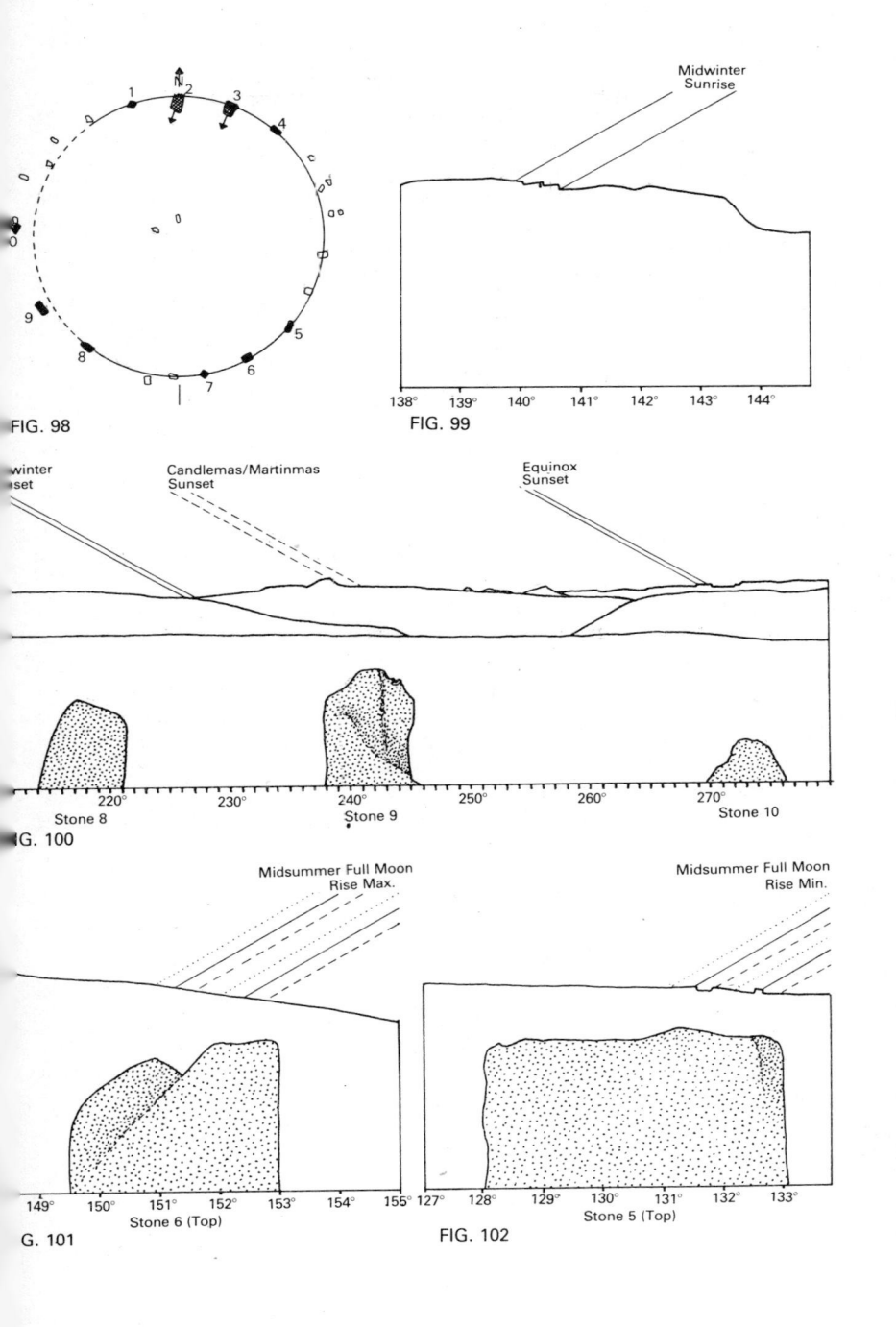

FIG. 99 — Midwinter Sunrise

138° 139° 140° 141° 142° 143° 144°

FIG. 100

winter set   Candlemas/Martinmas Sunset   Equinox Sunset

220° Stone 8   230°   240° Stone 9   250°   260°   270° Stone 10

FIG. 101 — Midsummer Full Moon Rise Max.

149° 150° 151° 152° 153° 154° 155° Stone 6 (Top)

FIG. 102 — Midsummer Full Moon Rise Min.

127° 128° 129° 130° 131° 132° 133° Stone 5 (Top)

ALIGNMENTS

This circle also has a large number of lines to the horizon, related to the stones and geometry:

Group A. Stones 8 to 10 and the main axis.

Stone 9, the main one of the group, aligns with Win Hill which was the position of the Candlemas/Martinmas sunset. The sun first touched the horizon at the peak of Win Hill and moved down its right slope; the last flash of light was on the more gentle slope above the point of stone 9. This stone is flanked by two smaller ones 8 and 10. Inside the arc defined by these two stones were a pair of solar lines marked by the horizon. Firstly, the midwinter sunset, where the last flash of light was exactly in the junction between Bamford Moor and Win Hill. Secondly, the equinox sunset, where the sun for one day only would set onto a small well defined part of Kinder Scout without touching its steep sides. This is also the approximate direction of the main axis of the circle.

Group B. Stones 1 to 4

This has two large stones 2 and 3 flanked by the other two. Stone 2 marks true north, but no reason has been found for the existence of stone 3.

Group C. Stones 5 to 7

Here there are two large stones flanking stone 6 which is smaller, this marked the direction of the midsummer full moon maximum which rose on a featureless horizon. (The setting position for the same day was marked by a change of gradient in Bamford Moor.) The moonrise at the minimum of its cycle was marked by prominent rocks on Stanage, above stone 5. Another line in this direction but this time not marked by the stones was the midwinter sunrise which was spectacularly marked by rocks on Stanage where a hole created a flash of light to the right of where the sun first appeared above.

To summarise, one group marks the sun, another the moon and the third north. Combined with the horizon, these mark the sun in the winter half of the year, and the moon at midsummer.

The Ewden Beck Circle, Broomhead Moor (SK.2381.9664)

This circle is well to the north of the main area of sites, and is unusual in its location. It is on a flat shelf of land just above the steep valley of Ewden Beck to the north, with Broomhead Moor rising to the south, and has virtually no good views to distant horizons. The circle is probably in this relatively low lying position because the higher moors with good views are all peat-covered and therefore not suitable.

This circle is easily found by following the footpath from the road until a small stream is crossed. Fork right down a small path at the side of the small stream gully. The circle surrounded by heather is just to the left after 150 yards. There are plans by the local parish council to keep the site vegetation-free.

The circle is unique in the Peak District in that it appears to be part of a defined complex. Running approximately east/west is a bank and ditch which cut off the shelf of land from the surrounding moor. This is nearly a mile long with a low bank and a ditch which has been deepened by flood waters following its course. These have never been excavated and are of unknown age, but two factors point to their connection with the circle. Firstly, it is not a defensive work as it has an internal ditch (from the moor side there is nothing to defend). Secondly, there are a large number of prehistoric features within the defined area but none without, a strong indication that it is earlier than at least some of these. Inside the area are the circle and at least seventeen burial cairns, most of these are small and look like typical mid Bronze Age features. All the cairns are to the south and west of the circle, but at one time there could have been more to the east where the land has been cleared to form a field.

The circle is badly disturbed, but enough remains to show it has many similarities to the Stoke Flat circle. It has a low bank which has an external diameter of 65 feet and is between 6 and 9 feet wide. There is little evidence of retaining rings except in the east where the slope made it necessary to build a strong outer

178 *Stone Circles of the Peak*

FIG. 103

FIG. 104

FIG. 105 From The Circle Centre

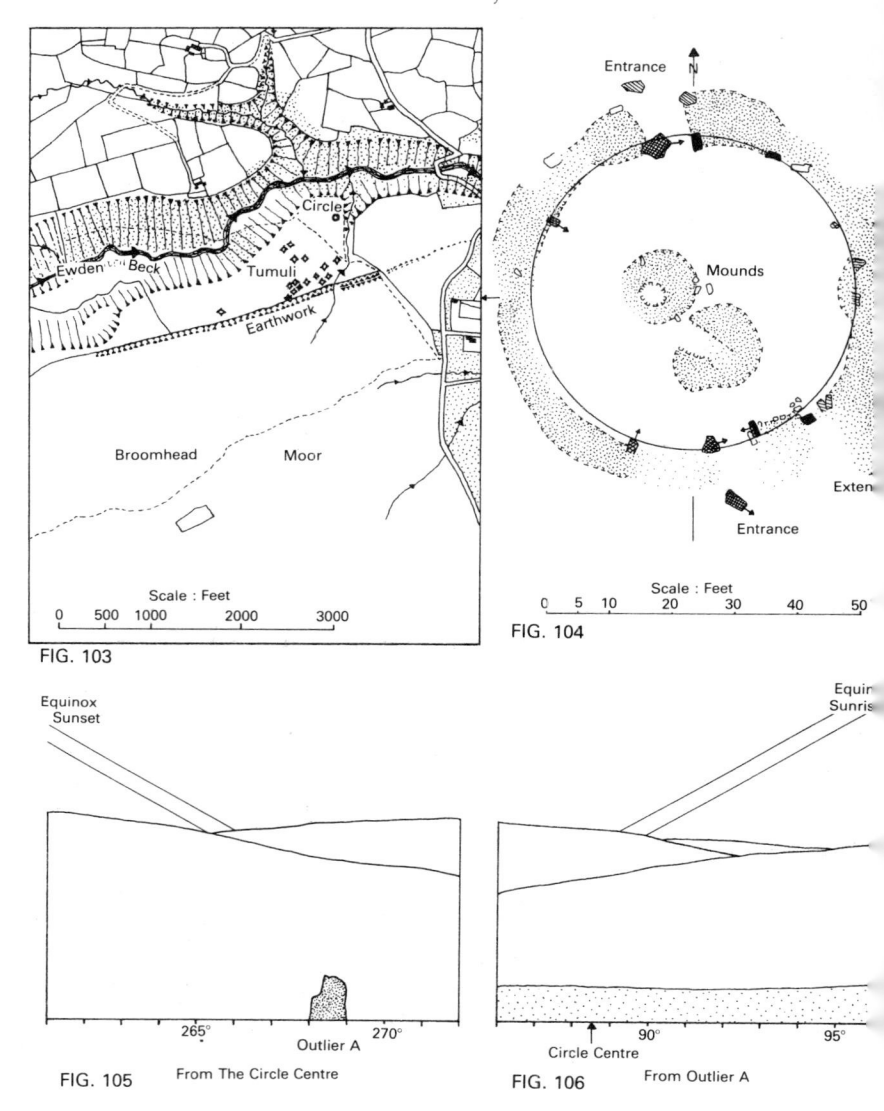

FIG. 106 From Outlier A

edge. The bank is broken by two entrances to the north and south which are 8 feet wide and flanked by standing stones. An unusual feature exists to the south-east where a ditch like area cuts through the bank from the outside, this is supported to the east by an extension of the bank which deviates from the ring.

The Northern Circles

The standing stones are badly disturbed, they fall into two groups all between 1½ and 2½ feet high. Firstly, those at the entrances with two on the inner edge of each entrance, a large stone near the outer edge of the southern entrance and possibly two at the northern one. Secondly, a ring of 4 or more smaller stones on the internal edge of the bank with a diameter of 47 × 52 feet. If only 4 stones originally existed they flanked the entrance stones; the others are only small and could be part of the retaining rings. In the centre of the circle are disturbed remains of two small cairns both about 12 feet in diameter. 130 feet from the circle to the west is a 2 feet high outlier which is now leaning.

GEOMETRY

The geometry cannot be reconstructed with any certainty as none of the standard types fit. It appears to be a circle flattened internally at both entrances, with dimensions of 76 × 70 × ¼MY, a circumference of approximately 240 × ¼MY and an entrance width of 12 × ¼MY. The outlier is 190 × ¼MY from the circle centre which is five times the circle's initial radius.

ALIGNMENTS

The horizon from the circle has only two junctions and both of these marked the equinox. Firstly that to the west which was the exact sunset and secondly that to the east where the sunrise just missed the junction but was marked by standing at the outlier and looking through the centre of the circle.

9

The Great Triangle

This construction is perhaps one of the most important geomantic structures rediscovered in Britain to date. It consists of a series of inter-connected triangles covering all the central area of the Peak District:

1) The Great Triangle. This is an isosceles triangle from Arbor Low to the Bull Ring and Wet Withers, with two equal sides of 10.415 miles[1]; the third is 9.145 miles with an angle of 52° 1' at Arbor Low.

2) A central axis from Arbor Low is orientated only 2° 58' west of true north. This extended northwards goes to the Peak Cavern, and is the balancing axis for the whole structure.

3) From the Bull Ring a line through the Peak Cavern goes to the top of Win Hill, and then on to the Hordron Edge circle. A right angle from the peak of Win Hill goes to Wet Withers forming a triangle with angles of virtually 30°, 60° and 90°, at the Bull Ring 29° 25' and at Wet Withers 60° 35 '.

4) An identical triangle to balance the one above to the base of the Edale Valley (see below). When this is extended it goes to a farm called Ringstones which is probably the site of a lost circle (further away than the Hordron Edge circle).

These constructions use points of various characters which at first seem incompatible, but when the nature of the macrocosmic geometry is understood, there is no conflict:

Henges—Arbor Low and the Bull Ring, the largest sites in Derbyshire.

Circles—Wet Withers, the largest circle and the Hordron Edge circle, possibly later constructions.

The Great Triangle

Natural Features—The construction uses two of the most prominent landmarks in the Peak. Win Hill is one of the highest in Derbyshire and is the termination of a long ridge from Edale Moor between the rivers Noe and Derwent. The ridge rises up to Win Hill with a flat top, but at the centre of the hill there is an uneroded band of harder rock which rises steeply to form the summit of the hill: from some angles this looks rather like a volcano. The Peak Cavern is the most impressive cave entrance chamber in Britain—330 × 102 feet and 60 feet high. This is below a high cliff which towers above it, situated at the top of a short steep-sided gorge. This entrance chamber was undoubtedly looked on with great awe by prehistoric man who from earliest times probably lived inside and worshipped the Earth Goddess there. It is so large that until relatively recently it had a row of cottages inside it. Further down the gorge is the Russett Well which is a natural spring constantly giving 4000 gallons per minute, this could have been sacred. Above the

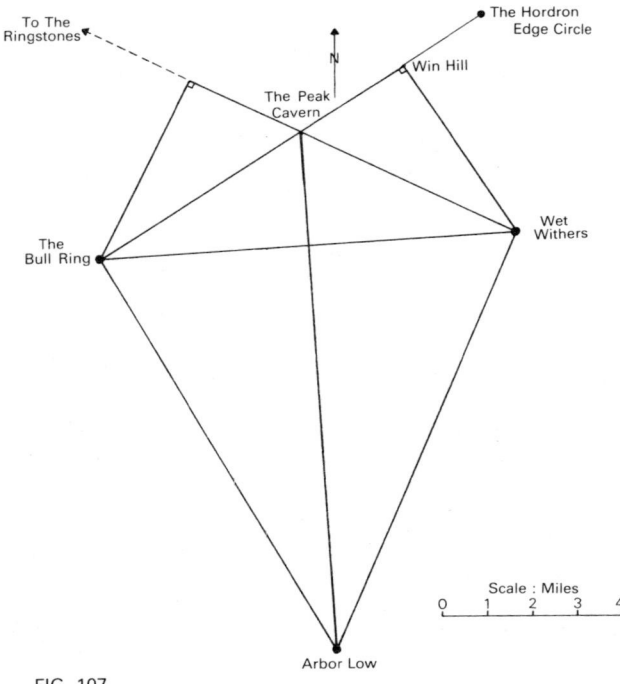

FIG. 107

cavern is the mediaeval Peveril Castle which is on a unique triangular piece of land, virtually inaccessible with cliffs on two sides and a very steep slope on the third.

Very few of the points are intervisible and to observe a complete line on the ground would involve 3 to 5 stages, for example Arbor Low to Longstone Edge, to Eyam Moor and then to Wet Withers. The only exception is Win Hill which is visible from Wet Withers and the Hordron Edge circle. Because of the present condition of the sites, it is difficult to say which of the lines are marked in the structures, but the present evidence is:

Arbor Low The Bull ring is very close to the cove orientation and is marked by stone 3 and the entrance edge. The central axis is marked by stone 4 and a prominent notch in the horizon. Wet Withers however is not marked.

Bull Ring This is too badly damaged but one of the angle changes is the approximate direction of the Hordron Edge Circle and the other points on this line.

Wet Withers This does not mark Arbor Low or the Bull Ring and the only line which could be significant is to the Peak Cavern which is the direction of the May Day/Lammas sunset in a prominent notch.

Hordron Edge Circle This has its main line to Win Hill marked by a stone and is the direction of the Candlemas/Martinmas sunset.

Faced with this evidence, notably the large distances and non-intervisibility it is inconceivable that prehistoric man designed and constructed these triangles, at the same time it is very unlikely that they are coincidence because of the geometric perfection which links the most important circles in the Peak with some of the more prominent natural features. The 'Great Triangle' is a classic case where the only plausible alternative is that the geometry is a natural phenomenon. One important question is how far were the builders aware of its existence. If this triangle is the most potent in the Peak District as is suggested, it follows that the largest circles would be built where they are by detecting the centres of power at intersecting points. The marking of lines from Arbor Low to points which are not visible indicates at least they could detect the direction of a power line, although the evidence at Wet Withers shows it was not always regarded as important. The different date of Wet

Withers indicates that if they ever achieved full awareness of the pattern, it must have arrived gradually.

Relationship to the landscape

Looking at the lines of the triangles balanced round the central axis (Arbor Low to the Peak Cavern) a definite series of opposites between Hill and Valley are revealed which in general terms works for 60 to 80 per cent of the total length. The balances are not absolute, but are what would be expected from an underlying force governing the development of the landscape, in conjunction with other forces which possibly work in contrary patterns. All the lines are shown as sections in the diagrams, and the main areas where the balance does not work are at the ends of the lines. This is because the circles all occupy similar positions; the Peak Cavern is the only rather ambiguous position, probably because it is on the balancing axis.

The main extreme balance points are:

Fig. 108: *Arbor Low to Wet Withers* balancing *Arbor Low to the Bull Ring* starting at Arbor Low they are:
(a) Bolehill/Upper Lathkill Dale, both distinct features.
(b) River Wye Valley near Ashford/Taddington Moor. These are half way along the line and are both very prominent features in the Peak District landscape.
(c) Longstone Edge/River Wye Gorge, both prominent landmarks. The rest of the line is distorted because the Bull Ring line follows a small tributary valley which does not reflect the surrounding landscape. Wormhill Moor to the side of the valley creates the correct balance with Middleton Dale.

Fig. 109: *Wet Withers to the axis* balancing *the Bull Ring to the axis*. This is not a very distinct line but it has the following:
(d) Abney Moor/Dam Dale and (e) Bradwell Dale/Dam Cliff. The points on the west are indistinct because of the rolling limestone moor with no prominent features.

Fig. 110: *Wet Withers to Win Hill* balancing *the Bull Ring to Edale Valley*. The first part of the line is confused because the Wet Withers line runs along the slope of Offerton Moor but the second half has good balances:
(f) Derwent Valley/Rushup Edge. Both important features.
(g) Win Hill/Edale Valley. Two absolute contrasts, the peak of a hill and an isolated sheltered valley bottom in the stream itself.

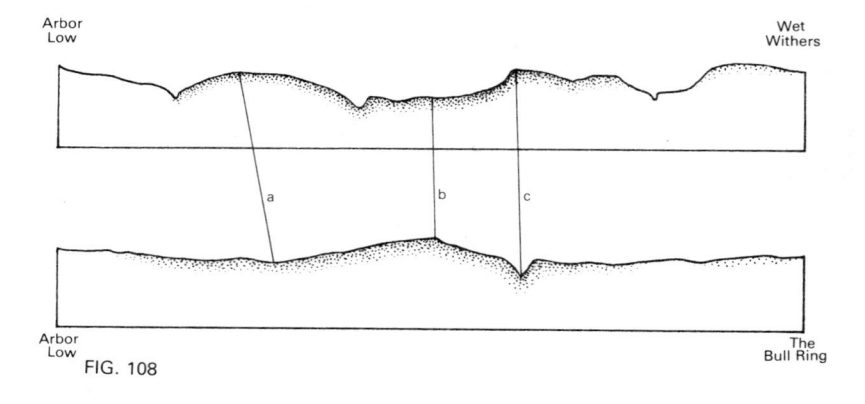

FIG. 108

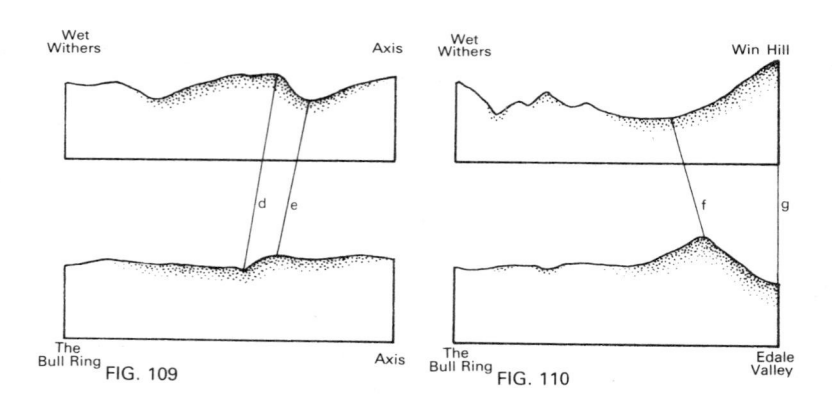

FIG. 109

FIG. 110

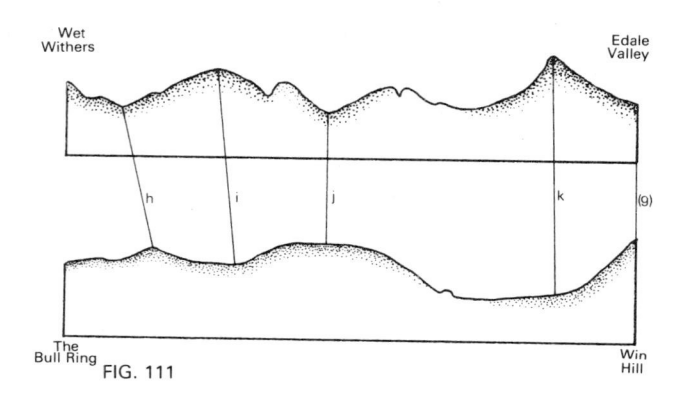

FIG. 111

Fig. 111: *Wet Withers to the Vale of Edale* balancing *the Bull Ring to Win Hill*. Starting at the circles, the main points are:
(h) Abney Clough/Bee Low and (i) Abney Moor/Perry Dale, all distinct features. (j) Hope Valley/Bradwell Moor. These are at the centre of the line and are two of the most important features of the area with the sheltered Hope Valley supporting a large population and the moor one of the most uninviting parts of the region. A confused area follows to the Peak Cavern with the line from Wet Withers running along the slope of the limestone plateau. (k) Mam Tor/Hope Valley. Mam Tor is a very impressive hill which dominates the western end of the Hope Valley, on its summit is the main hill fort in Derbyshire recently found to be Bronze Age in origin. The name itself means 'the mother hill', its balance point, the valley, was the main living area for the populations that built the fort and it contains the river Derwent, the largest of the area. (g) Edale Valley/Win Hill, already discribed.

These relationships with the landscape given above are one of the most convincing arguments that the triangles are not coincidence. They have a particularly significant balance in the right-angled triangles, where they define every main feature in the landscape: Peak Cavern, the Hope Valley and the River Derwent, the Edale Valley, Win Hill, Mam Tor and Rushup Edge; the only exception is Lose Hill which is ignored.

We do not know if prehistoric man was aware of all these relationships; but it follows that if he knew about the triangles, then he would have noticed the balances as he observed the lines.

The ideas covered in this chapter are still being developed. For work in hand at the present time, one should refer to Appendix C.

Appendix A. The Circles of the Peak District

a) Sites surveyed by the author

	1	2	3	4	5	6	7	8	9	10	11	12	13
Henges													
1	Arbor Low	1603.6355[1]	✓	295 × 280	2	✓	140 × 120	Egg	6	35 + 7	39 + 7	–	Part Excavated
2	Arbor Low II	1578.6335	✓	c 180?	?	×	c 90	?	?	–	?	–	Badly disturbed
3	Bull Ring	0784.7823[3]	✓	270 + 5	2	×	150 × 140	Egg?	?	–	?	–	Part excavated
4	Staden	0693.7211		190 × 175	2	×	152 × 136	Egg	?	–	?	–	Also a square enclosure
Circles													
5	Ewden Beck	2381.9664	✓	65 ± 1	2	✓	52 × 47	Complex Circle?	6?	11-14	15-16?	1-2	Badly preserved
6	Hordron Edge	2152.8685[1]	×	–	–	✓	53 × 50	Egg?	?	10	10?	–	–
7	Bamford Moor North	2088.8525	✓	98 × 93	×	×	80 × 74	Flattened D.	12	–	?	–	–
8	Bamford Moor Central	2146.8474	✓	36 × 30	×	✓	23 × 21	Ellipse?	?	–	?	–	–
9	Bamford Moor South	2211.8453	✓	98 × 93	×	×	26 × 23	Egg	?	–	?	4-6	–
10	Ciceley Low North	2752.8079	✓	64 ± 1	1?	×	84 × 79	Complex Egg?	?	–	?	–	–
11	Ciceley Low South	2751.8077	✓	92 × 81	1?	✓	49 + 1	Circular	4	–	?	–	Secondary part of 10
12	Offerton Moor West	2127.8055	✓	52	–	✓	75 × 60	Ellipse	4?	–	?	1?	Stones in C18
13	Offerton Moor East	2132.8057	✓	119 × 116	×	✓	38	Circular	4	–	?	–	Secondary part of 12
14	Wet Withers	2255.7900[1]	✓	44 × 41	×	✓	101 × 98	Complex Egg	6	10	16-18	–	Largest circle
15	Brown Edge	2883.7898	✓	63 × 56	×	✓	24 × 20	Flattened B	5	2	2	–	Excavated
16	Barbrook I	2785.7558[2]	✓	60 × 56	1	✓	47 × 41	Flattened B	5	12	12	8-10	–
17	Barbrook II	2775.7582	✓	97 × 88	0-2?	✓	49 × 45	Complex Flattened	6	7	9-10	–	Excavated
18	Barbrook III	2834.7728[2]	✓	77 × 70	×	×	86 × 77	Flattened A?	6	21	21-26	–	Ruined
19	Barbrook IV	2896.7561	✓	62 ± 2	?	×	62 × 53	Flattened B	5	–	?	–	Badly preserved
20	Barbrook V	2695.7515	✓	51	2	×	49 + 1	?	4	–	?	–	Badly damaged
21	Stoke Flat	2497.7679[1]	✓	48 × 46	38	×	Circular	4	9-15	?	–	Two rings of stone
22	Gardoms Edge	2746.7240	✓	44 × 39	X?	×	38 × 37	Ellipse?	?	–	?	–	
23	Gibbet Moor N.W.	2794.7067	✓	38 × 35	X?	×	32 × 28	Flattened B?	5	–	?	–	Parts of the
24	Gibbet Moor Central	2796.7065	✓	39 × 37	X?	×	26 × 23	Flattened B?	5	–	?	–	same monument
25	Gibbet Moor S.E.	2798.7063	✓	38-37	×	×	28 × 27	Flattened A?	6	1	1?	–	
26	Beeley Moor North	2777.6873	✓	51 ± 1	×	×	24-22	Circular?	4?	10-14	10-16	–	
27	Park Gate	2804.6851	✓	65 × 60	1?	×	38 + 2	Circular	5	–	?	2	Ruined
28	Beeley Moor Central	285.684[1]	✓	29 × 27	1	×	48 × 41	Complex Egg	5	–	?	–	
29	Beeley Moor South I	285.676[1]	✓	29-26	–	×	19 × 17	Flattened B	?	–	0	–	Excavated
30	Beeley Moor South II	285.676[1]	✓	50	2?	×	16-14	?	?	–	9	–	Badly preserved
31	Nine Ladies	2491.6349[2]	✓	48-44	2	✓	38 × 36	Complex Egg	5?	9	9	1	Outlier King Stone
32	Stanton Moor North	2495.6367	✓	78	2	×	33-30	?	3	2	?	–	Badly preserved
33	Stanton Moor Central	2480.6327	✓	–	1	×	65-63	Complex	3	3	?	–	–
34	Stanton Moor South	2471.6289	✓	57 × 51	–	✓	44 × 39	Complex	6?	3-7	3-11	–	–
35	Doll Tor	2383.6287	X?	–	–	×	19 × 14	Egg?	6?	6	6	–	Excavated
36	Nine Stone Close	2254.6264[2]	×	–	–	×	45-40	Circular?	4?	4	9	–	2 stones re-erected

b) Sites unlocated by the author

37	Bar Dyke	245.9452[2]	✓	75-70	?	×	64-58	—	—	—	—	?	—
38	East Moor	283.7332[2]	✓	60	?	×	45	—	—	—	—	?	—

c) Dubious Sites

39	Ford Hall	0841.8299	✓	56 × 52	1	×	49 × 45	Flattened A?	6	—	—	?	Possibly Tumulus
40	Dennis Knoll	2281.8404	✓	43-40	?	×	34-32	?	?	—	—	?	Plus central platform

d) Destroyed Sites[1]

41	Abney Moor I	203.804	✓	48	1	✓	33	—	—	—	9	—	Destroyed 1840-70
42	Abney Moor II	Close to 1	✓	?	?	✓	50	—	—	—	10	—	Destroyed before 1800
43	Eyam Moor	Close to site 14					Several described last century as small (possibly tumuli)						
44	Top of Riley	Probably 2277	✓	40 × 35	2	✓	Large	—	—	—	?	—	Destroyed before 1840
45	Seven Brides	Matlock Moor	?			✓	25	—	—	—	7	—	Recorded 1784 only
46	Cadster	02.792	✓			×	33 × 30	—	—	—	?	—	Recorded 1907 only
47	Morridge	04.532		40		×	?	—	—	—	?	—	Recorded 1850 only
48	Ringstones	006.896		Place name only									

Addendum:

A possible henge at Kniveton (SK. 2015.5006) has recently been brought to the attention of the author. This has been discovered by aerial photography and there is very little to see on the ground. Until excavation is carried out it is impossible to be certain of the nature of this site. It appears to consist of a circular bank with an internal ditch, with an overall diameter of approximately 350 feet. If this proves to be a henge, it fits with the trade route theory. It is a day's journey from Arbor Low on the main trackway southwards, in a position which would be a focal point for the population of the southern margins of the limestone plateau.

Key

1. Common name of the site
2. Map Reference (all SK.)
3. Existence of surrounding bank
4. External diameter (in feet)
5. Number of Entrances
6. Existence of standing stones
7. Diameter of ring of stones, or internal edge of bank (in feet)
8. Shape of ring
9. Number of sides of geometric figure
10. Present number of stones
11. Original number of stones
12. Number of outliers
13. Notes

Notes

[1] These map references have yet to be checked by a theodolite
[2] Marked on the 1″ O.S. map.

Appendix B
Symbolism of Numbers

This appendix is included to clarify the role of numbers in our conscious and subconscious minds, as basic expressions of truth and reality which go beyond any one religious sect. Because of their universal symbolic truth, they can be regarded as being the basis of the system of philosophy of the stone circle builders, although we can only guess how far these concepts had crystalised in their conscious minds.

Numbers 0 and 1
The difference between the two is that 0 is the unknown potential and 1 is its manifestation but in many ways they cannot be separated in the stone circles.

0 and 1
The whole, infinity, the absolute, the unbroken unity, the universe.

1 only
The basic unit, primordial matter, all things within itself. The beginning, the germ of all things. In relationship to further numbers it is the cause of all numbers and the beginning of diversity. The basic geometric symbol is the circle. (Further light is thrown on 1 in the sections on numbers 2, 3 and 10.)

Number 2
Duality, the division into opposites, polarisation. Many basic divisions exist, some of the more relevant ones are:

positive	:	negative	infinite	:	finite
active	:	passive	spirit	:	matter
male	:	female	life	:	form
sun	:	moon	life	:	death
day	:	night	truth	:	falsehood
sunrise	:	sunset			
summer	:	winter			
mountain	:	valley			
east	:	west			

Opposites obviously are the basis of any form of existence, but pure opposites cannot be reconciled and are therefore negative and static. 2 relates to 1 as an illusion, because all things are one and at the same time to 3 in relation to the world. 2 is also the beginning of the evolution of form and the basis of symmetry. The symmetry of all mammals. The geometric symbol is the cross. 2 is the only even prime number.

Number 3
The union of opposites, the synthesising power which opens the way for development and growth creating the basis for any material and spiritual world. The Trinity: The same the other and the esscence. Examples of basic trinities are:

same	:	opposite	:	union
positive	:	negative	:	neutral
body	:	spirit	:	soul
man	:	woman	:	child
sun	:	moon	:	earth
day	:	night	:	dawn/dusk
past	:	future	:	present

Obviously these trinities also relate to 1 and 2 and together they are 'the root of all things', to be considered as one number, with 3 the first number of positive energy and manifest reality. Other trinities exist which are more specialised, such as:

| new moon | : | full moon | : | old moon |
| virgin | : | wife | : | hag |

Also others which are specifically spiritual or physical. Three is also the creation of form, the 3 dimensions. There are two main geometric symbols for three, the triangle, and the vesica which represents the two opposite circles in perfect unity.

Number 4
The physical plane, finite reality, the world. The 4 elements: earth, water, air, fire, which can be put into modern terms as solid, liquid, gas and interchange. The 4 seasons: winter, spring, summer and autumn. The 4 directions: north, east, south and west. The 4 corners of the earth, the 4 winds, the 4 humours. From these relationships it follows that 4 can be regarded as the 'Foundation of solid reality'. The geometric symbols are the square, rhomb and the tetrahedron, the basic solid with 4 sides and corners.

Number 5
Creating a change of quality as matter is given life.
The 4 elements plus wood (symbolising the living world).
Birth, the material commencement of life.
The centre of numbers 1—9, the heart of things, man.
The birth of magic.

1 + 4, the infinite expressed in the finite. It follows that 5 is the creative power, 'The life force'. Other attributions are:
The 4 directions plus the centre (man).
The 5 senses—sight, hearing, small, taste, touch.
The 5 planets known to the ancient world:
Saturn ♄ Jupiter ♃ Mars ♂ Venus ♀ Mercury ☿
The main geometric symbols are the pentagon, the centred 4 ∴, and the four sided pyramid which is the link between 4 and 5 with four top faces plus the base and four corners plus the apex.

Number 6
A unity of opposite trinities, creating a static balance of harmony and proportion, a 'seal' of opposite forces, often seen as the combination of spiritual and physical trinities. Also the three dimensions related to man, the 4 directions plus up and down. The main geometric symbol is the hexagon often known as Solomon's Seal. The six sides of a cube. It is the only number with the properties of $1 + 2 + 3 = 6$ and $1 \times 2 \times 3 = 6$.

Number 7
This has always been known as a spiritual and mystical number. It is the point at the centre of six which is the link for synthesis between the two opposite triangles. 'The bridge between heaven and earth'. 'The stirring of the harmony making the accomplishment of all things possible'. Therefore the number of all creative acts and initiation. The completion of a cycle, bringing the development from 2 to 6 back to the perfection of 1. Symbolic rebirth, awareness. The beginning or the end.
Other attributions are:

The 5 planets plus the sun and moon. The 7 alchemical metals (known to Bronze Age man except iron; which was Gold ☉ Silver ☽ Mercury ☿ Tin ♃ Lead ♄ Iron ♂ possibly replaced by the alloy Bronze or some think flint), Copper ♀.
Natural phenomena: Colours of the rainbow, holes in the head, notes of music. A quarter of the basic lunar cycle, days of the week.

Seven is also known as the 'Virgin number' because it is not a product or factor of any other number in the decad. The geometric symbol is the seven pointed star, another is the centred 6 ∴.

It is the only basic number for a diameter of a circle to create an integral circumference if π is taken as $\frac{22}{7}$.

Number 8
The beginning of another cycle (after 1 to 3 and 4 to 7). Eight can be seen as double four with similar attributions but in a less basic form. An expression of the differentiation of definite forms caused by the duality of aspects of four; therefore also the harmony of the material universe. Another attribution is the seven planets plus the earth. Geometric symbols are the corners of a cube and the octagon.

Number 9
The trinity of trinities. A perfect balance which is the final consolidated union. The perfect man. The universal soul.
9 is also finality and judgement and at the same time representing change as the return to the beginning (number 10).

Number 10
The return to 1 as a beginning or on a more complex plane. The return as a completely enlightened man in harmony with the universe. The universe and all things arranged in it. Completion and rebirth.
7 + 3 all created things combined with the spiritual trinity. Man's fingers and therefore the basis of the number system.

Two other numbers are included as they have important basic attributions.

Number 12
The zodiac, the complete condition and influencing cycles of the manifest world (3×4, 2×6). 4 + 8 world and man combined and renewed.
$3 + 4 + 5 = 12$, cycles 1—3, 4—7, 8—12 sides of basic pythagorean triangle 3, 4, 5.
($1 \times 2 \times 3 \times 4 \times 5 = 120$ and sum of 1 to 15 = 120).

Number 13
The zodiac plus god; completeness, infinity.
The lunar months in a year.

Appendix C
The Zodiac

This is included to give a glimpse of an interesting direction present research is taking, which develops the information given in Chapter 9. It is included here because at the moment it is only theory. However, the more one looks at these observations, the more one intuitively feels they emphasise the landscape's structure. The notes have had to be kept brief; anyone who is interested in investigating further should if possible study the landscape in the field, or invest in a 1" Ordnance Survey Map.

From the centre of the structure described in Chapter 9, at a point on Bradwell Moor, is a series of radiating lines. These partition the whole of the Peak District into twelve equal parts based on the 'Great Triangle' and its axes, dividing the landscape into significant units. The lines are the main regions of weakness where water has cut into the uplands, while the areas between usually define the main blocks of moorland. The centre of this arrangement is not marked by anything of significance (neither are the centres of stone circles). For convenience the lines are lettered and the areas numbered in a clockwise order from north.

Uplands

The Limestone Plateau: This area is the most difficult to interpret because of its rolling nature with a lack of defined features in many areas, especially near the centre; however the following are important:
1) The high northern end of the plateau is defined by divisions 11 to 1. These moors pass into the slope to the east and the flat shelves around Eyam, fitting into divisions 2 to 4.
2) The high Longstone Moor is exactly defined by division 5.
3) Division 6 marks isolated hills running to the south namely Brushfield Moor, Fin Cop, Bole Hill and more importantly the whole south-eastern block of the limestone plateau.

FIG. 112

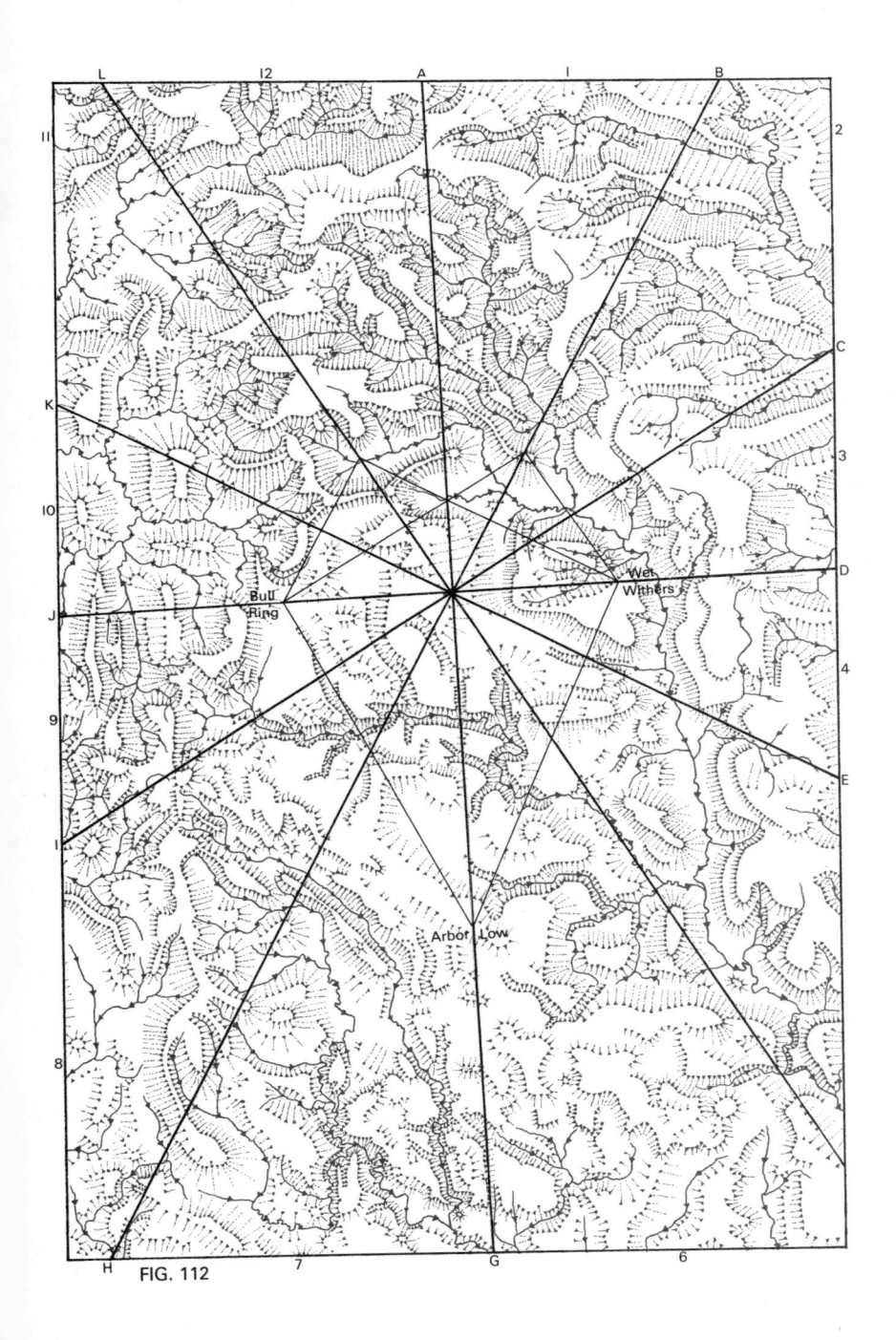

4) Division 7 defines the prominent Taddington Moor exactly and also the main area of high limestone ridges, these also fill division 8, but here form a much narrower strip.
5) Division 9 has very few features and defines the area where the limestone gently meets the high gritstone moors to the west.
6) Division 10 marks Bee Low and Gautries Hill.
7) The highest portion of the limestone, including the flat top of Bradwell Moor and Eldon Hill, are defined by division 11.

The Northern Gritstone Moors: This northern area is the highest in the Peak; it consists of a central area deeply dissected by narrow valleys, which is surrounded by vast areas of flat bleak uplands. Division 12 covers Kinder Scout, Edale Moor, Bleaklow and other moors in between. The eastern edge is well defined, but small areas of the moors run into division 11 on the west. Division 1 defines the Howden and Derwent Moors, with only a narrow ridge between them and Bleaklow. The southern end of Derwent Moor runs slightly into division 2. Dividing the northern moors from the Hope Valley to the south are two ridges which also fit with the divisions, the one between Edale Moor and Win Hill is exactly defined by division 1 and that between Mam Tor and Lose Hill by division 12.

The Eastern Gritstone Moors: The main block of moorland covers divisions 2 to 5 and has different characteristics in each area. Division 2 defines the large main shelf of Bamford Moor with the northern half of Stanage above it. In division 3 the shelves are dissected, with no large areas of flat moor, and above this is the high land of Hallam and Burbage Moors. Division 4 defines the widest area of moors with an unbroken shelf, with White Edge above this. Behind White Edge is the Barbrook Valley which has the only stream running from north to south across the main moors; this also creates the only major break in the moors which is between 4 and 5. Division 5 marks the narrower moors to the south which have broken shelves but a continuous main moor.

Between the main eastern moors and the limestone plateau are high isolated moors many of which also fit into the pattern. The largest of these is in the north and is a high moor which is virtually bisected by a deep valley, Bretton Clough. The northern half, Offerton Moor, is exactly defined by division 3, but the southern half Eyam Moor is one of the major discrepancies in the zodiac; its prominent southern ridge is only half way across division 4. In division 5 are a series of dissected shelves accurately contained although Calton Pasture in the south is higher than the others making the area unbalanced. In division 6 the fit is also not very good with the main area, Stanton Moor, half in 5 and the other areas not reaching the other side of 6.

The Western Gritstone Moors: These moors are much more dissected than those on the east and cover divisions 8 to 11. The only continuous area of moors is the Morridge/Axe Edge ridge which is defined by division 8. At the northern edge of 8 the moors suddenly drop to the lower Burbage Edge; division 9 contains this and Black Edge, with a narrow ridge between them, and also the high ridge from Shining Tor to Cats Tor to the west. The whole area has characteristic north/south ridges. Division 10 is very dissected and only contains isolated hills, such as Eccles Pike, and to the west the moors around Lyme Park. Finally division 11 defines the high ridge Rushup Edge/Brown Knoll, which links Mam Tor to Kinder Scout and also dissected moors to the west.

To summarise, the upland areas are often defined in one division but sometimes run through more. All however have distinct changes at the lines with the exception of Bradwell Moor. Only a few features do not fit with these divisions: Eyam Edge, Calton Pasture, the limestone plateau around the River Wye and western Kinder Scout. A series of prominent hills exist which are exceptions being placed on lines rather than between them: Win Hill line B, Lose Hill and Mam Tor lines A and L (slightly misplaced), Stanton Moor line F and Chinley Churn line K. It is interesting to note that Win Hill, Mam Tor and Stanton Moor were given special significance by prehistoric man.

River Valleys

The major valleys of the region also fit into the pattern in a similar way with changes of character occurring at the lines where there is also a distinct tendency for confluences to occur.

This main river in the Peak is the Derwent which runs from north to south. Its upper valley is very narrow and high with several major tributaries, which are exactly defined by divisions 12 and 1. The Derwent itself starts near line A and runs to line B where it joins with its main tributary; this comes from near line

A where the rivers Ashop and Alport join, the Ashop starting by line L. Just below line B the stream which divides the Derwent Moor from Stanage also joins the river. Downstream from B the river is in a valley which widens until near line C, where it joins the river Noe in the centre of the Hope Valley. The river Noe is the only tributary which starts in division 11, as a number of small streams which join together near line L, from here to line A it is in the wide isolated section of the Edale Valley. At A the valley changes direction and becomes slightly narrower eventually running into the wide Hope Valley and joining Peakshore Water at line B. This runs from the Peak Cavern on line A, although the valley itself runs into division 12 ending at Winnats Pass, an impressive dry valley gorge with high cliffs on either side and its top close to line L. From B the Noe continues through the wide Hope Valley to join the Derwent at C. Downstream the Derwent runs through the lower Hope Valley which gradually gets narrower to line D. A characteristic of this area is the large number of streams which join the river from either side, dissecting the gritstone shelves; these include the one in Bretton Clough which follows line D dividing the moors. The river takes a straight course through division 4, with unbroken moors on either side, until it reaches line E where there are two major breaks: to the west the limestone Stoney Middleton gorge which follows the line and then deviates to the north before joining the Derwent, on the east is the Barbrook break from where upstream it runs northwards to line D. Division 5 marks the main valley of the Derwent which is wide with relatively low-lying dissected land to the west. The river flows south until it approaches line F from where it turns towards the east until it reaches Matlock; here it enters a gorge, the southern end of which also touches line F from where the river follows the line out of the uplands of the Peak.

 The only large river which joins the Derwent is the river Wye which runs from west to east through the limestone plateau. This starts in division 9 as a number of streams running off the western gritstone moors which all come together near line I where they enter the limestone and form a steep-sided gorge. This continues through divisions 8 and 7 with a distinct series of curves at line H. In division 6 it develops a much more winding course until it leaves the limestone just before Bakewell at line F. From here it follows a straight course along the line until the river Lathkill joins it, then it goes east to join the Derwent misplaced from the line by Stanton Moor which has an unusual position noted above. The Lathkill starts in division 7 as a wide hollow with a series of shallow dry valleys, at line G the valley changes as a deep gorge starts with shelves high above it, this runs eastwards until it joins the Wye at F. The other river in this area is the Bradford which starts as a dry valley by line G. From here it takes a twisting course through the limestone till joining the Lathkill. A characteristic of division 6 in the whole of this area is the way the valleys take frequent right-angled turns. The only other main drainage system in the Peak is that of the Dove and Manifold in the south-west. These rivers are completely contained within divisions 7 and 8, with the narrow upper valleys in 8 which join together to create wider valleys in 7, which eventually pass into limestone gorges similar to that at Matlock before leaving the area.

The western side of the region is drained by a series of streams running off the moors. Division 8 contains the river Dane and its tributaries. Division 9 the river Goyt running northwards in a straight narrow valley, which changes suddenly into the wider dissected region of division 10, with many other streams joining it. This division also contains the only break through the moors onto the limestone from the west, Barmoor Clough. Defined in division 11 is a wide isolated valley between the limestone and gritstone above Perryfoot, with a large number of sinks where the water reaches the limestone. To the west is a dissected area of narrow valleys. Division 12 contains the long narrow valley of the river Etherow with its head at line A and entrance to a wide valley at line L.

The eastern side is drained by the river Don and its tributaries, with the Upper Don and Porter in 1 and 2 and the Loxley and Rivelin in 2 joining the Don by line C, which then continues downstream into 3, with the river Sheaf draining division 3.

These observations indicate that there is an underlying pattern governing the geological structure based on twelve divisions. This is the number of the zodiac and this whole structure may be similar to other zodiacs that have been proposed for other parts of Britain. The major difference between them is that the effect on the landscape in an upland region such as the Peak is more noticeable. The structure has been discovered from this effect rather than through the symbolic patterns of the others. These have not yet been found in the Peak District zodiac.

Notes

Chapter 2

1. Further south near Wirksworth (SK.2841.5421) is an isolated standing stone which is 7½ feet high; last century another was reported nearby. The 'Seven Brides' circle near Matlock which has now disappeared reputedly had a stone 7 feet high.

Chapter 3

1. The beginning of religion?
2. Its construction relates to the 'egg' at Wet Withers.
3. *Megalithic Sites in Britain* pp. 87-88.

Chapter 6

Stoke Flat Circle

1. Error of 0.58 inches.
2. Error of 0.72 inches.
3. Error of 0.87 inches.
4. Error—each side 3.28 inches too short.
5. Error—each side 4.1 inches too short.
6. Error—each side 4.92 inches too short.

Barbrook I Circle

7. *Megalithic Sites in Britain* pp. 66, 68.
8. 1.86 inches too long—hardly detectable, considering construction methods.
9. Actually = × 2.9572 giving 207.004 × ¼MY. This is 24.45 inches too short.
10. 38.09—error of 0.74 inches.
11. This deviation from a true circle was necessary because a circle with integral diameter and circumference cannot be divided into five equal whole numbered parts.
12. Error of 0.021 inches.

Notes

Barbrook II Circle

Wet Withers

Offerton Moor Circles

Ciceley Low Circles

13. In Chinese geomancy (fung-shui) it is stated that the ideal landscape should contain ⅗ yang and ⅖ yin.
14. Error of 14.09 inches.
15. Error of 10.02 inches.
16. Error of 38.2 inches.
17. Error of 3.92 inches.
18. Giving 220 MY when added together—possibly significant.
19. As 312 an error of 0.23 inches which is better than most ellipses.
20. 0.434 too long—error of 3.54 inches.
21. 0.402 too short—error of 3.28 inches.
22. Actually 5 inches too long.
23. Error of 9.76 inches.
24. Error of 7.44 inches.

Chapter 7

Nine Ladies

1. Actually 6.93—error of 2.34 inches.
2. Actually 13.86—error of 4.68 inches—detectable.
3. Actually 9.93 caused by error in BF and BG.
4. Actually 5.13—error of 4.37 inches.
5. Actually 13.13—error of 4.37 inches.
6. Actually 41.86—error of 4.62 inches.
7. Actually 7.02—error of 0.66 inches.
8. Actually 8.89—error of 3.74 inches.
9. Error of 4.37 inches.
10. Error of 2.34 inches.
11. Error of 4.37 inches.
12. Error of 4.37 inches.
13. Error of 2.34 inches.
14. Error of 0.66 inches.
15. Error of 3.74 inches.
16. Error of 4.37 inches.
17. Error of 2.34 inches.
18. Error of 4.37 inches.
19. Error of 4.68 inches.

Stanton Moor, Central

20. LM, LO 0.13 too short, error of 4.27 inches. MO 0.73 too long, error of 23.93 inches.
21. Actually 75.40, an error of 13.06 inches.

Stanton Moor, South

22. Actually 0.83 inches too long.
23. Actually 90.274°.

Park Gate Circle

24. Actually 65.47—error of 3.86 inches.
25. Actually 195.6—error of 4.91 inches.
26. Error of 9.79 inches.
27. Error of 3.98 inches.
28. Actually 9.39 inches too short.
29. Actually 42.43—error of 0.6 inches.

Chapter 8

Bamford Moor, South
Bamford Moor, North

1. Errors of 2.28 or 5.88 inches respectively.
2. Professor Thom's classification.
3. Actually 27.095—error of 3.09 inches.
4. Actually 89.436—error of 18.41 inches, note this is only 0.026 inches per foot.
5. Actually 54.2—error of 1.61 inches.
6. Error of 3.09 inches.
7. Actually 30.023—error of 0.19 inches.
8. Detectable error—3.09 inches.
9. Detectable error—18.41 inches.

Chapter 9

1. Error between the two of about 130 feet.

How to use the map references

All the references use the grid which covers Ordnance Survey maps throughout the country. The whole of the Peak District relevant to this work is within the division 'SK' denoting the part of the grid covering this area of Britain. The numbers which follow 'SK' are co-ordinates of the grid enabling the exact spot on the map to be found.

Most of the references given have eight numbers and these are divided into two halves of four each. (When a site's location is not known the same degree of accuracy only six numbers are used and divided into two groups of three.) The first four numbers determine the position along a line from west to east and the last four the position along a line from south to north, the site is where these intersect. Within both groups each number represents a position within a sub-division of the number before it into ten equal parts, e.g. To find SK.1279.3065 proceed as follows:

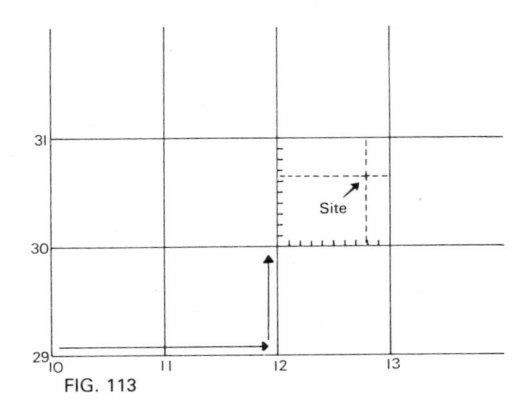

FIG. 113

Locate the square of the grid which contains the site from the first two numbers of each half: 12 and 30. Subdivide the square to find the exact point with the last two numbers of each half: 79 and 65.
Note: the last numbers of each half of 8-numbered references denote points which are 10 metres apart and therefore the site you are locating is fixed within 5 metres in any direction of the co-ordinates given, (with 6 numbered references ± 50 metres).

Keys to the figures

Maps

Small scale – figs. 1, 2, 112
- Rivers/streams
- Hills
- Valleys

Medium scale – Figs. 3-14, 56
- ○ Circles
- Earthworks
- + Tumuli
- Prehistoric clearance
- Escarpment Edges
- Rivers/streams
- Marsh
- Reservoirs
- Roads
- --- Tracks
- ······ Footpaths
- Woods
- Quarries
- Buildings

Large scale – Figs. 16, 24, 28, 78, 103
- Henges/earthworks
- ○ Circles
- ◇ Mounds
- · Stones
- Roads/tracks
- ===== Unfenced tracks
- ---·--- Footpaths
- Walls/hedges
- Streams
- Woods
- Quarries
- Buildings

Fig. 2 only
- o Henges
- • Circles
- + Possible sites
- × Lost sites

Figs. 4, 9 only
- • Medieval churches

Fig. 56 only
- Contours
- Geometry

Fig. 3 only
- ---- Tours

Fig. 13 only
- ---··--- Walls

Figs. 3, 4, 9 only
- Towns/villages

Fig. 16 only
- ○ Dewponds

Fig. 24 only
- Buildings and gardens

Plans

- Standing stones
- Leaning stones
- Fallen stones
- Possible stones
- Buried section of fallen stones
- Bank stones and rubble
- Banks/mounds – good condition
- Banks/mounds – badly-preserved
- Geometry
- ---- Possible/secondary geometry

Figs. 72, 76 only
- plus reconstructed stones

Fig. 76 only
- vertically set cist stones

Figs. 15, 17 only
- Fallen stones

Fig. 17 only
- Approximate original position
- Detached pieces of stone
- × Missing stones

Figs. 38, 72 only
- Balance points

--→ Celestial alignments

Alignments

The sun at solstices and equinoxes (Fig. 79)

The sun at midpoints of the year (within the range shown)

The moon at the solstices
- Solid lines – mean position
- Dashed lines – max. position (not Figs. 18-22)
- Dotted lines – min. position (not Figs. 18-22)
(Fig. 79)

Note: In most of these figures the rise and sets are shown as straight lines after leaving the horizon, in reality they have slight curves, only when these have any noticeable effect on alignments are they included.

- Stones from the centre of the circle
- Reconstructed stones
- Banks/mounds
- Stones and mounds at a distance

Fig. 79 only
- × Missing stones

Figs. 18-22 only
- Approximate height of the bank originally

Bibliography

General Reading

Burl, A.: *The Stone Circles of the British Isles*, Yale University Press, 1976.
Dames, M.: *The Silbury Treasure*, Thames and Hudson, 1976.
Hitching, F.: *Earth Magic*, Cassell and Co., 1976.
Michell, J.: *View over Atlantis*, Sago Press, 1969; *City of Revelation*, Garnstone Press, 1972; *The Old Stones of Land's End*, Garnstone Press, 1974.
R.I.L.K.O.: *Britain, A Study in Patterns*, 1971; *Earth Mysteries*, 1977, Research Into Lost Knowledge Organisation.
Thom. A.: *Megalithic Sites in Britain*, Clarendon Press Oxford, 1967; *Megalithic Lunar Observatories*, Clarendon Press Oxford, 1971.

The Peak District

Alcock, L. L.: "The Bull Ring Excavation", Proc. of the Prehistoric Society. N.S. Vol. 16, 1950.
Andrews, W. J.: "Bull Ring", Derbyshire Arch. Jour. O.S. Vol. 27, 1905.
Bateman, T.: *Vestiges of the Antiquities of Derbyshire*, 1848; *Ten Years Digging*, 1861.
Cox, J. C. (ed.): *Memorials of Old Derbyshire*, 1907 (Chapter by W. J. Andrews).
Gray, H.: "Arbor Low Excavations", Derbyshire Arch. Jour. O.S. Vol. 26, 1904.
Heathcote, J. P.: "The Nine Stones, Harthill Moor and Doll Tor Stone Circle Excavation", Derbyshire Arch. Journ. N.S. Vol. 13, 1939.
Matthew, T. A.: "Arbor Low and other Lows", Derbyshire Arch. Jour. O.S. Vol. 29, 1907.
Pegge, Rev.: "A Desquisition on the Lows and Barrows in the Peak of Derbyshire particularly that capital British monument called Arbelows", Archaeologia Vol. 7, 1783.

Radley, J.:	"A Ring Bank on Beeley Moor", Derbyshire Arch. Jour. N.S. Vol. 36, 1965; "A Bronze Age Ringwork on Totley Moor, and Bronze Age Ringworks in the Pennines", Arch. Jour. Vol. 123, 1966; "Origins of Arbor Low Henge Monument", Derbyshire Arch. Jour. N.S. Vol. 41, 1968.
Rooke, H.:	"An Account of Druidical remains on Stanton and Hartle Moor in the Peak, Derbyshire", Archaeologia Vol. 6, 1782. (Original notes and drawings kept at West Park Museum Sheffield.)
Thompson, D.:	*Official Guide to Arbor Low*, Ministry of Works, 1963.
Ward, T.:	*Victoria history of the County of Derby*, Vol. 1, "Early Man", Univ. of London, Inst. of Hist. Res., 1905-07.
Wood, W.:	*The History and Antiquities of Eyam*, 1842.

Index

alignments 50-6
Alport 69
Andle Stone 150, 154
Arbor Low 35-6, 39, 44, 53-5, 61, 63, 74-87, 119, 182, 186
Arbor Low II 36, 80, 186
Astrology, 58
Aubrey, John 13

Bakewell 18, 31, 61
Bamford North Circle 40, 44, 53, 72, 168-173, 186
Bamford South Circle 37, 40, 53-4, 71, 95, 162-7, 186
Barbrook I 40, 44-6, 53-4, 63, 65, 100-9, 117-9, 186
Barbrook II 36, 40, 44-6, 53, 55, 65, 110-113, 117-9, 186
Barbrook III 40, 66, 114, 115, 117-9, 186
Barbrook IV 40, 116, 117-9, 186
Barbrook V 40, 116, 117-9, 186
Bar Dyke 73, 186
Baslow 64
Bateman, Thos. 13, 151
Beeley Cairn 160
Beeley Moor 40, 159
Beeley Moor Central 44-5, 160, 186
Beeley Moor North 186
Beeley Moor South, 186
Bretton 67
Bronze Age 28
Broomhead Moor 177
Brown Edge Circle 36, 117, 186
Bull Ring, The 35-6, 63, 88-90, 119, 182, 186
Burbage Moor 135
burial mounds 37, 39, 153-4
Buxton 31, 63

Cadster 38, 186
Candlemas 52

Carl Wark Fort 69
Castle Ring 62, 158
Castleton 18
Chapel-en-le-Frith 32,
Chatsworth 18, 62
Chelmorton 63
Ciceley Low Circles 45, 54, 66, 68, 135-6, 186
climate 26
cloughs 25
Cove, The 78-9, 81, 87
Cork Stone 56, 154

dating 14
Doll Tor Circle 37, 56, 69, 150-2, 155, 186
Doveholes 63, 88
Druid's Inn 62

Eagle Stone 56, 67
East Moor Circle 186
eclipse 49
equinox 48
Ewden Beck Circle 37-8, 40, 72, 177, 186
Eyam 18, 68
Eyam Moor Circles, 40, 120, 186

Fivewells 18, 63, 90
Ford Hall Circle 38
Froggat Edge 66

Gardoms Edge Circle 66, 186
geomancy 180
geometria 122
Gibbet Moor Circles 186
Gib Hill 80, 86
Gray H. 74-9
Green Man 156

Haddon Hall 18, 62
Harland Edge 70
Harthill Moor 156

Hathersage 67, 71
Heaf, Eric 57
henges 33-6, 38-40, 74-93
Higgar Tor 55, 69, 71, 125-6
hill forts 30, 62, 69, 185
Hob Hurst House 69
Hope 31
Hordron Edge Circle 37, 55-6, 72, 174-6, 182, 186

Iron Age 30

King Stone 137, 139, 155
Kniveton Henge 186

Ladywash Mine 68
Lammas 52
ley lines 15, 58
life force 58, 182
Long Rake 61

Martinmas 52
Matlock 31
medieval field system 31, 61, 63, 67
megalithic rod 43, 45
megalithic yard 43, 45
Millstone Grit 32
Mompesson's Well 68
Monyash 61
moon's movements 48, 50
Morridge Circle 38, 186
Mother's Cap 56, 69, 124, 154

National Park 19
Neolithic 27
Nine Ladies Circle 37, 45, 62, 137-142, 155, 186
Nine Stones Close 53, 55-6, 62, 69, 155, 156-8, 186

Offerton Hall 67
Offerton Moor Circles 40, 44, 54-6, 67, 127, 128-134, 186
Old Woman's Stone 37, 164
Over Owler Tor 56, 69, 134

Park Gate Circle 53, 55, 69, 186

Peak Cavern 181
Peveril Castle 19, 182

rakes 23
Ringstones 38, 186
Robin Hood's Stride 62, 156
Romans 31
Rowsley 69

Saxons 31
Seven Brides Circle 137, 186, 198
solstice 48
Staden Henge, The 36, 45, 54, 91-3, 186
Stanage 18, 71
standstill 48
Stanton Central Circle 44-5, 146-8, 155, 186
Stanton Moor 37, 40, 56, 137-155
Stanton North Circle 148-9, 155, 186
Stanton South Circle 44-5, 146-8, 155, 186
Stoke Flat Circle 37, 44, 53-4, 66, 94-9, 186
Stoney Middleton 67
Stukeley, Wm. 13
sun's movements 48

Thom, Prof A. 11, 14-5, 41-7, 50-1 101, 115, 121, 139, 174
Tideswell 31
Top of Riley Circle 186

Upper Bradfield 72

vegetation 26

well dressings 18
Wet Withers 39, 45, 54-5, 68, 119-20, 182, 186
Win Hill 56, 181
Winnats 18
wobble 49

Youlgreave 31, 61